# ALL THE QUEEN'S MEN

GORDON DONALDSON

# ALL THE QUEEN'S MEN

*Power and politics in Mary Stewart's Scotland*

ST. MARTIN'S PRESS
NEW YORK

© Gordon Donaldson 1983

All rights reserved. For information, write:
St. Martin's Press, Inc., 175 Fifth Avenue, New York, NY 10010
Printed in Great Britain
First published in the United States of America in 1983

ISBN 0-312-02009-0

**Library of Congress Cataloging in Publication Data**

Donaldson, Gordon.
All the Queen's men.
  1. Scotland—Politics and government—16th century.
  2. Mary, Queen of Scots, 1542–1587.  I. Title.
    DA786.D66  1983    941.05   83-653
      IDBN 0-312-02009-0

# CONTENTS

*Preface*

1 Introduction: Rivalries and Loyalties  *1*
2 The Shaping of a Revolution  *9*
3 The Party of Revolution  *31*
4 The Queen and her Friends  *48*
5 The Queen's Enemies  *70*
6 The Queen's Party 1567–73  *83*
7 Conciliation  *117*
8 Conservative Revival and Radical Response  *132*

*Appendixes*

A. The Stewart succession before Mary  *155*
B. Surnames and territorial titles  *159*
C. The 'brain-washing expedition', 1550  *160*
D. Lairds in the Party of Revolution, 1559–60  *161*
E. The Hamilton and Dumbarton Bonds  *165*

*Genealogical Tables*

Hamilton and Lennox  *169*
The Queen's Maries and their kinsfolk  *170*
The Hamiltons and their allies  *172*
James VI and the Lennox family  *173*

*Notes*  *174*

*General Index*  181

*Index of Persons*  183

# PREFACE

I have to express my gratitude to Dr Rosalind Marshall and to Mr and Mrs A. W. Russell, from whose comments on a draft the final text has greatly benefited.

Satisfying portraits of Queen's Men are scarce. A painting of Châtelherault, for years their titular leader, has often been reproduced (for example in the present author's *The First Trial of Mary Queen of Scots* and *Who's Who in Scottish History*). From his doleful and elderly appearance (though he was only about 60 when he died) one must conclude that he had a depressing effect. The name of the Duke's heir, 'Young Arran', was long associated with a portrait which, it has now been demonstrated from a study of the costume, must be of later date; if a portrait in the Bibliothèque Nationale, titled 'Le Comte Darrant', is indeed Young Arran, he can have been no more prepossessing than his father, and in any event he faded from the scene so early that he hardly counts as one of The Queen's Men. A miniature in a private collection, titled 'Lord Hammiltoun', may be of Châtelherault's next son, Lord John, who was a leading Queen's Man, but it is not authenticated. A picture said to be of William Maitland of Lethington seems to be a mere modification of one of his brother John (whom admittedly he may have resembled). I thought only two portraits worthy of inclusion, a splendid Lord Seton (reproduced by permission of the Scottish National Portrait Gallery, which has been most generous with advice on the whole subject of iconography) and a Clouet of Kirkcaldy of Grange (from a private collection). The paucity of authentic portraiture may go some way to explain why The Queen's Men do not figure much in folk memory (a topic alluded to on p. 4).

Justice can be done to Châtelherault by a reproduction of his grandiose seal. An impression was made by the present Duke of Hamilton from the original matrix, preserved at Lennoxlove, and it was photographed for me by the Royal Commission on the Ancient and Historical Monuments of Scotland. It is likewise to the courtesy of His Grace that I owe the photograph of the Hall at Lennoxlove. The two facsimiles of documents are from the large collection prepared for inclusion in Sir William Fraser's family histories. The photograph of the Langside Monument was kindly given to me by the City of Glasgow Planning Department, and that of the Maitland Monument at Haddington by Mr G. Angus. The Bird's Eye View of the Siege of Edinburgh Castle derives from Holinshed's *Chronicles* (1577). The remaining illustrations are from photographs by the author, who takes this opportunity to acknowledge the practical help and professional advice he has had in this field from Mr Bill Weir.

# 1
# INTRODUCTION: RIVALRIES AND LOYALTIES

History is plentifully sprinkled with dynastic rivalries, and the human stage was well stocked with deposed sovereigns and pretenders long before republicanism drove monarchs into exile. England had its Wars of the Roses in the fifteenth century and Britain its Jacobite rebellions in the eighteenth; nineteenth-century France had Legitimists, Orleanists and Bonapartists; Spain its Carlists. There was a series of Wars of Succession – Spanish, Polish and Austrian – and the label 'The War of the English Succession' is sometimes given to the war which followed the Revolution of 1688–9 and the replacement of James VII and II by William of Orange.

As kingship in most European countries had from the middle ages been based (at times rather loosely) on heredity, it followed almost by definition that rival claimants were closely related to each other. An early example was the contest for the English throne in the middle of the twelfth century between Stephen and his first cousin Matilda. The Wars of the Roses represented the rivalry of the houses of York and Lancaster, who sprang from two brothers, sons of Edward III. When the English – or rather now the British – succession was disputed again, in the eighteenth century, the Old Pretender, for whom the Jacobites fought as James VIII and III, was second cousin to the reigning Hanoverian George I. The Carlist Wars in Spain started between the adherents of Don Carlos and those of his niece, Isabella II, and there was a similar struggle in Portugal between Dom Miguel and his niece Donna Maria da Gloria. The Bourbon and Orleanist claimants in France were unusual in that they had to go back five or six generations to find their common ancestor.

Scotland had no more than its fair share of such rivalries. At the end of the thirteenth century there were no less than 13 competitors for a vacant throne, among whom Edward I of England undertook to adjudicate. The complicated events which followed included a phase of something like civil war between the supporters of John Balliol and those of Robert Bruce, who was his second cousin once removed, and in the next generation the contest was resumed between Edward Balliol and David Bruce. Thereafter the Scottish succession showed remarkable stability, and for no less than ten generations, dating from the accession in 1371 of the first Stewart king, Robert II, each sovereign was succeeded by his eldest surviving child. Thus on the death of James V in 1542 his week-old daughter Mary was accepted, apparently without challenge, as Queen of Scots. This was the more remarkable because although by that time Europe had seen some notable female rulers – Margaret of Denmark, Norway and Sweden and Isabella of Castile – there were lingering doubts about the acceptability of a queen regnant and about the possibility of the transmission through females of a hereditary right to a throne. Besides, Scottish experience had shown that even within a purely male succession there were areas of possible dispute. The tenure of the Scottish throne by the reigning line had more than once been under threat in the fifteenth century, and the regularity of the parent-child pattern conceals the debatable ground which still existed, in Scotland as elsewhere, within a succession which was broadly hereditary.[1]

While the right to a crown depended on blood relationship, there was a shadow of doubt as to whether it had to be a lawful relationship, to the exclusion of those who were of illegitimate birth or descent. It was not only in earlier centuries and in backward societies that illegitimacy proved to be no insuperable bar to kingship, for in the second half of the fourteenth century Castile and Portugal each received an enduring new dynasty when a bastard seized the throne. Bastards had no reason to be deterred from making claims. Some of the 13 competitors for the Scottish throne at the end of the thirteenth century were descended from illegitimate offspring of kings, and in late sixteenth-century Portugal, when the house of Aviz (itself founded by a bastard) came to an end and there were seven claimants to the throne, one of them was Dom Antonio, Prior of Crato, illegitimate son of the late king's brother. That such claims were becoming increasingly unrealistic was illustrated when the Duke of Monmouth, an illegitimate son of Charles II, challenged the right of his uncle James VII and II in 1685, for, despite the intensity of feeling against the Roman Catholic James, the Protestant champion Monmouth got little support and would have got even less had he not claimed (as indeed Dom Antonio had done, though with less conviction and less credibility) that his parents had been married.

But besides actual bastards there were claimants over whose legitimacy there hovered some uncertainty, arising from the complex medieval marriage laws – laws with which many did not manage to comply and breaches of which could be covered by papal dispensations which were in their turn open to challenge. It is in such shifting sands that the origin lies of the York-Lancaster rivalry in England and the contemporary Douglas-Stewart rivalry in Scotland.[1] When in 1455 the Earl of Douglas denounced James II as 'him who calls himself king of Scots'[2] he was (though apparently not on his own behalf) disputing the right of James to be king. In the next reign Douglas was associated with a challenge to James III by his brother the Duke of Albany, who styled himself 'Alexander IV, King of Scots'. All in all, there were plenty of illustrations of the pitfalls which surrounded the succession and of the chances and changes which might arise in the somewhat fleeting reigns and even lives of monarchs. James III was in the end dismissed from the throne by a party which had his son and heir, and not his brother, as its figurehead. At that juncture James (after explaining sadly 'I was your king this day at morn') in the words of parliamentary record 'happinit to be slane' – rather conveniently, for, had he lived, civil war might well have continued between the father's party and the son's.

When Mary, Queen of Scots, was deposed in 1567 in favour of her son, James VI, she did not happen to be slain. Armed conflict between her adherents and those of James went on intermittently until 1573, and the cessation of hostilities did not bring to an end controversy, conspiracy and negotiations, which continued for most of the remaining 14 years of Mary's life. Such a contest between parent and child was not without parallel. After all, James VII and II was deposed in favour of his daughter Mary and her husband William of Orange, so that the original Jacobites and Williamites were partisans of father and daughter. Perhaps the closest resemblance to the survival of the dethroned Mary alongside her son is to be found in Spain. When Isabella II was deposed in 1868 experiments were made with a republic and with a king of foreign extraction, but after that Isabella's son was made king as Alfonso XII while his mother was still alive, and indeed she survived him by 18 years.

While the protagonists, the actual claimants, in dynastic rivalries were usually related to each other, and sometimes very closely related, the contests were more than mere family quarrels. It was not uncommon for a 'Pretender' to have the support of a foreign power, and internal disputes became the reasons or pretexts for conflicts between nations. Apart from the international 'wars of succession' already mentioned, a foreign power was often ready to stir up trouble by patronising a claimant. This was an old story in Anglo-Scottish relations, for just as Scotland supported Lancaster against York and took up Perkin Warbeck when he claimed the crown worn by Henry VII, so England supported the Earl of Douglas when he renounced his allegiance to James II and the Duke of Albany when he threatened James III. In the Jacobite phase, France, Spain and Sweden all at one time or another lent support – very sparingly – to the Stewart Pretenders. In sixteenth-century Portugal the Prior of Crato received help from France and England and in nineteenth-century Spain Britain supported Isabella while more reactionary powers helped to finance Don Carlos.

Within a land where the succession was in dispute, pretenders were apt to find support in areas remote from the centre, backward in their economic and social structure, inhospitable in their terrain, sometimes divergent racially and linguistically from the bulk of the population and perhaps with separatist tendencies. Thus in Spain the northern provinces of Biscay and Navarre were strongly Carlist, in France the Bourbons found devoted followers in the eastern fringes of Vendée and Brittany, and in the United Kingdom Jacobitism had more support in parts of the Scottish Highlands and in western and north-western England than it had elsewhere. The areas which tended to support pretenders were apt to be the refuge of conservative or reactionary ideas, and of course conflicting political principles were associated with at least some of the dynastic quarrels. It may never have been quite true that the rivalry of *de facto* rulers with pretenders who asserted their *de jure* sovereignty was no more than a cloak for the furtherance of personal ambitions or political principles, but it is unquestionable that behind each party there usually lay convictions which went beyond mere dynastic claims and not infrequently had religious as well as political bases. The association of Scottish Jacobitism with the Episcopal Church and of English Jacobitism with Roman Catholicism, and the contrary association of the Hanoverian cause with Protestantism in England and Presbyterianism in Scotland are obvious examples. Similarly, in France the Legitimists and in Spain the Carlists stood for ultra-conservatism, clericalism and what their enemies would have called obscurantism. Indeed when there was a disputed succession the *de facto* sovereign usually represented if not a liberal or democratic element at least a less conservative element; in contrast the *de jure* case meant support for something like the indefeasible rights of the sovereign by descent. This was inevitable, for the rejection of a prince whose hereditary rights were sound implied a belief in an element of selection or election of a monarch and in the right of the people or their constitutional representatives to choose one.

Historical assessments of the movements in favour of *de jure* monarchs, movements to which the term 'legitimist' may reasonably be applied – though that term begs the question as to which party really had law on its side – have been affected by two factors. One is the 'success bias' which afflicts historical judgment. Historians like to be on the winning side, they seldom admit that things went wrong, and consequently the failures of history get a bad press. Therefore revolts (which failed) tend to be treated with a certain contempt, whereas revolutions (which succeeded) meet with acclaim. On the other hand, though this time in the eyes of the inexpert observer rather than the professional historian, certain legitimist movements have attracted something of the glamour which is apt to attach to lost causes. This has been intensified through association with remote and picturesque regions and societies. There is something 'romantick' about Vendéens and Carlists and certainly not least about Highland Jacobites. Yet, curiously enough, while so much glamour has attached to Queen Mary herself, relatively little of either serious study or sentiment has been attracted by those who kept her standard flying for years after her abdication in 1567. One reason may have been that the military operations included few actions which have found vivid narrators who would impress them on the popular imagination; another may have been that the Marian party was a somewhat heterogeneous body and that it never had a leader possessed of the dash of Montrose or Dundee. But a third may well have been the absence of Mary herself from the scene, after her flight to England in 1568. She assuredly had all the capacity for adventure that her descendant Charles Edward displayed in 1745–6, and had she been actively involved in the campaign or lurking in various parts of Scotland under the protection of devoted followers, rather than languishing in an English prison, one can imagine that the term Marian would have been as familiar and as evocative in history and literature as the term Jacobite. As it is, I recall only once finding that a reference to 'the Hamiltons' elicited (from an unexpected quarter) the immediate response, 'The Hamiltons were Queen's Men'. But one distinguished and gallant twentieth-century Hamilton, General Sir Ian Hamilton, wrote: 'Every Hamilton the wide world over should remember that he has the honour to be connected with every other Hamilton and that he himself is of the very same blood as those who stood by their beautiful Queen on that evil day when the Glaswegians, led by a Murray, were firing at her with their new-fangled cannon'.[3] The general was ill-informed about the nature of Scottish surnames (which are no proof of blood relationships), but he was making an attempt to attach to the Marians something of the glamour of the Jacobites.

Most of the features characteristic of dynastic disputes elsewhere can be detected also in the quarrel between the supporters of Queen Mary and those of her son. The international setting was shaped by relations with France and England, each of which from time to time strove to control Scotland, from which England's security could be threatened. In the 1540s England, 'the auld enemy', had intermittent success in dominating Scotland, and when in 1548 the Scots turned to their 'auld ally' for help to liberate them from English garrisons, the result was a phase of domination by France which culminated in 1559 in a personal union of the two crowns under 'Francis and Mary, King and Queen of France and Scotland'. The Scots then turned to England for help to evict the French occupying forces, and after Elizabeth Tudor intervened in their favour in 1560 it was agreed that both French and English forces should withdraw. Yet Scotland was still in danger of being a satellite: Queen Mary, back in Scotland in 1561, to some extent represented French influence, the reformers and their political supporters represented English influence, and both during her remaining years as Queen and in the early years of her son's reign English and French agents were active in Scotland and Scottish factions constantly appealed to France and England for help. Thus, after Mary's deposition, her party had support, up to a point, from France and later from Spain, while the King's Party had support – however hesitating and grudging – from England.

The geographical distribution of the two parties within Scotland was not simple – far less simple than it was to be in the Jacobite episode – and one of the things to emerge from a study of the Queen's Men is how widely they were spread throughout the country, so that any generalisations must be heavily qualified. The main interest lies in the dividing lines not so much between territories as between great families, with their followers, and familial attachment did not always coincide neatly with topography.

The structure of the following of a great Scottish family was complex, but some study of it is vital to an understanding of politics, because a very large proportion of the population aligned themselves not according to their personal opinions – if they had any – but according to their attachment to the greater men whose views carried most weight. Such attachments may be thought of as consisting broadly of a series of circles of relationships, though some of the circles were intersecting rather than concentric. Closely surrounding the magnate at the centre were two circles: first the obvious one of the immediate family, living together in a home, and then the 'household' in the sense of servants. Usually when a man of even modest standing was involved in any kind of trouble he would be supported by half a dozen or a dozen 'servitors'. No doubt these included the genuine domestics, and there is ample testimony that every Scottish family of standing had enormous numbers of such employees, serving in return for board and lodging, which a landlord could readily furnish from the rents he received in kind. Observers often commented on this, and a visitor in 1618 spoke of nobles keeping 30, 40, 50 or more servants, besides giving alms every day to three or four score poor people at the gate.[4] But, besides 'servitors' who were innocent domestics, others might be hired ruffians who were engaged because of their strong arms and their skill with weapons. It may be doubted if the 24 'gentlemen' in the household of Kennedy of Bargany, an Ayrshire laird, would qualify for that designation today.

5

Beyond the immediate family and the household there was the extended family, a group consciously and definably related by blood. How far it reaches out is a matter of speculation. It has been suggested that it may have been delimited by the degrees of kinship within which marriage was forbidden by canon law. In 1215 the forbidden degrees had been reduced from seven to four, and as the counting was done by inclusive reckoning this meant that any couple with a common grandfather or great-grandfather could not marry. This was reasonable enough, though few people were able to identify all their great-grandparents and it was all too common for a couple who wanted to have their marriage annulled to 'discover' that they had married in ignorance of a relationship which would invalidate their marriage. However, for the purpose of attachment within a 'following' it would be sufficient to be able to reckon the paternal male ancestry back three generations, and most people could do that.

Beyond the extended family lay other families or family-groups, comprising the cadet branches of the main line, usually connected to it by an identifiable common ancestor and of course sharing its surname. Going still farther, beyond people demonstrably related by blood, there was the association created by a common surname which did not necessarily denote kinship. By the sixteenth century the great majority of people in Lowland Scotland had surnames, and we hear much of social groups which were based on surnames, but such groups were far more elastic than groups based on blood, because people could be incorporated into such a group by the simple process of adopting the appropriate name. Not only could a tenant adopt the surname of his landlord – and frequently did – but the surname of a leading man could be applied, almost generically, to his followers, so that when we hear of activities by large numbers of 'Murrays' or 'Douglases' it would be rash to believe that everyone involved was actually called by one of those surnames. The surname was a convenient label, and in the minority of James V, when the Douglas Earls of Angus were out of favour, it was suggested that Douglases should change their name to Stewart and so shed a stigma.[5] So much emotional loyalty seems to have focussed round the surname that King James VI remarked, 'I would there were not a surname in Scotland, for they mak all the cummer [disturbance]'.[6]

While men could thus adopt a surname to indicate their attachment or allegiance, the significance of the surname may not always be at once apparent, owing to the titles of peers. Although most 'Lords' – that is, peers below the rank of Earls – were known by their surnames, every Earl was known by a territorial designation. Equations like Douglas and Angus, Kennedy and Cassillis, must constantly be kept in mind.[7] Fortunately few of the territorial titles happened to be also common surnames, but there is at least one hazard: Crawfords are not to be found in the following of the Earl of Crawford, who was a Lindsay and was followed by Lindsays.

There were still farther ties, beyond kinship and surnames. There were territorial links, the relationships between a magnate and his feudal vassals who held land by charter of him as their superior, and, at a lower level, his tenants holding by lease. Contrary to what has often been said, it is clear from rent-rolls that tenants not only often retained their holdings for long periods but commonly passed them on to their heirs, and this created a tradition of hereditary service to some great family. Similar to such ties by tenure were the ties created by bonds of manrent, whereby a lesser man undertook to serve a greater man and take part in his quarrels, in return for protection. All in all, there were plenty of clients of one kind or another who were accustomed to serve the magnates out of traditional loyalty, out of fear, or out of hope of reward. Something of the pattern created by those various ties is explicit in a remission granted early in 1566 to the 2nd Earl of Arran, head of the house of Hamilton, and his dependents, who were classified into those of his surname, the servitors of his household, 'wagers' whom he paid for their armed assistance, men 'depending of old on the house' of the said earl, the tenants and dwellers on his lands.[8] The document lists nearly 300 persons under those various heads, and this was not exceptional. In the 1580s a Highland chief went visiting – apparently with quite peaceful intent – accompanied by 86 followers, and the Master of Hay, heir of Lord Hay, had an entourage numbering 48.[9] When violence was intended, the numbers could be readily increased. The Hamilton remission just mentioned shows this, and the Master of Glamis, whose social and economic level was far below that of the Earl of Arran, could muster about 240 men for a private feud.[10]

One reason why the Queen's Men do not fall into a simple territorial pattern within which those complex followings could exist and operate is that magnates were not infrequently at feud, or at any rate at variance, with their neighbours, and some such rivalries were among the most persistent features of the period. Perhaps the greatest of them, that between Hamilton and Lennox (who were always on different sides), was essentially dynastic, but the families were neighbours in the Glasgow area. More definitely territorial was the series of rivalries among Argyll, Atholl, Huntly and Moray, which extended right across the country: Atholl and Argyll were almost always at loggerheads, Atholl and Huntly frequently so, and Huntly never had easy relations with his other neighbour Moray. In Fife, Lord Lindsay and the Earl of Rothes were quarrelsome neighbours who were often in opposite camps. Local disputes in Angus no doubt had something to do with the divided party allegiances which were so conspicuous there. On the other hand, the fact that there were few feuds in East Lothian may explain why there was so much uniformity of opinion there, and in the Borders, while feuds were numerous and vicious they did not always hinder political co-operation. The contrasting pattern of the habitual alliance of two families is commemorated in the lines:

> Home and Hepburn, hald ye together,
> If ye dissever ye shall rue it for ever.

It is easy to see why, although followings under the leadership of magnates played a large part in constituting the parties and factions of the sixteenth century, and not least the Queen's Men and their opponents, we do not find in Scotland the conspicuous territorial loyalties familiar between rival claimants for thrones in other countries. There is more similarity in the ideological pattern, with the Marian party cast for the conservative role. If it had a political principle, that was surely the acceptance of legally constituted government or authority. It was true that, if precedent counted for anything, the succession to the Scottish throne could at any time be determined by statute, but on the other hand the regularity and continuity of the succession, generation by generation, must have been detrimental to the concept of statutory definition and have greatly strengthened the cause of a reigning monarch against a challenger. If Mary's supporters did not wholly repudiate a right of deposition they at least denied that the deposition of Mary was justified. Yet we need not believe that all the Queen's Men had argued the rights and wrongs of the case against her, for some of them took a simpler view: as long as she had been on the throne, they had been habituated to her rule, and after her deposition – or rather her extorted abdication – she was still in their eyes a lawful ruler. Thus, while attachment to Mary as an individual is not to be ignored, not all 'Marians' saw the contest in personal terms. James's supporters – who, incidentally, could not in the nature of things be moved in any degree by personal attachment to an infant or at best a precocious boy – perforce took their stand expressly on the contention that a sovereign could lawfully be deposed and that Mary justly deserved deposition.

That the Queen's Party thus stood for a conservative attitude in internal politics is plain enough, but the issues between Queen's Men and King's Men do not admit of a single or simple explanation, either personal or political. What they did amount to, what motives prompted men to align themselves as they did, should emerge in this book. Some of the political attitudes involved, and in particular attitudes to the monarchy, were deeply-rooted in the national consciousness and reflected centuries of history (or, more often, what men imagined to have been history). Religious dissensions contributed to the conflict, but were only in small measure responsible for shaping the two parties, because neither on religion nor on attitudes to foreign powers was the issue clear-cut. Queen's Men and King's Men certainly did not equate neatly with Roman Catholics and Protestants or with Francophiles and Anglophiles. There were many shades of ecclesiastical opinion rather than a simple division between Roman Catholics and Protestants, even although the final session of the Council of Trent, which concluded in 1563, had at last defined exactly what beliefs the papacy expected of its supporters. Besides, while there were in the King's Party only a few men of Roman Catholic sympathies, there were vast numbers of Protestants in the Queen's Party. After all, Roman Catholics and Protestants were not yet, if they ever were, automatically attached to one or other of the political schools of thought, and it may be assumed that at least some of the Protestants who were in Mary's party were there because their political outlook was conservative. At the same time, some of the divisions in Scotland which helped to shape the situation in which the two parties confronted each other had arisen from the progress of the Reformation and its effects on Scotland's foreign relations. To that extent, the origins of the alignment can be found in the generation or more during which some Scots had begun to adhere to reformed doctrines and to challenge the traditional roles of England as the 'auld enemy' and of France as the 'auld ally'.

# 2
# THE SHAPING OF A REVOLUTION

*1525* Statute against Lutheran literature
*1542* Battle of Solway Moss
Death of James V
Accession of Mary
*1543* Arran Governor
Treaty with Henry VIII concluded and then repudiated
*1544–5* Scotland invaded by Hertford
*1546* Burning of George Wishart
Murder of Cardinal Beaton
*1547* Battle of Pinkie
English occupation of south-east Scotland
*1548* Queen Mary sent to France
*1554* Mary of Guise Governor
*1557* 'First Bond' of Lords of Congregation
*1558* Accession of Elizabeth Tudor in England
*1559–60* Insurrection in Scotland
*1560* Treaty of Berwick
Treaty of Edinburgh
'Reformation Parliament'

Protestantism had a firm footing in Scotland long before a parliament met in 1560 to abolish papal authority and forbid the celebration of the Latin mass. Some recent assessments have underestimated the strength of the attachment to the cause of reform and have even suggested that when the religious change was officially made it was no more than a matter of manipulation for political reasons. This reinterpretation is not merely the result of one of those changes of fashion which periodically afflict historical writing. The fact is that in the later twentieth century concepts of moral guilt are at a discount and the doctrine of sin has become unfashionable. Nowadays the church, instead of calling sinners to repentance, seems to devote a lot of its resources to reaching an accommodation with sin – without repentance – and to lend its patronage to social and political programmes based on appeals to envy, hatred, malice and all uncharitableness. Thus few now have any appreciation of the despair of those who admit to being 'miserable sinners' and of the solace which they can find in the Passion of Christ. It was not so in the sixteenth century.

No one has yet attempted to write the history of religious thought in Scotland, and very likely the material is insufficient to present anything like a complete picture. Yet we are not without information as we approach the period of the Reformation. A volume issued by the Scottish Text Society, called *Devotional Pieces in Verse and Prose*, contains a variety of items which were known in Scotland in the late fifteenth and early sixteenth centuries. They were not all of native composition, some had been written at earlier dates, some were based on Latin models, but their acceptance in Scotland shows the trend of Scottish piety in the two generations when the Reformation was taking shape. The consciousness of sin is all-pervasive and the remedy which is offered is contemplation of the Passion and its details, in describing which there is no squeamishness. Early sixteenth-century Scots vernacular is not easy to follow, and quotations must be presented in modernised form, though the moving vividness of the original is thereby lost. Thus:

> Through Thy mercy and this memory
> Of Thy pains and the sorrow
> Grant that the remembrance of Thy passion
> Be to me full remission.

or:

> If you your life in sin has led
> To ask me mercy be you not dread
> For the least drop I for you shed
> May cleanse you soon
> And all the sin this world within
> That you have done.

This thought could find expression and practice within contemporary orthodoxy, and the obsession with the Passion was manifested in devotion to the Holy Blood, with which altars and fraternities were associated,[1] and in representations of the instruments of the Passion, for example at the collegiate church of Seton. But it was also true that it was hard to reconcile some of the devotional thought with official teaching, and, while some continued to invest in masses for the souls of the departed, misgivings must have been caused and clerical eyebrows raised by lines like these:

> Continual and devout meditation of the Passion is better than to fast a year on bread and water and daily scourge himself until the blood run, or daily read a psalter.
> Suppose all holy church pray for a man, he may get more grace himself for remembering of the Passion.
> Devout remembrance of the Passion is better than our Lady and all the saints prayed for him.

Such emphasis on individual, personal faith was in line with teaching outside standard orthodoxy. And such teaching existed. Hardly anything is known of the enduring influence of the earlier movements of reform which had reached Scotland in some strength with Lollards from England and Hussites from Bohemia in the early fifteenth century, but certain radical views did here and there survive. The 'Lollards of Kyle', Ayrshire gentlemen who were in trouble with the authorities in 1494, were accused of holding some extremely irregular opinions, and even some of their milder tenets were startling enough: 'After the consecration in the mass there remains bread. . . . The mass profiteth not the souls that are in purgatory. . . . We should not pray to the glorious Virgin Mary, but to God only'.[2] Any surviving Lollardy would receive fresh vitality from the German reformation. Luther's defiant issue of his theses against indulgences took place in 1517 and within eight years the Scottish parliament legislated against the import of Lutheran literature. Scotland had strong commercial links with

Germany, the Low Countries and the ports on both sides of the entrance to the Baltic, where Scottish merchants not only traded but settled in significant numbers. There was any number of channels by which the ferment caused by Luther's revolt could affect at any rate the coastal burghs of eastern Scotland. The doctrines which were being disseminated are represented in 'Patrick's Places', a digest of evangelical theology attributed to Patrick Hamilton, who was executed for heresy in 1528 after associating with Lutherans in Germany. They put sharp emphasis on the Passion as the one remedy for sin, with the reiterated proclamation: 'Christ bought us with His blood, Christ washed us with His blood, Christ came into the world to save sinners, Christ was the price that was given for us and our sins, Christ has made satisfaction for us and our sin'. The stress was on the futility of works and the necessity of faith, by which alone sinners are justified: 'Whosoever thinketh to be saved by his works, denieth Christ is our Saviour, that Christ died for him. . . . To what end should He have died for thee, if any works of thine might have saved thee?'[3] Here, with complete assurance, was the message that men had been craving, and it was a message fatal to the mass, which was bound to be denounced as idolatrous (because it involved the worship of a wafer), blasphemous (because it put something else in place of Christ's work on Calvary) and derogatory to the majesty of God and the mediation of Christ (because it set up the priest as a mediator between God and man). The whole paraphernalia of the medieval system was under threat.

Between 1525, when parliament passed the act against Lutheran books, and the opening of Mary's reign 17 years later, there was a whole series of incidents – iconoclastic outbreaks, violence against clergy, disturbances in churches, prosecutions for heresy and a few executions – as well as expressions of contempt for the irregular lives of priests and for superstitious devotion to relics. The evidence, while not sparse, is almost fortuitous in the sense that we have few relevant archives of ecclesiastical courts and have to rely in the main on information about cases in which the crown took action, either by prosecution or (more frequently) pardon.[4] Yet it yields almost 100 names, mainly in connection with incidents between 1538 and 1543. At that stage the Reformation was, as we should expect, essentially an east coast phenomenon: about a fifth of the names are from Dundee, a quarter from the Firth of Forth area, about a third from Angus, Mearns and Aberdeenshire. Less than a tenth come from Glasgow and Ayrshire, where Lutheranism may have counted for less than the lingering influence of Lollardy. The recurrence of certain names, especially in Dundee, where there were three Annands, three Wedderburns, two Patersons, two Rollocks and two Fleshers, may point to the existence of something like family 'cells'. While most of the culprits were relatively insignificant socially, some noble and lairdly families which were to have a persistent Protestant tradition were represented: a son of the Earl of Glencairn had a remission for heresy in 1539, a son of Lord Ochiltree had one in 1537 for casting down an image in the church of Ayr, and a list of persons guilty of heretical inclinations includes the Earl Marischal, the heir of the Earl of Rothes and over a dozen lairds.

The 1525 statute against Lutheran writings was ratified by parliament in

1535 with an addition to the effect that anyone who had such books must hand them over to the bishop within 40 days,[5] and in 1541 parliament issued a code of nine acts which would have been unnecessary if earlier legislation had not been worse than fruitless: the sacraments were to be respected; the Blessed Virgin was to be the object of worship, honour and intercession; papal authority was not to be impugned; 'kirks and kirkmen' were to be reformed (the former in their fabric, the latter in their 'habit and manners'); 'congregations or conventicles to commune or dispute of the holy scripture' were prohibited; heretics, even if they abjured, were to hold no public office; assistance was not to be given to fugitive heretics; informers were to be rewarded; and statues of saints were not to be 'cast doun' or otherwise treated irreverently.[6] These statutes give a fair idea of what was going on in the later years of James V.

It is safe to assume that by this time some of the verses which were later included in the collection of *The Good and Godly Ballads*[7] were circulating, to reinforce at a popular level the reformed theology of preachers and to bring the spiritual solace which, as the *Devotional Pieces* prove, men had been seeking.

> Where I could not the Law fulfil,
> My works made me no supply,
> So blind and weak was my free will,
> That hated the verity:
> My conscience cast me ever in care,
> The Devil he drove me to despair,
> And hell was ever before my eye.
>
> God had great pity on my woe,
> And above measure showed me grace....
> To His beloved Son he said,
> The time of mercy draws near
> To save man and the fiend invade;
> Therefore, my heartly son so dear,
> Go free them from the fiend's feud;
> You must overthrow sin, hell and death,
> Then man restore both whole and strong.

There is again preoccupation with the Passion:

> For us that Blessed Bairn was born
> For us He was both rent and torn
> For us He crowned was with thorn,
> Christ has my heart aye.
> For us He shed his precious blood,
> For us He was nailed on the rood,
> For us He in many battle stood,
> Christ has my heart aye.

And the Passion was linked with the Eucharist in a manner habitual in both medieval and evangelical thought:

> Our Saviour Christ, King of Grace,
> With God the Father made our peace

> And with His bloody wounds fell
> Has us redeemed from the hell.
>
> And He, that we should not forget,
> Gave us His body for to eat
> In form of bread, and gave us syne
> His blood to drink in form of wine.
>
> Who will receive this sacrament
> Should have true faith, and sin repent:
> Who uses it unworthily
> Receives death eternally.

It is noticeable that the words of the second stanza echo the phraseology of an item in *Devotional Pieces*: 'He ordained His precious body to us as sacrament in form of bread'. These early Scottish Protestants, who risked their fortunes and their lives, might have paraphrased the Declaration of Arbroath: 'It is not for power or riches or material security that we contend, but for Redemption alone'.

It is not likely that the hearts of a vast number were so touched by the evangelical message that it provided the most important motive in their actions, but at the same time there was an all but universal belief that every human activity and all public policy must be fitted into the context of a scheme for man's salvation. This was generally taken for granted and few if any would have publicly denied it.

By the later 1530s impetus was coming not only from the other side of the North Sea but also from the other side of the Border. Hitherto Scots who did not know Latin and wanted to understand the Bible had had access only to translations which circulated in manuscript, but in 1526 Tyndale's translation of the New Testament into English became available and in a matter of months it reached Scotland.[8] Before many more years passed, Henry VIII, though far from favouring anything like Protestantism, had thrown off papal authority and was dissolving the monasteries. It had long been evident that there was in Scotland a political party which might be called anglophile, and in the last years of James V's minority (1526–8) a pro-English administration had been headed by Archibald Douglas, 6th Earl of Angus, who had married Margaret Tudor, sister of Henry VIII and widow of James IV. The belief that there might be a better future in peace with England than in the traditional hostility was reinforced when England provided an example of ecclesiastical change and also furnished a refuge for a number of Scottish reformers who were in trouble with the authorities at home. That the religious influences on Scotland were now Anglican as well as Lutheran appeared in the articles on which Sir John Borthwick was indicted in 1540: besides reading the works of Lutheran divines he had approved the 'English heresies' and urged them on his fellow-countrymen.[9] Nor was the association of Scottish reformers with Henrician England merely underground or surreptitious. From time to time Henry sent envoys to James pressing him to follow the example of England, and negotiations for a meeting between the two kings implied that Anglo-Scottish agreement in ecclesiastical policy was under consideration. Here can be seen the first indications of the concept of ideological conformity as one element in a satellite relationship between the two countries. James rejected Henry's proposals, and the close attachment to France which he formed by his two successive French marriages intensified resentment among anglophiles and reformers alike, so that before his death in 1542 there were clearly two parties – a reforming and anglophile and a conservative and francophile. How strong the former was at this stage it is hard to say. To adopt phraseology which has been used in speaking about the reformers in Italy,[10] we know about the 'diers' – the handful of Protestant martyrs – and about the 'flyers' who recanted or took refuge in England or on the continent, but we can only guess at the number of 'liars' who were successful in concealing their views. There is, however, a story which crops up in three sources, apparently independent of each other, [11] to the effect that there was a 'Black List' of noblemen and gentry disaffected to the church, a list prepared by the clergy and put into the hands of the King, partly by way of a threat and partly to tempt the acquisitive monarch to act against heretics as he had acted against others whose wealth excited his cupidity. Had such a list survived, it would have been the first of many lists which indicate party alignment over the next 40 years or so, but anyone who studies the records of individuals and families from the late 1530s onwards can make an intelligent guess as to the names which would have been on such a list.

Ecclesiastical disaffection apart, the events which closed James's reign in 1542 reflect a clear lack of enthusiasm, to say no more, for papal policy. In December 1538 the Pope at last ordered the execution of his bull excommunicating Henry VIII, and it looked for a time as if a crusade would be launched against schismatic England by the Emperor and the King of France (with his ally Scotland). But with the renewal of friction between France and the Empire the coalition dissolved and all that came of the grand design was an Anglo-Scottish war in which the Scots were not only unaided but divided. When James V mustered his army, some who attended did so only 'to show their obedience, against their hearts',[12] but many did not attend, and, while absence from 'the host' was not unusual, this time the absentees included a significant number of men, mainly lairds in Angus, Kincardineshire and Aberdeenshire, who were guilty also of disputing on the scriptures and reading forbidden books and who had a subsequent record of attachment to the reforming cause. It is incredible that this group was unique or that the inhabitants of other eastern districts, like Fife and East Lothian, did not hold similar opinions. When the reluctant force assembled by James V did ultimately engage the English at Solway Moss (24 November 1542), few Scots were killed but 1200 were captured. Borderers (who always saw their own private advantages in Anglo-Scottish war) slew some of their compatriots, robbed others and – so it was said – seized some nobles and turned them over to the enemy. If some nobles did indeed surrender rather than die in the service of a king in whom they had lost confidence it need occasion no surprise, but one reason for their disaffection, as for the absence of others from 'the host', may have been that Scotland was adventuring on behalf of the papacy against an England which had rejected Roman supremacy. Certainly Lord Maxwell, who was accused of deliberately fomenting the panic which led to the rout, was soon to appear as a champion of the vernacular Bible. Attachment to the Reformation did not in itself involve commitment to any particular political policy, and we shall see how, in later years, reformers were often divided in their political allegiance, but at this stage the issue was so clear-cut that Protestantism and advocacy of amity with England were inseparable.

However, leaving aside any 'Black List', and behaviour before and at Solway, the conclusive proof that there had already been strong support for pro-English and reforming opinions in the lifetime of James V is the fact that, almost immediately on his death, it was possible to form an administration committed to a measure of reform and ready for close alliance, indeed union, with the anti-papal England of Henry VIII.

James died three weeks after the defeat of his army and the crown fell to his week-old daughter Mary. The divided state of the nation was at once illustrated by a contest over the regency. The obvious candidate was James Hamilton, 2nd Earl of Arran, who was heir presumptive throughout the reign and was to end his chequered career as the figurehead of Queen Mary's Men in their war against the supporters of James VI. The Hamilton family, which is believed to have originated in Northumberland, was established in Scotland before the end of the thirteenth century. The foundation of their fortunes was laid when their ancestor received from King Robert Bruce certain lands in West Lothian and Lanarkshire, including the estate of Cadzow (pronounced Cadyow), which came to be known as Hamilton and which remained with the family for over six and a half centuries until pressure of taxation led to its disposal. The grant by Bruce was a reward for joining him after his victory at Bannockburn – a piece of opportunism which not many of the line were to be clever enough to imitate, for they were often on the losing side. But there was to be one more outstanding example of successful opportunism, on the outbreak of the campaign between James II and the 9th Earl of Douglas in 1455, when Lord Hamilton, who had been a supporter of his neighbour Douglas, suddenly deserted him and so, as a chronicler remarked, 'left the Earl of Douglas all begylit'.[13] Hamilton was rewarded for this *volte-face* by a confirmation of his existing estates and a grant of more, but an additional reward came some years later, when he married the Princess Mary, daughter of James II. She had previously been married to Thomas Boyd, who had been created Earl of Arran, and the son of the Hamilton marriage was elevated to an earldom of Arran in 1503. The island of Arran, which was to remain with the family for four centuries, gave them the lymphad or galley which figures on their coat of arms and brought their territories into the fringe of the Highlands, where they were neighbours of the Campbells, Earls of Argyll.

The royal marriage had not at first brought the Hamiltons very near the throne. James III, whose sister Lord Hamilton had married, had three sons; in the end only one of them, James IV, survived, but by that time he was already a married man with the prospect of a family. Besides, James III also had a brother, and that brother's son, John, Duke of Albany, was nearer the throne than the Hamiltons. But the Hamilton prospects improved, if that is a suitable way to represent the catastrophes which overtook the senior lines. When James IV was killed at Flodden he left only a baby son, and a second boy, born posthumously, lived less than two years. Besides, by that time the Duke of Albany, though married for some years, had no family. The prospective failure of the Albany line brought the Hamiltons nearer to the throne, and they became closer still when the Duchess of Albany died without children in 1523 and Albany himself did not marry again and died in 1536. It was at that point that the Earl of Arran – by this time the 2nd Earl, who had been born about 1516 and succeeded his father in 1529 – was for the first time actually heir presumptive. The King married in 1537 and after his first wife died childless married again in 1538; he started to raise a family, but his two sons died in 1541 and when James died in 1542 he left only the fragile life of an infant daugher between Arran and the throne. One need not believe that Arran was coldly calculating or that he would have wished for the extinction of the senior line; but the Hamilton family must surely have watched these rapid changes with alternating hopes and dismay.

It was Arran, then, who was the obvious candidate for the governorship when James V died. But his claim was challenged by Cardinal David Beaton and the conservative party, almost certainly because Arran was believed to be unsound in religion – not without reason, to judge from his claim that for five years he had considered the Pope to be no more than a bishop 'and that a very evil bishop'.[14] Arran had the support of a batch of lords who had been captured in the rout at Solway and released on giving undertakings to further Henry VIII's designs in Scotland, and also of that veteran English agent Archibald Douglas, 6th Earl of Angus, who had headed a pro-English administration in the 1520s. When his ascendancy was brought to an end by James V in 1528 Angus had taken refuge in England, whence he now returned. Arran and the anglophiles were too strong for the Cardinal, who was put under restraint, and when parliament met in March, attended by 12 earls and 18 lords – one of the largest attendances between 1513 and 1567 – it authorised commissioners to treat for the marriage of the infant Scottish Queen to Henry's five-year-old son Edward and passed an act permitting the reading of the Bible in the vernacular. The act (against which the prelates protested) was introduced by Lord Maxwell, who had been accused of disloyalty at Solway and had since been primed by Henry. Both central and local government authorised the preaching of 'the true Word of God', there was said to be a great demand for religious literature from England, and the Bible, which people claimed to have been reading in secret for years, emerged from concealment 'to be seen lying upon almost every gentleman's table'.[15] The authorities did not intend to encourage radical tendencies any more than their mentor Henry VIII did, but there were unauthorised attacks on ecclesiastical establishments in Perth, Dundee and Edinburgh, laymen seized revenues of religious houses, and writings defaming 'all estates both spiritual and temporal' were in circulation.[16]

Arran's 'godly fit', however, did not last. As was to appear again and again, he was the most irresolute of men, and at this point he was peculiarly vulnerable to pressure. The parliament of March 1543, which formally declared him Governor, also pronounced him 'second person of the realm' and entitled to succeed to the throne, failing Mary and her issue. Arran needed such a declaration, for he was the child of a marriage which had followed a divorce whose validity was open to question, and consequently his legitimacy could be challenged.[17] The man most likely to challenge it was Matthew Stewart, 4th Earl of Lennox. Lennox's grandmother and Arran's father were children of Princess Mary, daughter of James II, by her marriage to Lord Hamilton, and if Arran was not legitimate then it was Lennox and not he who was heir presumptive. It was at this point that the Hamilton-Lennox rivalry, which was to be one of the leading features of the events of the next 40 years, first became acute. Lennox, after many years in France, now returned to Scotland as a kind of object lesson to Arran, and Cardinal Beaton, head of the ecclesiastical judicature in Scotland, could point out to Arran that it was in his power to deal with matters like legitimacy and validity of marriages. Another actor who was to play an important part in coming years also arrived from France at this juncture – John Hamilton, Arran's half-brother, Commendator of Paisley and later Beaton's successor as Archbishop of St Andrews. John possessed the resolution which Arran lacked and he threw his weight behind the blandishments of the Cardinal. Within a few months the Governor abjured his lapse from orthodoxy and joined forces with Beaton and the conservatives. A parliament in December rejected the proposed English alliance, reaffirmed the alliance with France and passed a fresh act against heresy: because 'there is great murmur that heretics more and more rises and spread within this realm, sowing damnable opinions contrary to the faith and laws of holy church', the ecclesiastical authorities were exhorted to take action and were promised the Governor's support.[18] The *volte-face* could not have been more complete.

In a divided nation, the new policy, like the previous one, commanded a good deal of support, not only from Beaton and the churchmen. Two earls who, although they had attended the March parliament, had not approved of the admission of that English agent, Angus, to the council, or of the confinement of the Cardinal, turned up in December with seven other earls, besides nine lords, while seven earls who had been present in March were absent in December. Thus, while the administration in general won the approval of those who had opposed the diplomatic and ecclesiastical policy adopted in March, it lost those who had favoured it, and the latter, who stood out against the reactionary line in politics and religion now being taken by Arran, clearly represented pro-English and anti-Roman opinion. The Earls of Angus, Cassillis and Glencairn (who all declined to attend Mary's coronation a week after Arran's capitulation to the Cardinal), as well as Lords Somerville and Maxwell, were clearly of this mind, and they were joined by that newcomer to the political scene, the Earl of Lennox. He had come back from France to bolster up the French and conservative party against Arran, but the Hamilton-Lennox hostility was such that when Arran's policy changed Lennox became a champion of the English cause. There was soon talk of his marriage (which took place in 1545) to Margaret Douglas, Angus's daughter by Margaret Tudor, sister of Henry VIII and widow of James IV. Lennox thus became the husband of a woman who, failing Henry's own issue, stood next to Mary Stewart in the English succession. As son-in-law of Angus and nephew by marriage of Henry VIII he was cast for leadership of Scottish anglophiles.

Early in 1544 Henry defined what he expected from his Scottish supporters, headed by Lennox, Angus, Cassillis and Glencairn: they were to cause the Word of God to be preached, to endeavour to put Mary into Henry's hands and have him made Protector during her minority, and to secure him in the possession of certain Border strongholds. In return, he would send an army to co-operate with them, and on their victory Lennox was to be Governor. This involved the concept of a satellite administration, established with the aid of English arms and bound to England by a common ideology. It would be easy to make too much of the ideological commitment, and perhaps safer to speak of the Angus-Lennox faction rather than of a Protestant, or even of an anglophile, faction. Yet, whatever the precise motives, when the faction was in arms against Arran two or three times at the end of 1543 and in 1544 it had massive support. We have the names of some hundreds of men who were subsequently either prosecuted or pardoned for being on the losing side at this point, which is the first occasion when it is possible to compile lists substantial enough to construct from them some analysis of party alignment.

The faction which challenged Arran's reactionary policy was under the leadership of the Earls of Angus, Lennox, Glencairn, Cassillis, Huntly, Rothes, Crawford, Erroll, Morton and Marischal and Lords Lindsay, Glamis, Innermeath, Somerville and Gray, and the composition of its lower echelons was determined by the structure of Scottish society and the nature of the followings of great men. It is not surpising that the Douglases of Borg, Drumlanrig, Pittendreich, Pumpherston and Whittinghame followed Angus, head of the Douglas kin and name, or that Buchanans, whose home was in the Lennox area, followed the Earl of Lennox. Territorial influence may sometimes have extended beyond the direct power of landlords or feudal superiors, for one sees the hand of Lord Gray, and perhaps also of Lord Glamis, in the presence of lairds from the sheriffdom of Forfar (of which Gray was sheriff) and from adjoining east Perthshire – Carnegies, Maule of Panmure, Charteris of Kinfauns and perhaps Moncrieff of that ilk. It is less easy to account for a group from what may be called southern Perthshire – Drummonds, Murray of Tullibardine, Haldane of Gleneagles and Stirling of Keir. The appearance of a good many Fife lairds – Balfours, Colvilles, Learmonths, Sandilands of St Monans and Wemyss of that ilk – may have been due to the influence of Lord Lindsay, who was sheriff of Fife, but one wonders how far some of them were moved mainly by animosity against Cardinal Beaton, whom they were to conspire to murder within less than two years. Angus's own sphere of influence lay not in the sheriffdom from which he took his title but mainly in the south-east, and this may have had something to do with the support his faction had from Cockburns, Homes, Haigs and at least one Ker (Cessford), as well as Johnstone of Elphinstone and perhaps Dundas of that ilk. Glencairn and Cassillis would be responsible in the same way for the presence of Ayrshire lairds, especially their own cadets of the names of Cunningham and Kennedy, as well as Dalrymple of that ilk and Pollock from adjoining Renfrewshire. In the far south-west,

Maxwells took the line which the reforming and anglophile Lord Maxwell had taken, and continued to adhere to it after he had changed sides.

One striking feature of Lennox's operations at this stage was the unwonted participation of a number of Highland chiefs, who at that period seldom took part in civil strife in the Lowlands; but this was not purely civil strife, for Henry VIII sponsored what was in effect a separatist administration in the Western Highlands and Islands, based on a lingering loyalty to the once semi-independent lordship of the Isles (which had been annexed to the crown in 1493). West Highlanders, with their habitual disregard of the claims of the crown to their loyalty, were prepared to be Henry's tools, and among the men who were subsequently found guilty of treason were MacLeods of Harris and Dunvegan, the Captain of Clanranald, Cameron of Lochiel, MacKinnon of Strathordale, MacNeil of Barra, Macleans of Duart, Lochbuie, Coll and Ardgour, MacQuarrie of Ulva and two lairds in the old Stewart territory of Bute – James Stewart, the sheriff, and Bannatyne of Kames – who may have found it congenial to follow a Stewart Earl of Lennox. On no occasion in the period were the Highlanders as united in support for a purely Scottish faction as they were at this point under the auspices of Henry VIII.

Leaving the Highlanders aside, a great many of the names which appear among the supporters of Angus and Lennox at this stage will recur again and again in later lists at each crisis, and there seem to have been cases where an allegiance which was to endure had already been established. Certainly some of those supporters of Angus and Lennox were consistently faithful to the reforming cause in later years, and a fair amount of the support came from areas which were already much influenced by reforming thought – Angus, Fife, East Lothian and Ayrshire. Principles and policies seem even to have outweighed some familial attachments: the Hamiltons of Briggs, Crawfordjohn, Fingalton, Haggs, Humbie, Innerwick, Orbiston and Millburn, most of whom were to have clear records as Protestants, did not support Arran, head of their house, when he abandoned the reforming cause, but fought alongside his dynastic rival, Lennox.

Conflicting ideologies and the traditional affiliations among Scots were not the only factors which were operating. Material inducements were held out by England on the one hand, by the Scottish civil and ecclesiastical authorities on the other. Henry's distribution of pensions, which had started at a modest level of £100 or £200 and soon rose in a competitive market to the level of £1000, may have produced at least professions of support for him, but the Cardinal had ecclesiastical property at his disposal to win professions of allegiance to the church, and Arran's administration could offer pensions to rival Henry's. Then in 1544 and 1545 Henry had recourse to a policy of frightfulness, with devastating invasions of south-eastern Scotland under the Earl of Hertford, and their results are hard to assess: they could hardly win friends, but some Scots became collaborators with the English out of fear, and others, blaming the Cardinal and Arran for bringing such attacks on the country, returned to support for the English alliance. Events in February 1545 give a glimpse of the diverse influences which shaped alignment. Angus, converted to patriotism by a pension from the Scottish government, led a force to victory over the English at Ancrum, and Lindsay and Rothes imitated his return to Scottish allegiance; but some Scots, including Douglases who bore Angus's name and at least one Highland chief, MacNeil of Gigha, fought on the English side. Lennox himself did not desist from support for Henry, and, appointed lieutenant by the English King, continued operations in the south-west. If some Scots were thus won back to loyalty to their government, others capitulated to pressure put on them to return to professions of orthodoxy. The Cardinal and Arran were trying to persuade Rothes, Gray, Ogilvy and Glamis to abandon their heretical leanings, and it was at this point and a little later that Huntly, Gray, Argyll, Stewart of Doune and Arbuthnott, and no doubt many more, received charters and similar grants in return for promises to support the church. Argyll, besides, received lands forfeited by Lennox.[19]

It must not be thought that support for either the religious policy which Arran had adopted during his 'godly fit' or for the marriage of the Scottish Queen into a schismatic English dynasty necessarily involved any rejection of the essentials of orthodox theology. After all, in the same year as Henry VIII's Archbishop of Canterbury had superintended the publication of a new version of the Bible, which was to be placed in all churches, Henry's parliament has passed the Six Articles, upholding transubstantiation, communion in one kind, clerical celibacy, vows of chastity, private masses and auricular confession. Thus it was quite logical that Scottish landowners like Hay of Yester and Ogilvy of Findlater should continue the endowment of collegiate churches, and when so late as 1546 Lord Fleming, who had supported the English marriage in 1543 and took part with Angus and Lennox against Arran in 1544, founded the collegiate church of Biggar – the last of the Scottish collegiate churches – he was not inconsistent and his action was in line with that being taken in the England which the Scots proposed to imitate. At the same time, whatever success the government might have in diverting support from Angus and Lennox, and however strong the attachment to traditional beliefs and devotion, it was not possible to check the growth of heretical views, which were liable to punishment in Henrician England just as they were in Scotland. There were some more executions, all at Perth, in 1544 – the number of victims is given variously from four to six – and in or about April 1545 Lord Methven urged that an attempt should be made to reconcile 'all great gentlemen that be ignorance are of ill mind towards holy church, because it is now doubtsome to punish by the law'; what he meant was that too many influential men were now favourable to heresy for punitive action to be effective and that conciliation was the only possible course.[20]

The combination of political, ecclesiastical and economic motives from which disaffection sprang was well illustrated, in the very years of Hertford's invasions, by the activities of George Wishart. A kinsman of the laird of Pittarro, in Angus (who had been in trouble for heresy in 1542), Wishart now came from England to preach, it seems with comparative freedom and wide acceptance, in Montrose, Dundee, Perth, Fife, Leith, East Lothian and 'the westland'. These were already reforming centres, for the east coast had felt the impact of the Lutheran reformation and the people of Leith had already been reported to be 'all good Christians',[21] while the 'gentlemen of Kyle' who welcomed Wishart may have been the sons or grandsons of those Ayrshire lairds who had professed Lollard tenets 50 years earlier. Besides, the merchants in the burghs had a distaste for English wars which disrupted their trade, and lairds in Angus, like Wishart of Pittaro and Erskine of Dun, and lairds in East Lothian, like Crichton of Brunstane, Douglas of Longniddry and Cockburn of Ormiston, welcomed Wishart as they had opposed the Solway expedition, partly because they were conscious of the economic advantages of peace with the southern neighbour and the disadvantages of devastating invasions. 'The greatest fervency', it was said, 'appeared in the Mearns [Kincardineshire] and Angus, and Kyle and Fife and Lothian, but chiefly the faithful in Dundee exceeded all the rest in zeal'.[22]

Wishart was in the end apprehended and burned, but very soon his prosecutor, David Beaton, was murdered and the castle of St Andrews was held by the murderers and by radicals (including some priests) who were attracted to a centre of possible revolution. The slaughter of the primate in his own castle shook the whole ecclesiastical system, and Wishart's fate, far from being a deterrent, stimulated further agitation, especially as his teaching had represented something more extreme than either Lutheranism or Henrician Anglo-Catholicism, so that we now hear of 'sacramentaries' who denied the Real Presence. At any rate, a fortnight after Beaton's death the privy council expressed the fear that 'evil disposed persons will invade, destroy, cast down and withhold abbeys, abbey places, churches, as well parish churches as other religious places, friaries of all orders, nunneries, chapels and other spiritual men's houses' and prohibited the despoiling of ecclesiastical buildings and their contents.[23] And some seven months later the council received from the bishops, on behalf of the whole church, a complaint that 'sundry parts of this realm, which has been ever Catholic since the beginning of the faith to these days, are now infected with the pestilent heresies of Luther, his sect and followers, and so persevere unpunished, until diverse of them are become sacramentaries and especially against the blessed sacrament of the altar, others of them, abjured and relapsed, banished of old, now come pertly, without any fear, not only in the far parts of the realm but also to the court and presence of your lordships and sometimes preach openly and instruct others in the said heresies'. The response of the council was to ask the churchmen for names, so that action could be taken. And on the same day the council passed an act against those guilty of obstructing ecclesiastical officers in the discharge of their duty by tearing up bishops' letters and assaulting, threatening and chasing those who strove to execute them, 'in great contempt of holy church'.[24] The picture is one of general insecurity for the church and churchmen.

St Andrews Castle ultimately fell to a French force and the murderers of Beaton and their associates were sent to captivity in France, a punishment which, whatever its intention, did nothing to endear to them or their friends the cause of France and the papacy. In September 1547 came an English invasion under Scotland's old enemy Hertford, now Duke of Somerset and Protector in the minority of Edward VI. The Scots were heavily defeated at

Pinkie and English garrisons installed at a number of strongholds in southern and south-eastern Scotland, from Broughty Castle near Dundee southwards. The army which met the invaders at Pinkie had been a large one, but the fact that churchmen were conspicuous in its ranks, fighting under a banner entreating God to look favourably on His afflicted spouse, the Church, can hardly have contributed to its unity, and there was an atmosphere of mistrust which probably contributed to defeat, as it had at Solway five years before. The English occupation has been likened to the creation of an English 'Pale' such as existed in Ireland, and it provided an unprecedented opportunity for the extension of English influence and the nurturing of English sympathisers in areas where, so it was said, the English already had 'maniest favourers'.[25] This was unquestionably one of the most significant and formative episodes in the whole century, and one about which we are uncommonly well informed, thanks to the reports in the English State Papers and the entries in the Register of the Privy Seal relating to the many Scots who had collaborated with the occupying forces. While there is good evidence in general about the existence of reformers or even of a reforming party earlier, the ample information at this stage shows that farther foundations were now laid of loyalties among individuals and families which were to persist for decades.[26]

Possibly some of the collaborators were moved not so much by positive attachment to England as by a negative lack of confidence in the military prospects of their own smaller, poorer and disunited country. Absenteeism from the army rose to what seem to have been unprecedented levels, for over 1300 names of persons prosecuted for failure to join 'the host' are recorded between about 1548 and 1551. It would be going too far to see in this any sort of conscientious objection – not of course in the sense of pacifism but in the sense of a lack of conviction about the Scottish cause. A lot of men may simply have become weary of the incessant musters – there were four or five in the years 1548–9 – and perhaps felt that they had had their share and would not dislocate their lives yet again. It might be reasonable to argue that the absentees were not over patriotic, but it would be going too far to argue that they were actually unpatriotic, still less that they were actively pro-English. At the same time, this state of mind was not so far removed from one of ready acquiescence in an occupation.

As to active collaborators, we have about 1000 names, and there were so many unnamed dependents that a list of certain groups of Borderers was computed exactly at 5395. There were, besides, hundreds of men from the Highlands and Islands who were taking part in raids in return for payment by the English. The collaborators were chiefly in the areas where the English had garrisons, from Broughty Castle southwards, with heavy concentrations in Lothian, Berwickshire, the other Border sheriffdoms of Roxburgh, Selkirk and Peebles and the south-western shires of Dumfries, Kirkcudbright and Wigtown; but Angus and Mearns had a higher figure than either Fife or the total for Dunbartonshire, Renfrewshire and Lanarkshire. Some merely gave 'aid and comfort' to the enemies of the realm, by supplying them with food and drink, but others went farther. They entered into formal 'assurance', as it was called, with the English, in effect transferring their allegiance, adopting the English badge of the red cross and becoming known as 'sworn Englishmen'.

Clearly there were various motives. These men were in occupied territory, undefended by their own government (which, however, some of them had done little enough to help when it essayed defence), and a foreign garrison could exert considerable material pressure on the inhabitants of the surrounding countryside. Englishmen who were not loved may have been feared, but there was an element of prospective financial gain. Few may have been as candid as Sir George Douglas, who carefully calculated the offers he had from the French King, the Scottish Governor and the Scottish Queen-Dowager and said that £1000 would make it worth his while to join the English. But others understood that when the English suppressed the Scottish abbeys those wealthy livings would be distributed among their supporters, and they blatantly made applications along those lines to Somerset almost as if he were in full control of Scotland. Some, while less blatant in their material interests, were attracted to collaboration because they thought they lived 'in more wealth and quietness' under English rule and were unwilling to exchange it; an English captain boasted that Scots said their country had not been in such good order for 20 years. It would appear, however, that some Scots welcomed disorder, to the extent that they took the opportunity to join the English against families with whom they were themselves at feud; the Kers of Ferniehirst and Cessford used English help to turn on their enemies the Scotts of Buccleuch and Branxholm, while other collaborators, like Heriot of Trabroun, Broun of Colstoun and Douglas of Longniddry, were also enemies of the Scotts (though not all the Scotts, for their part, adhered consistently to the national side).

Yet collaboration with England was inseparable from a degree of sympathy with the Reformation. Every English garrison was, and was seen to be, a source of inspiration and instruction for reformers, and those who wanted to put their attachment to England beyond challenge were loud in their professions of the reformed cause. Religion was never far, if not from their hearts, at any rate from their lips. Sometimes the formal undertaking of 'assurance' included a specific renunciation of 'the usurped power of the bishop of Rome' or a specific commitment to be 'setters forth of God's word'. The Earl of Glencairn, who already had a long record of attachment to England, promised to raise, in support of the cause, 1000 of his 'friends and surname' and 1000 more 'favourers of the Word of God'.[27] It is no more surprising, in view of the record of the town of Dundee, that a declaration signed by the magistrates promised that they would be faithful setters forth of God's Word and would be true to King Edward. The English did their part by burning all the 'idols' in the church of Dundee, and their commander reported that he was 'daily cried on by Dundee and by the lords and gentlemen for a good preacher, Bibles, Testaments and other good books'.[28] That collaboration extended to religion as well as politics was plainly brought out in James Henryson's 'Godly and Golden Book for concord of England and Scotland' (1548), outlining the kind of ecclesiastical settlement which might be achieved in a united kingdom and anticipating several points of the programme which the Scottish reformers were to propose some years later: farmers were to enjoy their own teinds (*anglicé* tithes), criminal clerks were to be tried in secular courts, the poor were to be relieved, education in schools and universities was to be fostered, parish churches were to be repaired and the episcopate was to be strengthened through the appointment of suffragans, especially in the Highlands and Islands, where 'many souls perish' for lack of pastoral care.[29] This tenderness for the Highlands suggests that some of the chiefs there who had been such active collaborators with the English had made a special plea for attention, but this and similar complaints about the state of religion there find some support in the gravestones of the period, which seldom show Christian symbolism or piety and on which the poor Latinity of the inscriptions suggests a degree of illiteracy. Whatever the pro-English chiefs may have thought, it is hard to believe that the rank and file were moved to follow them by attachment to Protestantism or any other religion. So far as the Lowlands were concerned, in the period of the English occupation of the south-east (1547-9), the official English Reformation had not yet proceeded very far – the first, extremely conservative, Prayer Book belongs to 1549 – yet there was already much pressure for more sweeping changes, largely by disciples of Zwingli and other continental reformers who were far more radical than Luther, and no doubt some extreme ideas were being imbibed by Scottish collaborators.

It is true, and hardly surprising, that some collaborators were suspected of insincerity. One English agent deplored to Somerset that some gentlemen were 'feigning themselves favourers of the Word of God more for your pleasure than for God's sake.' In July 1548, by which time a French force had arrived to stiffen the Scots, the English reported a massive decline of support: Borderers once willing to serve the English garrisons now temporised, and one agent wrote that whereas previously 'all the Lothians and gentlemen between Edinburgh and Berwick' had been friends, now they were 'most sovereign enemies' and victualled the French camp. In 1549 (after the English withdrawal from Scotland) a Scot drew a distinction between 'the godly, who love the marriage and union and would spend their lives and all they have' but who were mostly small people and few in number, and the majority, who professed to favour union but only for the sake of material advantage. Yet, however mixed and various the motives of the collaborators, it is not open to doubt that religion was one element. It is not difficult to pick out individuals who gave ample evidence of their attachment to the Reformation even when they were under no pressure from English garrisons: James Skea had fled from Orkney in 1547 'for fear of burning for the Word of God'; John Rough, who ministered to the English garrison at Dumfries in 1548, was later a Protestant martyr in England; Crichton of Brunstane, Douglas of Longniddry and Cockburn of Ormiston had harboured Wishart; David and George Forrest, also in East Lothian, were to attend Knox's preaching in 1555; Alexander Whitelaw of New Grange in Angus, who at this stage was said to be responsible for drawing Lord Gray and others 'to the faith and opinion of England', was later to be an active agent of Knox; and Robert Lockhart, an enthusiastic collaborator, had been influenced by his master, Meldrum of Fyvie, who had been noted as a heretic in 1544, and he attended Knox's preaching in 1555. Moreover, it must be remembered, in assessing the sincerity of the collaborators, that they were running the risk of future trouble with their own government should the fortunes of war go against England, and when the English did withdraw there were in fact some executions of collaborators, notably Melville of Raith, while Ormiston, Brunstane, New Grange and some burgesses of Dundee were forfeited. The great majority of those who were convicted of collaboration – 700 or so – got off lightly, as was the Scottish custom, and a few fled to England. Some of those 'flyers' received pensions from the English government, absorbed the increasingly radical views which soon reached England from Strasburg, Zurich and Geneva, and returned to take part in the Scottish Reformation a decade later. All in all, there is plenty of evidence of the truth of Lord Methven's opinion at the time that the disaffection in Scotland and the attachment of so many Scots to England arose largely from the fact that 'part of the lieges have taken new opinions of the scripture'.[30]

It was only with French help that the English had been driven out, and the price of French assistance had been the despatch of the young Queen to France with a view to her marriage to the Dauphin. Moreover, France was clearly pursuing a policy of extending its influence among the leading Scots, through the agency largely of Mary of Guise, the Queen Mother. As a measure of conciliation, she brought about the release of the gentlemen who had been taken as prisoners to France after the fall of St Andrews Castle, and honours were available for Scottish nobles: Angus, Argyll, Arran and Huntly were admitted to the Order of St Michael, and Arran was elevated in addition to the dukedom of Châtelherault, with a rich income. More was to come, when in 1550 Mary went on a visit to France. She took in her train a large number of men who seem for the most part to have been of Protestant inclinations and, on their record, anglophiles. The episode has been dubbed 'a brain-washing expedition', but the offers of financial inducements to the visitors were so evident that it was reported that the King of France 'bought them completely' and there is good evidence that former pillars of the English and reforming cause, like Glencairn, became French pensioners.[31] It is no mere cynicism to say that these impecunious Scottish peers were prepared to accept pensions with complete impartiality from either England or France, often without doing much to earn them.

Yet the realm was still, as it had been since 1543, under its native Governor, Arran. During his term of office the Hamilton family reached the peak of its fortunes. 'Fortunes' was the word, because apart from political power Arran seems quietly to have appropriated the vast wealth, estimated at 300,000 livres, left by James V. Irresolute though he often was, there were two points on which Arran was constant: his rights as heir presumptive must be safeguarded and no questions must be asked about his financial transactions. Besides wealth, he had a status which was unique, for dukes had always been extremely rare in Scotland and the only dukedom ever created for anyone other than a king's son had been a short-lived dukedom of Montrose conferred on the Earl of Crawford in 1488. Châtelherault was invariably designated, simply but quite adequately, 'The Duke'. As Governor he signed 'James G.', and after he demitted office he signed 'James', like a prince. His grandeur, not to say grandiosity, is visible in his seal, surely the most impressive yet used by any subject in Scotland.³² Although Arran could hardly have resisted heavy French pressure, he clearly had a degree of freedom of action. This he used, in conjunction with his half-brother John, who had become Archbishop of St Andrews in 1549, to enter on a policy designed to offer something to the reformers without alienating conservatives and to win for the house of Hamilton a measure of support which might enable it to fight off French dictation. Church councils passed statutes aimed at tightening up discipline among the clergy and improving (very slightly) the salaries of parish priests, and a *Catechism* was issued which expounded justification and the Eucharist in such a way as to satisfy moderate reformers. The *Catechism*, besides, was silent about the Pope, and in 1550 the Scottish privy council proposed that 'all benefices within the realm of Scotland, excepting bishoprics only, be provided within the realm' and not at Rome.³³ Arran had nothing to learn about the existing powers of the crown to nominate to prelacies, but it was only in the face of some papal reluctance that he had obtained the wealthy abbeys of Arbroath and Paisley for two of his sons, and, while one half-brother had become archbishop of St Andrews, he had not prevailed on the Pope to concede the archbishopric of Glasgow to another half-brother (who was fobbed off with the poor bishopric of Argyll). It was understandable that he wanted to extend his control over ecclesiastical promotions, but it is not clear how far the privy council recommendation of 1550 was operative. Applications continued to flow to Rome, but no investigation has yet been made of the extent to which they were effective unless applicants obtained appointments by Scottish authorities as well, and it would seem that the crown began to make appointments without reference to Rome at all. Archbishop Hamilton, besides, had powers which enabled him to carry out a number of functions traditionally reserved to the Pope, though it seems that some Scots spurned his jurisdiction and continued to take their suits to the court of Rome.

The concessions of John Hamilton may well have encouraged further weakening of ecclesiastical order, but this was not the intention. There was even in 1550 one more execution of a heretic, and in 1551 parliament passed acts to check indiscipline. One of them, against 'perturbation in the kirk', fulminated against interruption of 'preaching of the Word of God, stopping the same to be heard', which was certainly a new emphasis and might suggest that disturbances were now caused by ultra-conservatives rather than by friends to the Gospel, and that already services not in accordance with medieval orthodoxy were being conducted. Another act of 1551 related that printers 'daily and continually print books concerning the faith, ballads, songs, blasphemies, rhymes as well of churchmen as temporal men' and proposed to institute a kind of censorship by the bishops.³⁴ The terms of this act point to the circulation of material like that in *The Good and Godly Ballads*, with their mixture of scurrilous abuse of the clergy and moving affirmations of evangelical faith.

Archbishop Hamilton's reforming statutes, had they been implemented, would have amounted to more than mere tinkering with the ecclesiastical machinery, and it is conceivable that the country might have moved gently into a religious settlement which would have satisfied moderate reformers without involving revolution and – so long as the Archbishop's brother was Governor – without involving the loss of independence to France. When, at the instance of France, Arran was superseded as Governor by Mary of Guise in 1554 it was soon apparent that Scotland was to be an instrument of French foreign policy, dominated by France and used as a base from which attacks might be mounted against England, but the change of governor had no immediate effect on the ecclesiastical situation. Mary was not disposed by temperament to be a persecutor and could not afford to be one while John Hamilton was still primate and the Hamilton interest, around which any opposition to her was likely to focus, stood for compromise. Besides, concessions to the Protestant agitation in Scotland might help to win concurrence in French political and military objectives and might even encourage disaffection in England against the Roman Catholic reaction now being conducted by Mary Tudor (1553-8) and her Spanish husband, Philip II, with whom France was at war. The policy of conciliation was demonstrated by marks of royal favour to men like the Earls of Cassillis, Argyll, Glencairn and Morton, Lord James Stewart (after 1557 the eldest surviving illegitimate son of James V), Crichton of Brunstane, Kirkcaldy of Grange, Cockburn of Ormiston and Erskine of Dun, several of whom were by this time becoming open supporters of the Reformation. Mary may not have 'bought them completely' as the French King was reported to have done in 1550, but she showed how patronage could be used.

All in all, the reformers had a good deal of latitude, of which they took full advantage. There were evidently more disturbances: in 1554 protections had to be issued to the Blackfriars and the Charterhouse – the very institutions which were to feel the first blast of the revolution when it started in 1559; in 1555 there was an act against 'insolent and evil persons' who ate flesh in Lent; in the summer and autumn of 1558 there were riots in Edinburgh focused on the image of St Giles; and by the end of that year images were being destroyed in the diocese of Aberdeen. But activity was not only of this negative nature; there was also positive dissemination of the reformers' message by energetic preachers, some of whom had been refugees in England but returned home once Mary Tudor's persecution started. Among their influential supporters were the Earls of Glencairn, Argyll and Morton, Lord Lorne (Argyll's son) and Erskine of Dun, who in the 'First Bond' about the end of 1557 pledged themselves to 'labour . . . to have faithful ministers . . . to minister Christ's evangel and sacraments'. A few months later 'the lords and barons professing Christ Jesus' made arrangements for Protestant worship in churches as well as 'quiet houses',[35] and the Earl of Argyll entertained a preacher so ostentatiously that Archbishop Hamilton felt it necessary to remonstrate with him. Support came not only from the magnates but from local authorities, notably the town councils of Dundee, St Andrews and Ayr. There had already been several half-secret congregations or 'privy kirks', especially in east coast burghs, but now what would have been called 'the face of a public kirk' was beginning to show itself, with clergy of parish churches conducting services according to the Prayer Book. Presently a third reforming council was called and the clergy of the diocese of Aberdeen were bewailing the growth of heresy and imploring their bishop to set an example by dismissing his concubine and refraining from associating with men who were 'suspect contrarious the faith'. Whether the progress of Protestantism at unofficial or semi-official levels could in itself have ultimately produced a revolution it may be hard to say, but it would surely either have done that or provoked repression which in turn would have produced a violent reaction. The latter course was what in the end happened, but the religious issue was not the only one creating unrest in the late 1550s.

All the Queen Regent's mildness and conciliation in religion were powerless to counteract the resentment caused by secular policy, as French troops were introduced to garrison Scottish fortresses like Dunbar, Inchkeith, Broughty, Blackness and Eyemouth, Frenchmen were appointed to certain offices of profit and the French ambassador – or we should rather say 'resident' – was constantly at the Dowager's side. It had often been shown in the past that when Frenchmen came to Scotland in any numbers they were unpopular – partly, it may be suspected, because their extravagant tastes and standards were too high for a poor country and partly because they were arrogant and contemptuous towards their thrifty hosts. As early as 1555 a statute related that seditious persons had raised among the common people murmurs and slanders, speaking against the Queen, sowing evil reports concerning the French King's subjects who had been sent to Scotland 'for the common weal and suppressing of the old enemies furth of the same' and tending to create sedition between the Scots and the French.[36] But worse was to come when it became evident that the Scots were expected to pay for fortifications on the Border and to risk their lives in expeditions into England. The government met with flat refusals from the nobility, who had no wish to see another Flodden or Solway Moss. It could well be argued that the main stimulus to revolt in the late 1550s, when the reformers were largely getting their way in religion without revolt, came less from religion than from the resentment which was building up against the government's pro-French policy.

Yet in the end religious disaffection rather than political unrest was the immediate cause of the outbreak, which is usually dated from the arrival of John Knox in Scotland in May 1559. Knox had preached to Cardinal Beaton's murderers in St Andrews Castle in 1546 and on its fall he had been sent as a convict to the French galleys. On his release he had found a home in the Protestant England of Edward VI, but under the threat of Mary Tudor's persecution he fled to the continent, where he ministered to a congregation of English refugees at Geneva. Elizabeth's accession (17 November 1558) and the indications that England would again reject the papacy encouraged exiles, including Knox, to return. He had been absent from Scotland for 12 years except for a few months in 1555–6, and he wanted to enter England again, but Elizabeth declined to receive the author of a recent book against *The Monstrous Regiment of Women*, and Knox made for Scotland, where he landed on 2 May 1559. His return coincided with a crisis which had been foreseen and which indeed had been advertised in advance, and it is hard to avoid the conclusion that an explosion was inevitable, Knox or no Knox.

On or before 1 January 1559 there had appeared on the doors of Scottish friaries a 'Beggars' Summons', warning friars to surrender their properties to the poor on 12 May following. Coincidentally, Mary of Guise, who found that the Scots disobeyed her order to return to their religious allegiance at Easter (26 March), summoned the leading preachers to appear before her on 10 May. They did not go, and their lay supporters rallied in arms to their defence. It was on 11 May that Knox preached at Perth a sermon 'vehement against idolatry' and the result was to set off a wave of looting of friaries and other churches. It at once became evident that the militancy had the backing not only of the burgesses of Dundee and Perth but of the 'gentlemen' of Angus and Mearns and of the 'congregation' of Ayrshire, and 'the brethren from all quarters' came flocking into Perth. The force with which the Earl of Glencairn hastened from Ayrshire matched or even exceeded the 2000 men whom he had boasted of being able to muster in 1547. It was at this point that 'the Lords of the Congregation' became the leaders of an army, and there followed a year of intermittent military operations. Desertions from the government were so frequent that the French 'resident' complained, 'You cannot tell friend from enemy, and he who is with us in the morning is on the other side after dinner'.[37] But the insurgents made a poor showing, partly because their volunteer forces had to face a substantial body of French regulars. It was only with English help (promised by the treaty of Berwick in February 1560) that the rebels were able to blockade the great French stronghold of Leith and cut off the chance of reinforcements from France. Scotland's satellite position had never been more plain. Politically viewed, the Scottish rebellion was only an incident in Anglo-French hostility, and it was appropriate that the war was ended (after the opportune death of Mary of Guise in June) by a treaty between England and France, concluded at Edinburgh in July. When military operations began in 1559 an English observer had remarked acutely, 'There is great appearance of battle, but many of those with the Queen being of like religion and kindred with the other faction, it will likely end without battle'.[38] Few Scots were willing to be killed for the sake of a government and a religion in which they had lost faith, and the most serious fighting seems to have been between English and French, with few Scottish casualties.

The treaty of Edinburgh provided for the withdrawal of French and English troops from Scotland, leaving the Scots to settle their own affairs. The treaty itself was accompanied by 'Concessions' from Francis and Mary to their Scottish subjects which represented an additional success for the revolution. There was to be no revival of French domination either by armed occupation, the holding of Scottish offices by Frenchmen or control of Scottish foreign policy; machinery was proposed for the appointment of a council designed to represent the sovereigns and the estates; a parliament was to be called, but it was not to deal with religion, which representatives of the lords were to discuss with the King and Queen. This rearguard action, in so far as it was designed to curb the power of the revolutionaries, failed. In practice the Lords of the Congregation remained in control as a kind of provisional government and it was they who took the initiative in calling a parliament (whether with or without a formal royal summons). When parliament met in August, it passed acts forbidding the Latin mass, abolishing papal authority and adopting a reformed Confession of Faith, and the envoy sent to France was to ask simply for royal ratification of the legislation – which was not forthcoming.

Elizabeth's intervention had been ostensibly for political ends – to save Scotland from subjection to France (and thereby safeguard England's northern frontier) – but her own subjects and many of the Scots saw it as a move in the ideological war between the Reformation and papalist powers. The outbreak of the Scottish revolt in 1559, if it is dated from Knox's sermon at Perth, on 11 May, had taken place, by what surely seemed more than a happy coincidence, three days after Elizabeth had finally given her assent to the Acts of Supremacy and Uniformity. Inevitably the strongly anglophile flavour which the Scottish reform movement had had since the 1530s was reflected in Scottish worship. Use was made of the English Book of Common Prayer (the official English service-book) and of the Book of Common Order (the book compiled for English refugees in Mary Tudor's reign and preferred by the more radical). The majority of the metrical psalms which were printed with the Book of Common Order for use in Scottish churches were the work of English translators. 'Readers' in Scottish parishes (who were not allowed to compose their own sermons) used the Book of Homilies, originally prepared in England in 1543, published in Edward VI's reign and authorised by the Archbishop of Canterbury in 1562. The only printed Bible the Scots ever knew was in the southern form of English and not in their own northern version of the tongue. It is not surprising that the Scots upheld the authority of the English archbishops ('whom', they said, 'God of His providence and mercy hath erected as principals in ecclesiastical jurisdiction within the realm of England') and denounced the first English nonconformists (who were told, 'We wish your consciences had a better ground').[39] The English intervention in Scotland in 1560 was therefore almost a classic example of a short-lived military effort designed to set up an administration favourable to the politics and ideology of the master power.

# 3
# THE PARTY OF REVOLUTION

*1560 Feb.* Treaty of Berwick
*June* Death of Mary of Guise
*July* Treaty of Edinburgh
*August* 'Reformation Parliament'
*Dec.* Death of Francis II
*1561 Jan.* First Book of Discipline approved
*August* Mary arrived in Scotland

It need hardly be said that simple thirst for the Gospel, significant though it was for the few who found 'the strait gate and the narrow way which leadeth unto life', was not the predominant motive of the party which carried through the revolution of 1559–60. But even among the many who preferred the wide gate and the broad way there were religious motives, to the extent that they believed in a church which had a mission to fulfil and they had views on how it could best perform its task. There was something like unanimity, even among those who were theologically conservative, that much was amiss in the ecclesiastical system, because many clergy were lax in their lives and inattentive to their duties, the wealth of the church was distributed almost in inverse proportion to the value of the work done, and in particular the parishes and their ministry were shamefully neglected. Others sought redistribution of endowments from less altruistic motives, for lords and lairds regretted the pious munificence of their ancestors and were now, by a variety of methods, recovering some ecclesiastical wealth for their own pockets. Hard-working burgesses saw the prelates and the monasteries as 'idle bellies', that is, consumers and not producers of the wealth which was not easy to come by in Scotland except through hard work.

Leaving aside those who were moved by religion, there was more than one political consideration which counted. In the first place, the insurgents appealed to patriotic resentment against the French. There had been an illuminating conversation between the 3rd Earl of Cassillis and the Earl of Westmorland in the summer of 1557, when England, with its Queen, Mary Tudor, married to Philip II, was a satellite of Spain, and Scotland, with its Queen betrothed to the Dauphin, was equally a satellite of France. When the Englishman taunted the Scot with being tied to France, Cassillis retorted, 'By the mass, I am no more French than you are a Spaniard.' Westmorland admitted, 'Marry, as long as God shall preserve my master and mistress [Philip and Mary] together, I am and shall be a Spaniard to the uttermost of my power', but Cassillis affirmed, 'By God, so shall I not be French, and I told you once in my lord your father's house, in King Henry VIII's time, that we would die, every mother's son of us, rather than be subject unto England'.[1] This remarkable assertion of independence from England and France alike was striking as coming from Cassillis, who, despite his asseveration 'By the mass', had been an anglophile and friend to reform. There was an even more revealing remark in September 1559 by the Earl of Argyll, who was heavily committed to the reforming cause: the French, he said, 'are come in and sitten down in this realm to occupy it and to put forth the inhabitants thereof and likewise to occupy all other men's rooms [estates] piece and piece, and to put away the blood of the nobility'. And, it was added, he 'makes the example of Brittany'.² That was the crucial point. Two generations earlier the Duchess Anne of Brittany had married first Charles VIII and then Louis XII, kings of France, and, despite safeguards, the duchy had been merged in the French monarchy. Now the same was to happen in Scotland; the French and Scottish crowns were joined with the marriage of Mary to the Dauphin and his accession to the French throne in 1559, and the prospect for a Scotland ruled by their descendants was the loss of national identity.

In June 1559 the insurgents claimed that the nation's independence had been threatened by Mary's marriage, and the arrival in August of additional French troops, accompanied by their families, gave more specific grounds for alarm. Argyll was not alone in believing or alleging that Frenchmen were to be planted in the 'native rooms' or hereditary estates of Scottish proprietors, while the 'just possessors and ancient inhabitants' were to be evicted.³ How the patriotic appeal was weighed against religious allegiance was indicated when in October 1559 the Earl of Arran, who had recently joined his father, Châtelherault, at the head of the insurgents, wrote to Lord Sempill. Sempill had a fairly consistent record of conservatism: he had supported the monks of Paisley against heretics in 1545 – not without reward, for he received a charter of the bailiary of the abbey: and he fought against England at Pinkie, where he was taken prisoner. At a more personal level he was at feud with the Protestant and anglophile Glencairn, and he evidently felt no revulsion against the ecclesiastical system on the ground that his daughter was the mistress of Archbishop Hamilton. His support for Mary of Guise against the Congregation, and his determination to maintain the mass, were so patent that Knox described him as 'a man sold under sin, an enemy to God and all godliness'.⁴ Yet Arran was not without hope that Sempill, 'albeit peradventure . . . nocht resolute in your conscience towards the religion', would nevertheless support the insurrection 'for the common wealth and liberty of this your native country'.⁵ The appeal was in vain, and the Congregation tried force instead: Sempill was unhappily placed in Renfrewshire, between the militant Glencairn in north Ayrshire and Arran's Hamiltons who now had a firm grip on Paisley, with the result that 'the western lords' (no doubt headed by Glencairn) besieged his house of Sempill in 1559 and Arran besieged it again in 1560. Nationalist resentment against France had failed to move Sempill, but burgesses and lairds elsewhere were swayed by the attraction of the economic advantages of peace with England, which seemed inseparable from the reformed cause.

The other political issue, besides relations with France and England, which affected attitudes to the revolution was the question of the future government of Scotland. The two points were closely related because the very existence of the administration of Mary of Guise depended to some extent on its connection with France, but the resentment provoked by French domination had to be weighed in the balance against the attraction of lawfully constituted authority. Despite ample and fairly recent precedent for setting up a rival to the reigning sovereign, and precedents from earlier times for statutory redefinition of the succession, the unfaltering transmission of the crown from parent to child for two centuries meant that loyalty to the reigning sovereign was by this time a strong card. Mary of Guise's most effective propaganda weapon, on John Knox's admission, was the accusation that the insurgents' purpose was revolutionary and treasonable. She said that they had rejected an offer of freedom of conscience pending a decision by parliament on the religious issue and were instead bent on overthrowing 'the authority' and transferring the crown from her daughter. In practice, the insurgents' proceedings did seem to contradict their claim that they contended only for 'the Evangel' and did not aim at 'inobedience to the prince or usurping of higher powers'. Even their protest in July 1559 that 'we have yet made no mention of change in authority, nor has it even entered our hearts'[6] had an air of qualification about it, and there is no doubt that some were indeed thinking, then or shortly thereafter, of superseding the absent Queen, married as she was to the King of France and perhaps unlikely ever to return to Scotland. The two possible candidates were Mary's half-brother, Lord James, the eldest surviving bastard of James V, Commendator of St Andrews Priory and later Earl of Moray, and James Hamilton, Duke of Châtelherault, lately Governor of the realm and still heir presumptive. Cecil thought Lord James 'not unlike either in person or qualities to be a king soon',[7] but although recent experience in other countries showed that the elevation of a bastard could not be ruled out, it was something that had not happened in Scotland in historic times, and everyone knew that the Hamiltons would never accept Lord James; on the other hand, the Duke lacked the 'person or qualities' to make him attractive as a possible king. What happened, as a provisional step, was that in September, when Châtelherault's son and heir found his way home from France, where he had been more or less a hostage for ten years, the Duke joined the insurgents to become their figurehead, and in October Mary of Guise was declared to be suspended from the regency.

Even this step, let alone the supersession of the Queen, did not appeal to all those who contended for 'the Evangel' or all those who were concerned primarily to see the end of French domination, and the insurgents had to trim accordingly. They were also under some pressure, at least by implication, from Queen Elizabeth, from whom they expected, and ultimately received, armed assistance, but who, seated as she was on a throne acquired only a year before and under some threat from rival claims, had a strong prejudice against rebellion. When, in February 1560, by the treaty of Berwick, England agreed to help the Scottish rebels, the latter affirmed their continued obedience to Francis and Mary. The treaty put its emphasis on the liberation of Scotland from France, but from that time the Scottish insurgents repeated that they did not intend political revolution and laid their stress on the religious issue, about which the treaty had been silent. This move not only reassured Elizabeth but avoided the dissension which would have been inevitable had either Lord James or a Hamilton been put forward as an alternative to Mary. A bond signed at Leith on 27 April 1560, undertaking to set forward the Reformation, condemning the French occupation and promising obedience to Mary and Francis, was signed by about 140 persons, including a dozen peers, some commendators and about 30 lairds.[8]

The leaders of the rebels were trying, with a fair degree of success, to be all things to all men – men whose personal, familial and dynastic interests were at variance and whose ecclesiastical sympathies ranged widely, but who were held together by at least the prospect of maintaining the nation's independence under its hereditary rulers and relying on English help to protect it against French domination. Reformers of every shade of opinion and even ecclesiastical conservatives were prepared to unite on a basis of opposition to France provided that lawfully constituted government was maintained. The burgh of Aberdeen, for example, explicitly made its support of the Congregation conditional: the rebels must not 'enterprise any purpose against the authority'.[9] It required subtle argument to justify the constitutional position of the insurgents. The provisional government of the Lords of the Congregation had no legal basis and when the parliament met its acts were passed in the name of 'the three estates' without the customary reference to 'Our soverane lady'. However, the scruples of those who were tender about the rights of 'the authority' seem to have been satisfied by acknowledgment of the formal sovereignty of Francis and Mary without demanding obedience to them in practice.

In view of the need to overcome the objections of ecclesiastical conservatives on one side, it is plain that the insurgents would not have put the emphasis they did on 'the Evangel' had they not been convinced that it would draw popular support on the other side. And the operative word is 'draw', not 'create'. After a generation of Protestant teaching, inconoclastic outbreaks and growing ecclesiastical instability, there had been intense activity in the two or three years before 1560. When we recall the existence of the 'privy kirks' and the action taken by local authorities at the beginning of 1559, not only before there was sanction or direction from the centre but even before rebellion broke out at all, we realise that when the insurgents made an appeal on religious grounds they had good sense on their side. Mary of Guise herself believed in the summer of 1559 that the greater part of the kingdom agreed with those who preached the Gospel.[10] The notion that the Reformation was not a popular movement, but something carried through by a clique of nobles making religion a cloak for their own selfish ends and in defiance of majority opinion, and that Protestantism took root only after a parliament had legislated in its favour, cannot be entertained. On the contrary, the religious issue and the social and economic ideas of the reformers, which some would now call the theology of liberation, probably rallied a lot of popular support which arguments about foreign policy and constitutional rights, however much they appealed to the magnates, would not have gained. One can see how easily the poor could be convinced of the inequity of prelatical wealth and – once they learned the scriptures – the contrast between the lordly prelates of the sixteenth century and the humble apostles of the first whom they claimed to represent. It was certainly a delicate balance between appealing to ecclesiastical conservatives on patriotic grounds and appealing on religious or socio-religious grounds to the 'rascal multitude' of the towns and the 'poor labourers of the ground' in the country, but the tactical work was good. What resulted, although it was not an agreement artificially engineered among formally organised groups, was something which can not unreasonably be called a coalition.

The unity was not only maintained, but if anything rather enhanced, by the events of July and August 1560, when the treaty of Edinburgh provided for the withdrawal of the French and English troops, and a parliament approved of Protestantism in a theological sense but made no commitment to any particular programme for either polity or endowment. Reformers of all shades of opinion were satisfied, those who were anxious to maintain the ecclesiastical structure because they could operate it to their material advantage were not antagonised, and, it was clear, even many who had conservative inclinations in religion were not alienated. And all this had been achieved without disinheriting the lawful Queen or becoming an English-occupied country.

The occasion for further controversy about the Queen's rights receded. At the same time, the situation was more like an armistice than a peace, and no one could know what might happen or how opinion might shape if Mary attempted to reverse the decisions of the parliament or make a renewed bid for control by fresh armed intervention from France. The insurgents, temporarily victorious, therefore decided to secure their position by a formal and lasting agreement with England. The recent revolution had been, besides much else, a triumph for the Hamiltons. Châtelherault and his son James ('Young Arran') were at the head of the provisional government, and this position, if not the throne itself, might continue to be theirs should Mary perhaps decide not to return to a country which had firmly rejected French policies. This strengthened the case for the marriage to Elizabeth of Young Arran, a prospective heir to the Scottish throne, and this proposal gained wide support even from some who had not been enthusiastic for the recent revolution and others who had actually withheld their assent from it. The scheme envisaged permanent alliance, and perhaps union, with an England which had in the previous year repudiated papal authority and had replaced the mass by the Book of Common Prayer. This could not be reconciled with allegiance to the papacy and could not have been acceptable to anyone who was in any real sense a 'Roman Catholic', yet it was supported by the Archbishop of St Andrews and five bishops.

It may be hard to explain why members of a party which had just rebelled against the consequences of rule by 'Francis and Mary, King and Queen of France and Scotland' should now entertain the possibility of rule by 'James and Elizabeth, King and Queen of England, Scotland, France and Ireland' (for so they would have been styled), with its equal loss of Scottish identity. The Protestants who favoured the match may have been prepared to sacrifice national pride for the sake of the security of the Reformation, and to that extent religion may have been stronger than patriotism, but no such consideration explains the support from ecclesiastical conservatives. Calculation that because Scotland would this time supply the King in the joint sovereignty therefore his wife would be subject to him might have been excusable at the time, naive though it seems in the light of what we know of

Elizabeth's personality. Perhaps the feature that emerges most clearly is the width and depth of the desire for Anglo-Scottish amity. At any rate, whatever the motives, the agreement on the Arran-Elizabeth match probably represented the peak of unity, the maximum extent of 'coalition'.

An attempt to analyse the state of opinion in the crisis of 1559–60 and assess the degree of support which the revolution enjoyed can draw on three documents in particular. There is first the bond of 27 April 1560, already mentioned, pledging support for the 'reformation of religion according to God's Word'. Second is the record, including the sederunt, of the parliament of August 1560. The third list of names relates to a sequel, arising from the fact that the parliament, although repudiating Rome, had said nothing about institutional change within the Scottish church. There was already in existence a 'Book of Reformation' enunciating proposals for the organisation and endowment of a reformed church, but conflict with vested interests led to delay, controversy and revision. It was not until a convention in January 1561 that what we know as 'The First Book of Discipline' was approved by some nobles and lairds who, however, added the qualification that existing holders of ecclesiastical offices who had joined the reformers were to continue to enjoy their emoluments for life provided that they contributed to the support of ministers.[11] Far fewer subscribed the Book of Discipline, which touched their pockets, than had approved the August legislation, which did not, but the discrepancy may not be due only to material considerations. One simple fact is that fewer would attend the convention than the parliament. The latter had presumably been formally proclaimed (though it cannot have had the customary 40 days' notice), it had marked the termination of armed conflict, and the season had been a favourable one for travelling. A convention had less formality than a parliament and usually fewer members, and this one took place in the depth of winter and in a less critical situation.

There is a fourth list, of supporters of the proposal that Elizabeth should marry Young Arran – a very important test of opinion – but as it is defective its value is limited.[12] Another list of significance is the sederunt of the gathering which some consider to have been the first general assembly of the reformed church. This names only six ministers and 40 laymen, but meetings from 20 to 27 December (with an adjournment to 15 January) were even less attractive than those of the convention just referred to, especially to people who had not yet capitulated to the radicals' condemnation of Christmas festivities.[13] More valuable as a supplement to our three main lists is a bond subscribed at Ayr in September 1562 by 'a great part of the barons and gentlemen' of the sheriffdom, undertaking to maintain 'the holy Evangel'. While some of the signatories had possibly been converted since 1560, the list at least confirms the Protestantism of those among them who had apparently already been with the insurgents in that year.[14]

All in all, the sources yield over 200 names of lords and lairds and make it plain that the party of revolution made a good showing among peers and other notables. At its head stood the Duke of Châtelherault and his son Young Arran. They gave the party respectability rather than leadership, for the Duke was 'so unconstant, saving in covetousness and greediness, that in three moments he will take five purposes',[15] and his son was soon to show signs of mental instability. More effective was Lord James Stewart, the future Earl of Moray, in whom Cecil had discerned kinglike qualities. Among the earls who gave their support the most enthusiastic were Argyll, Glencairn, Morton, Rothes and Menteith, with Marischal not far behind. The Earl of Huntly seems to have done his best, as his descendants were more than once to do later, to sit on the fence. As head of the Gordon kin and name he held a position which was indicated (though perhaps not until later times) by the nickname 'Cock of the North'. He had carried himself with suitable *panache* when at Pinkie he wore a suit of enamelled armour, but now he was an ageing man of 50 who within a couple of years was to die suddenly, probably of apoplexy. He vacillated in 1559 and although he signed the bond of April 1560 after the insurgents made it clear that they did not plan political revolution, he did so with reluctance. He alleged that in the north the French had persuaded nobles and clans to contend for the French authority and 'the auld manner of religion' and that this made it necessary for him to have certain guarantees before he committed himself. This may have been no more than an excuse, to justify the indecision or lethargy of which contemporaries, as they waited day after day for him to appear in the camp at Leith, were well aware, and some explicitly described the Earl as 'wily', but his attitude is understandable at a time when the success of the revolt was by no means assured, and the tale he told can hardly have been wholly improbable. It was said that when he finally agreed to sign the bond he did so in secret.[16] Huntly's cousin Sutherland, and the Earl of Crawford, seem also to have had reservations, but did not stand aside; the Earl of Erroll appears to have been detached, but his heir, the Master, was a member of the party. Among the lords, the most militant were Ruthven, Gray, Boyd, Cathcart, Yester, Herries, Innermeath, Lindsay, Livingston, Ochiltree and Ogilvy of Airlie; Home, Drummond, Erskine and Forbes were less involved but not hostile. The bishops who gave strong support were Alexander Gordon of Galloway (brother of the Earl of Huntly), John Campbell, Elect of the Isles (a kinsman or client of the Earl of Argyll), James Hamilton of Argyll (a half-brother of Châtelherault) and Adam Bothwell of Orkney, whose origins were middle-class but who was related by marriage to Protestant lairds. The 16 or so commendators or titular abbots and priors who turned up at the parliament of 1560 presumably approved of its proceedings and assuredly, with one or two exceptions, never gave any sign of attempting to reverse them. The important point about the commendators, as about the bishops, is that they were to a great extent integrated with the lay notables: two of them (Arbroath and Kilwinning) were Hamiltons, kinsmen of Châtelherault – and indeed there was a third Hamilton commendator, Paisley, but he was John, Archbishop of St Andrews; one (Deer) was a Keith, kinsman of Marischal; one (Coupar), who immediately on the outbreak of the revolt in May 1559 lost no time in 'putting on secular weed',[17] was a Campbell, kinsman of Argyll; two (Jedburgh and Newbattle) were Kerrs; two (one holding Dryburgh and Inchmahome, the other holding Cambuskenneth) were Erskines; three (Holyrood, Coldingham and Inchcolm) were Stewarts; the commendator of

Inchaffray was Alexander Gordon, Bishop of Galloway.

Social distinctions apart, the most striking characteristic of the party of revolution is that it contained an impressive proportion of men whose stance in 1560 could have been predicted from their past records and to whom the ecclesiastical and political convulsion was the fulfilment of hopes they had cherished for 15 years or more. At the parliament their spokesman was the sexagenarian Lord Lindsay, from Fife: 'The old Lord of Lindsay, as grave and goodly a man as I ever saw, said, "I have lived many years, I am the eldest in this company of my sort, now that it hath pleased God to let me see this day where so many nobles and others have allowed so worthy a work, I will say with Simeon *Nunc Dimittis*"'.[18] The most committed earl was surely Glencairn, whose career almost epitomises the whole anglophile and reforming movement over 20 years or more. His brother had been in trouble for heresy in 1538; he himself had been a Solway prisoner, a pensioner of Henry VIII and one of those 'suspects' whom the Dowager had taken to France in 1550. He entertained Knox in 1556 and signed the 'First Bond' in 1557, in 1559 he had brought a force from his own country in Ayrshire to defend the Protestant preachers, he was a party to the deposition of Mary of Guise and to the treaty of Berwick, he was at the parliament of 1560 and he took forceful action against 'idolatry'.

No other earl had quite as consistent a record as Glencairn, but several peers had been conspicuous on the pro-English and reforming side long before 1559. James Douglas, 4th Earl of Morton, was a nephew of the 6th Earl of Angus (husband for a time of Margaret Tudor), who had headed the anglophile administration in the last years of James V's minority, and after his uncle's eclipse in 1528 he lurked in obscurity during James's personal reign. In Mary's minority he joined Angus in opposing Arran's reactionary policy in 1544, and his father supported Wishart in 1546. When Angus switched to the anti-English and patriotic side, his nephew followed him, with the result that he was taken prisoner and spent two years in the Protestant England of Edward VI, where he tasted an official reformation and acquired an English accent and diction much as John Knox did. He succeeded to the earldom of Morton in right of his wife in 1548 but was not prominent again in Scotland until he signed the 'First Bond' in 1557. By that time he had vastly increased his influence by becoming 'tutor' or guardian to his nephew the 8th Earl of Angus, who was a minor, for this gave him the management of the Angus estates and a claim to the allegiance of all Douglases. Though one of the most significant figures in the whole century, and ultimately an outstandingly successful regent for James VI in the 1570s, Morton has never been the subject of a full investigation of the charges of ruthlessness and avarice which have clung to him. His alleged 'licentiousness' – he had four known illegitimate sons – is at least capable of some explanation, for his wife had been insane for 22 years before she died. (She was, incidentally, a sister of the mother of 'Young Arran', who may be presumed to have inherited his mental taint from his mother.)

The Earl Marischal, whose sea-girt stronghold of Dunnottar, south of Aberdeen, surely exposed him to any Lutheran winds which blew from the continent, had been accused of heresy in 1543, had favoured Mary's marriage to Edward, associated with Glencairn against Arran in 1544, supported George Wishart and undertook, on behalf of Henry VIII, to act against Cardinal Beaton. He joined the national rally in the Pinkie campaign but in the next year was once more reported to be pro-English, in 1550 he was one of the 'suspects' taken to France by Mary of Guise and in 1556 he welcomed Knox's preaching. In 1561 he was one of the rather select group of notables who went so far as to subscribe the Book of Discipline but he seems to have had some doubts about the claims of the reformers to dictate to the Queen. Patrick, 4th Lord Gray, had been taken prisoner at Solway and committed to the care of the Archbishop of York, but he was back in Scotland in time to attend the parliament of March 1543, which approved of the vernacular Bible and the marriage treaty with England. The fact that Cardinal Beaton thought it worth while to give him a charter on condition that he supported the Church (20 October 1544)[19] may suggest that he was considered worth buying, but the Cardinal wasted his money, for in 1547 Gray adhered to England in the Pinkie campaign. He was one of the first to join the reformers when the rebellion started in 1559. John, Lord Innermeath, had sat in the parliament of March 1543 which approved the vernacular Bible and the English marriage and at a later stage he had been a collaborator with the English; he was at the parliament of 1560 and approved the match between Arran and Elizabeth. Alexander, 5th Lord Home, head of a leading Border family with some reputation for unreliability in previous generations, had been a prisoner in England for some time after Pinkie, but, after succeeding his father in 1549, he was taken to France by Mary of Guise in 1550 and was one of those who were at that point 'bought completely' by the French King, with a pension of 2000 livres. It looks as if his inclinations had been towards England and Protestantism, and he cannot have been ill pleased to sit in the parliament of 1560 and support the Arran-Elizabeth match. Andrew Stewart, Lord Ochiltree, who took his title from lands in the Protestant stronghold of central Ayrshire, had a brother who was in trouble for heresy as far back as 1537, his father had supported the anglophile and reforming programme in 1543 and he himself had been one of Knox's hosts in 1555.

There were a good many lairds in the party of revolution whose constancy in the English and reforming cause paralleled that of even the most committed of the peers.[20] Henry Balnaves of Halhill, for example, who had embraced the reformed faith in the 1530s, had been active in the moves in 1543 towards Protestantism and the English alliance, he had been in St Andrews Castle with Beaton's murderers and had then shared Knox's servitude in the galleys. Several others had given an early indication of their views when in 1544 they had adhered to Lennox and Angus in supporting the English alliance and the cause of reform which Arran had abandoned: Caprington, Stair, Drumlanrig, Morphie, Houston, Dunrod, Loudoun, Tullibardine, Torry and Bonnington. Some had themselves been in trouble for heresy in the 1540s: Phillorth, Lauriston, Pittarro; others had supported Wishart: Lefnoris, Bar, Dun and Calder. Cumnock, like Balnaves of Halhill, had been among those who held the castle of St Andrews after Wishart's execution had been avenged by the murder of Beaton. A great many had been active collaborators with the English occupying forces in the later 1540s: Colstoun, Meadowflat, Kinnaird, Dundas, Briggis, Fingalton, Innerwick, Wauchtoun, Trabroun, Applegarth, Elphinstone, Johnstone, Cessford, Ferniehirst, Garlies, Drummelzier. Some of those collaborators, who at the time had been stimulated by their enthusiasm for England – or their fear of the consequences for them in Scotland after their treason – to take refuge south of the Border, were now back home and triumphant. The outstanding example of this group was Cockburn of Ormiston, who in 1559 was conveying £1000 from the English government as a subsidy for the Scottish insurgents, only to lose it when he was ambushed by one of the few nobles then still loyal to Mary of Guise. Some of those who now emerged as successful revolutionaries had of course been in the party whom the Dowager had – all in vain – taken to France in 1550 in the hope of curing them of radical ideas: Crawfordjohn, Letham and Tullibardine. More recently, some of them had entertained Knox when he preached in Scotland in 1555; Kinyeancleuch, Gadgirth and Carnale. One of the places where Knox had preached was Calder, in West Lothian, where there was something like a Protestant 'cell', under the auspices of the Sandilands family, renowned for piety both before and after the Reformation. As patrons of the parish they had built one of the few late medieval parish churches in the country and they had recently selected a committed reformer as parson. The laird was Sir James, who had been associated with that conspicuous anglophile, Angus, in the 1530s, had opposed the government's proposals for taxation in 1555 and supplicated Mary of Guise on behalf of the reformers in 1558; and the parson was John Spottiswoode, who had been ordained in England by Archbishop Cranmer and was later to be superintendant of Lothian in the reformed ministry. The laird's eldest son, John, had been in Wishart's company in 1546; his second son, James, who was 'preceptor of Torphichen' or head of the order of St John in Scotland, had visited France in 1550 along with Spottiswoode, apparently among the 'suspects' who were to be exposed to French influence.

There were many in the party of revolution whose family relationships made their attitudes predictable. Some were simply following in their fathers' footsteps, notably the Earls of Argyll and Rothes. Archibald Campbell, 4th Earl of Argyll, had married a sister of the 2nd Earl of Arran (Châtelherault), and this may explain why in the 1540s he had stood by Arran against Lennox. The fact that he had a charter from Cardinal Beaton on the understanding that he would act against heresy may suggest not that he was a loyal supporter of the Church but that, as with others who received similar grants, his loyalty required material encouragement. Before his death in 1558 he had signed the First Bond of the Protestant lords. His signature was accompanied by that of his son, who had been educated at St Andrews under teachers favourable to the Reformation and who, after succeeding as 5th Earl, remained a consistent supporter of the Congregation. The Argylls were the only West Highland magnates who were regularly immersed in national affairs, but their ancestral lands bordered on the Firth of Clyde and so were within easy reach of the central Lowlands, where they themselves had properties and connections. George Leslie, 4th Earl of

Rothes, once a Solway prisoner, had been associated with Angus and the pro-English party in 1544; three of his sons were involved in the murder of Beaton and he himself joined the murderers when they held St Andrews Castle thereafter; a fourth son, Andrew, who succeeded as 5th Earl in 1558, was a full participant in the activities of the insurgents in 1559-60. There are several other examples, notably in Angus, of the links which kinship created among the revolutionary party. Robert Arbuthnot of that ilk was in the company of the father of his first wife, that active reformer Erskine of Dun (who had signed the First Bond) and also of the brother of his second wife, the Earl Marischal. Lord Gray was in partnership with his father-in-law, Lord Ogilvy, James Haliburton turned out with his nephew George, the young laird of Pitcur, whose 'tutor' or guardian he was, and both Walter Lundie of that ilk and Robert Graham of Morphie were accompanied by their sons. If our evidence were fuller it might disclose that the inheritance of opinions could go back more than one generation, but the solitary, though arresting, example is that of Adam Reid of Barskimming, who signed the Ayrshire Bond of 1562: an earlier Adam Reid of Barskimming had been one of the 'Lollards of Kyle' in 1494.

It is always easy to identify affiliations indicated by surname, whether or not blood relationship or direct descent was involved. Eight Hamilton lairds were out in a quarrel which, whatever its ideological appeal, was likely to advance the dynastic interest of their head, James Hamilton, Earl of Arran and Duke of Châtelherault; and half a dozen Cunningham lairds followed the Earl of Glencairn, head of their name. Nor is it surprising that half a dozen Douglas lairds adhered to the anglophile cause of which Archibald Douglas, 6th Earl of Angus, had once been a champion, and the effective head of their name was now James Douglas, 4th Earl of Morton, who was 'tutor' to the 8th Earl of Angus in his minority. There were three Gordon lairds in company with George Gordon, Earl of Huntly. The Campbell Earl of Argyll had the company of two leading cadets, Glenorchy and Loudoun (one from Argyll, the other from Ayrshire), as well as half a dozen lesser Campbell lairds. Lord Ogilvy was followed by four Ogilvy lairds from his own district of Angus and by one or two from farther north. Four Home lairds were in the field with Lord Home, and Ker of Cessford, who took his cue from Home,[21] was followed by four other Kers. It is equally evident that if the head of a family was hostile or lukewarn to the revolution, lairds of his name tended to be at any rate not conspicuous in it. Thus Kennedys, although they had their home in that strongly Protestant area, Ayrshire, on the whole followed Gilbert Kennedy, 4th Earl of Cassillis who, unlike his father, was unsympathetic to the revolt, but one Kennedy laird signed the Leith bond of April 1560, another signed the Book of Discipline and a third signed the Ayrshire bond in 1562. Hugh Montgomery, 3rd Earl of Eglinton, was another Ayrshire peer of conservative views whose influence was like that of Cassillis; three Montgomerys did indeed, like him, attend the 1560 parliament, but only one had sufficient enthusiasm to sign the Ayrshire bond in 1562. However, while blood relationship, the name and customary affiliations were powerful, it would seem that just as ideology occasionally prevailed against them so it could transcend traditional feuds, because although Kers had feuds with Scotts and Rutherfords, yet all three of those families (or rather, names) were represented among the insurgents, and Rothes and Lindsay for once laid aside their habitual feud.

The territorial pattern is instructive, too, and brings in men not immediately connected with noble houses.[22] Over a score of the individuals in our lists came from Angus and Mearns, where Protestantism had taken root early and was by this time reinforced by family ties. About a dozen came from Aberdeenshire and adjoining areas, but in Moray and farther north there were hardly any notable insurgents. The East Lothian area, another conspicuous nest of reforming and anglophile opinion, likewise yields about a dozen names, and Midlothian and West Lothian each added seven. The Borders, to the south of East Lothian, shared something of that area's enthusiasm and produced nearly 20 names. Fife and Kinross, where there had been much Protestant activity in coastal burghs like St Andrews, made a showing of two peers (Rothes and Lindsay) and a dozen lairds. The figure for Ayrshire is exceptionally high, and that sheriffdom was in more than one way a special case. It was the one area in the west which had been strongly affected by the Reformation, and thanks to the bond of 1562 we are particularly well informed about it, with three peers (Glencairn, Boyd and Ochiltree) and about 30 others. The dividing line was slight between Ayrshire and Renfrewshire, to which some of the lairds who signed the Ayrshire bond belonged, but there were two or three other identifiable Renfrewshire names. East of Ayrshire was the seat of Hamilton influence in Lanarkshire, from which came a total of 16. The more remote south-west, from Dumfriesshire to Wigtownshire, perhaps reflected the attachment of Lord Maxwell to the reforming cause in the 1540s and also the influence of English operations in the area at that time, when there was a goodly number of collaborators there, and it now produced several significant names. But the farther we move from the east coast and the English frontier the more signs of support for the Reformation dwindle. In the eastern and southern fringe of Perthshire there seem to have been few insurgents. The region of Argyll, despite the leadership of the Earl, produced few names, and probably not many of the people there were as much affected by what was happening in the Lowlands as was the Earl, with his Lowland properties.

The geographical pattern discernible in the attitudes of lords and lairds can be detected also in the burghs. Twenty-two burghs were represented in the parliament of 1560, easily the largest attendance recorded in this reign. The number included nearly all the significant burghs on or near the east coast, to the number of 14 – Inverness, Banff, Aberdeen, Montrose, Forfar, Dundee, Perth, Cupar, Kinghorn, Inverkeithing, Stirling, Linlithgow, Edinburgh and Haddington. In the Borders, an area affected as much by the tradition of collaboration with the English as by Protestant thought, there were three – Peebles, Jedburgh and Selkirk. From the west there were only five, two of them in Ayrshire – Glasgow, Ayr, Irvine, Kirkcudbright and Wigtown. Significant though these figures are, even they do not represent the total burghal enthusiasm for the Reformation, because St Andrews and Brechin, two of the places known to have had 'privy kirks' before 1560, did not send commissioners to the parliament, and Leith and Dunbar, likewise unrepresented in parliament, were among the places represented at the so-called first general assembly in December 1560.

It is thus beyond question that there was a fairly cohesive and well-rooted body of committed opinion on the revolutionary side. It is more difficult to assess conservative strength. It has often been pointed out – rightly – that there was a considerable amount of vitality in the old religious system, to the extent that right down to the 1550s it was still receiving fresh endowments. In the burghs both gilds and individuals were giving money to enable chaplains to serve at the numerous altars in the town churches, and in the country lairds were still showing an interest in their collegiate churches, alike expressing the consciousness of sin and the craving for redemption which caused others to turn to 'the Evangel'. They would not have done so had they not continued to believe in the efficacy of masses. The friars, or some of them, still had a good record as theologians and preachers, and the Observant Franciscans, in particular, were still faithful to their obligations, including that of poverty. These were, it may be said, signs of health. It is a mistake to believe that health is further indicated by some institutional changes made in the sixteenth century, such as the creation of new canonries and of cathedral and diocesan dignities – even a totally new constitution for the cathedral of Orkney. Institutional change may be a sign not of vitality but of spiritual bankruptcy: in the twentieth century the 'answer' to every problem is to set up a new committee, a new board, a new council, a working party, all of which have the result mainly of diverting energy and money from the congregations, where the church's real work should be done. So, in the sixteenth century, the elaboration of cathedral and diocesan organisation was carried out directly at the expense of the parishes, which were further impoverished to find money for new institutions. A lot of what was done was no more than fiddling while Rome was burning. Besides, little of the vitality, which was in itself real enough, was reflected in the character and work of the prelates who should have provided leadership.

It is hardly surprising that in 1559–60 the opponents of the rebellion lacked both cohesion and resolution. It was abundantly clear before the end of 1559 that the Queen Regent's supporters had been sadly depleted: on 10 November it was reported that only the Earl of Bothwell and Lords Borthwick and Seton were still at her side, and Bothwell was there out of loyalty and not because he opposed the Reformation. Seton, at least, remained faithful and fought alongside the French troops in Leith after the English army arrived to lay siege to it in April 1560. Obviously, although Mary of Guise had the advantage of representing lawfully constituted authority, the nationalist and religious appeal of the revolt outweighed that consideration in most minds once the notion of superseding the reigning sovereigns had been dropped from the insurgents' programme. And, after the Queen Regent was removed from the scene by her death on 11 June 1560, even those whose attachment to her had persisted were in difficulty. Who and what were they now to fight for? The young Queen was in France, married to the French King and perhaps unlikely ever to return; the success of the revolution, with English support, was assured; there seemed no future in continued opposition to the administration which had been set up by the successful insurgents and which, at the time of the treaty of Edinburgh in July, received at least *de facto* recognition from the lawful sovereigns. It is not surprising that in July James Beaton, Archbishop of Glasgow, packed up and went off to France, taking with him the archives of his see as if to close a chapter of history.

There are conflicting accounts of what happened in the parliament of August which abolished papal authority and the mass and adopted a reformed Confession of Faith. Knox has it that 'there were present . . . a great number of the adversaries of our religion' and that they 'were commanded in God's name to object, if they could' against the Confession, but that among the lords and lairds only Atholl, Somerville and Borthwick voted against it and the bishops 'spake nothing'.[23] Randolph, the English ambassador in Edinburgh, reported quite differently that Cassillis and Caithness (whose names are not in the sederunt) alone said 'Nae'.[24] To confuse us still farther, Archbishop Hamilton implied that Cassillis, Caithness, Crawford, Atholl, Eglinton, Home and Gray absented themselves to avoid having to vote,[25] yet all of them save Cassillis and Caithness are recorded as present and Gray at least had shown all the signs of attachment to the Reformation. The only indication, apart from that manifestly erroneous assertion by the Archbishop, that there might have been something like intimidation, is a clause in the 'Concessions' by Mary and Francis in July, to the effect that, when parliament met, 'those who were in use to be present' should be entitled to attend, which may have been designed to safeguard the rights of the prelates; but in practice those who had the courage to attend and oppose the Confession – whether they were laymen or clerics – apparently suffered no ill consequences. The one thing that is clear is the complete lack of leadership on the conservative side. We have two reports on the attitude of the Archbishop and the Bishops of Dunkeld and Dunblane. One was that 'thus far they did liberally profess, that they would agree to all things that might stand with God's Word, and consent to abolish all abuses crept in in the church not agreeable with the scriptures; and asked longer time to deliberate'; the other is that the Archbishop said of the Confession that 'as he would not utterly condemn it, so was he loth to give his consent thereto', and Dunkeld and Dunblane concurred. A few weeks later the primate was reported to have 'given over his mass and received the common prayers' (that is, the English Prayer Book).[26] This evidence of hesitation on the part of the bishops agrees well enough with suggestions that their attitude discouraged conservatives. The Earl Marischal, Knox said, declared that it confirmed him in his worst suspicions about the Roman Church and in his attachment to the reformed faith, and Randolph told the same story: 'The Lord Marischal said, though he were otherwise assured that it [the Confession] was true, yet might he be the bolder to pronounce it, for that he saw there present the pillars of the Pope's Church and not one of them that would speak against it'.[27] A few weeks later Randolph gave additional information about the alignment of the nobles: Cassillis, he said, remained obstinate against the Reformation; Atholl's opposition was due partly to his feud with Huntly, who (though not in the parliament) had lent his name to the insurrection; Eglinton, whose wife was a daughter of Châtelherault whom he wanted to divorce, 'loves his wife so well he will do nothing for her father's sake', in other words would take the opposite side from the Duke; and Marischal had now left the parliament, an action deplored by his son.[28]

Other evidence, besides what we know about the parliament, likewise indicates a lack of confident, principled or consistent opposition at this stage. Atholl, Somerville and Borthwick may have voted against the Confession, as Knox says, but Somerville had signed the insurgents' bond in April and all three supported the Arran-Elizabeth marriage proposal later in the year. As already explained, that proposal had strong religious implications, for if the marriage took place it would commit Scotland to Protestantism, yet, despite their hesitation about the Confession, the Bishops of Dunkeld and Dunblane supported it, as well as Archbishop Hamilton, to whose dynastic interests it meant so much. The three other bishops who supported the proposed marriage – John Campbell, Elect of the Isles, James Hamilton of Argyll and Alexander Gordon of Galloway – were all committed Protestants.

Weighing all the evidence, it is possible to recognise certain opponents of the religious revolution. Cassillis and Eglinton, on their earlier and later records, fall into this category, and it was not for nothing that Eglinton was later characterised as 'a rank papist'.[29] With them we may bracket a few absentees from the parliament – Montrose, who was to be the only peer to attend Mary's first mass when she returned in 1561, Oliphant, whose sympathies seem always to have been conservative, Seton, who, after his consistent support of Mary of Guise, had gone off to France like Archbishop Beaton (though unlike Beaton he returned), Sempill, one of the few who (so far as we know) suffered materially for his refusal to join the Hamiltons, and perhaps Fleming, whose uncle the commendator of Whithorn likewise absented himself from the parliament and was later prosecuted for saying mass. Huntly, whose hesitation about signing the insurgents' bond in April has been described, repeated in June his allegation about the strength of conservatism in the north and implied that he was under some pressure from local opinion;[30] he pled sickness for not attending the parliament in August; he did not, so far as we know from a defective record, approve of the Arran-Elizabeth match; and before the year was out the inconstant man was reported to have set up the mass again.

Conservatives could take courage from the fact that the legislation of 1560 was at best of doubtful validity, for it had been passed by a parliament forbidden to deal with religion and it would be open to challenge unless or until Mary ratified it – which she never did. At the worst (from their point of view) it forbade the mass and abolished papal authority, but went no farther in defining law and practice. Consequently, no one could say it was now illegal for bishops to exercise their traditional functions, and they sometimes did so. And, despite the act against papal authority, litigants and supplicants continued to have recourse to Rome, while some notaries continued to insert the pontifical year in their instruments. Of course it would be naive to suggest that the men who did so were 'Roman Catholics'; they were simply continuing practices which had assuredly been legal and might still be legal, in a situation where it was hard to say what was and was not so. They were no more 'Roman Catholics' than the drafters of crown gifts of ecclesiastical revenues, who continued for another generation to declare that such gifts were to be as valid as if provision had been made at Rome. Yet this all meant that the old system continued to have some of the attractions of established authority.

New hope was injected into the conservative ranks when Francis II of France died, for this meant that Mary was now more likely to return to Scotland: a revival of courage among the 'papists' was one of the ways in which, as Knox said, 'The King's death made great alteration'. Randolph reported a meeting at Dunbar on 10 December 1560 (by which date it would be known that Francis was desperately, perhaps mortally, ill, though not that his death, on the 5th, had taken place), attended by Lord Home, his brother the Abbot of Jedburgh, Sir Andrew Ker of Cessford, William Ker, parson of Roxburgh, Rutherford of Hundolie, Ormiston of that ilk and the lairds of Langton and Greenhead. Besides, Randolph went on, Huntly, Sutherland and Eglinton were privy to the meeting and Ruthven (who had not been in Edinburgh since the parliament) was very friendly with Home. Eglinton's matrimonial affairs continued to be a barrier between him and his father-in-law Châtelherault: his wife accused him of impotence, though since his wife had left him 'he hath gotten a wench with child', and the Duke was pressing for a divorce, in the hope that his daughter might then marry Cassillis.[31] If the Dunbar meeting was as sinister as Randolph thought, it would suggest that some who had supported the revolution now had second thoughts, and, although we hear nothing farther of the results of the meeting or of other activities of 'papists', the presumption may be that some such group, no less than the provisional government of the Lords of the Congregation, were preparing to put their case to Mary as her return became ever more likely. In June 1561 there was word of the activities of 'most wicked papists'[32] and later in that year Huntly made his famous boast that he could set up the mass again in three shires – which Lord James denied to be in his power.[33]

There was a limited challenge to the reformers on theological grounds, which must have existed in 1560 and 1561 although some of the evidence does not appear until two or three years later. Quentin Kennedy, uncle of the Earl of Cassillis and Commendator of Crosraguel, whose *Compendious Tractive* (1558) appealed to the traditions of the Church and to the authority of the early general councils – but not to the Pope – against the foundations which reformers laid on the scriptures and on private judgment, challenged John Knox to debate and had a disputation with him at Maybole in September 1562. Ninian Winyet, a Linlithgow schoolmaster, in *Certaine Tractatis* (1562) posed questions which searched out weaknesses and inconsistencies in the reformers' position and resolutely upheld the concept of a personal succession in the ministry from apostolic times. Numerous priests were to be prosecuted for saying mass in 1563 and 1569, and no doubt there were many others who said mass but escaped prosecution. And there may have been an uncounted multitude of layfolk who could say, 'My heart gives me to the mass and therefore I can not come to the communion'.[34] That remark was of deep significance. Granted the existence of a body, perhaps a growing body, of opinion prepared to challenge the revolution, the conviction remains that there was confusion and lack of clear belief on the conservative side. Was a stand to be made for the kind of non-papal catholicism towards which the Scottish church had been moving, or for the ultramontanism of the Counter-Reformation? The Council of Trent had not yet finished its deliberations, Roman Catholic doctrine was not yet defined. The evidence from later years, when even conservative bishops were very reluctant to have dealings with papal envoys, suggests that there were few real papalists. In the circumstances, were the so-called 'papists' very clear in their own minds about what they stood for, except for their attachment to the consolation they were accustomed to receive from the mass?

# 4
# THE QUEEN AND HER FRIENDS

*1560 Dec. 5* Death of Francis II
*1561 Jan.* First Book of Discipline approved
*August* Mary returned to Scotland
*1562* Huntly's rebellion: Corrichie
*1565 July* Mary married Darnley
*August–Sept.* 'The Chaseabout Raid'
*1566 Mar.* Murder of Riccio
*June 19* Birth of Prince James

Already before Mary's return in August 1561 the revolutionary coalition, if such it had been, was showing signs of breaking up. Members of its more conservative wing, who had sacrificed their religious preferences 'for the common wealth and liberty of their native country', now seemed likely to make common cause with resurgent 'papists'. But even among convinced Protestants there was dissension, partly because diverse influences, English as well as continental, had helped to shape their opinions. Knox was almost alone in having been directly inspired by Calvin at Geneva, and there were other leading divines who had come under the milder influences of Lutheran Germany or Scandinavia, Zurich and England and had never been near Geneva; several, indeed, had never, so far as we know, been out of Scotland. Thus 'divers men were of divers judgments' as Knox admitted, certainly on forms of worship and quite possibly also on church government. Principles apart, conflicting material interests had led to division on the financial proposals of the Book of Discipline, which appealed to the more altruistic but not to those whose minds ran on their own aggrandisement and thought the proposed endowment of the reformed church and its ministers much too lavish: many lords, they protested, had not so much to spend, and the scheme was 'a devout imagination'. There was no need for Mary or anyone else to 'split the reformers'.

Concurrently with the debate on the Book of Discipline there were the first signs of dissension on the need to define the attitude to be taken to Mary, for the death of Francis on 5 December 1560 made it likely that she would return from France. The coalition had not been directed either ostensibly or in reality against Mary personally, but against the crown as the agent of France and of Rome, and revolt against a Regent ruling under French direction was not necessarily going to shape relations with a young Queen present among her subjects. Another way in which the King's death 'made great alteration' was that it was followed by Elizabeth's rejection of the suit of Young Arran and the revival of the idea – which had been mooted long before – that he should marry Mary. There had been a remarkable consensus on the Arran-Elizabeth match, because by perpetuating the English alliance it would secure Scotland against a renewed threat from France, but the Arran-Mary match, while it was of course warmly entertained not only by the Hamilton interest but also by Elizabeth and by ardent Scottish Protestants because it would commit Mary to the Reformation, did not commend itself to those who were less enthusiastic about tying her hands on the religious issue or about elevating the Hamiltons. Arran, before his return to Scotland in the autumn of 1559, had been influenced by French Huguenots and, despite (or possibly because of) his mental instability, was far more resolute than his father, Châtelherault. He aligned himself with the Geneva-inspired Knox and the more radical wing of the reformers. Thus, should Mary come back still an adherent of a faith now condemned by parliament, extremists, including Knox and Arran, were determined to countenance no celebration of mass either publicly or privately. However, more moderate men, who, as it turned out, were prepared actually to defend by force Mary's right to have mass in her chapel, were headed by Lord James, who, although himself attached to the reformed church, was too realistic a politician to agree with Knox and Arran. The other leading 'moderate' was William Maitland of Lethington – 'Mitchell Wylie' or Machiavelli to his Scottish contemporaries. He had been appointed by Mary of Guise, in December 1558, to the office of Secretary of State, which, with those of Chancellor, Treasurer and Comptroller, formed the core of the executive of the Scottish crown. Lethington may not have cared so little for religion as to declare the devil to be 'but any bogle [scarecrow] of the nursery', but his mind was undoubtedly 'somewhat more given to policy than to Mr Knox preaching',[1] and his eyes were never deflected from the grand design of Anglo-Scottish concord. The question of the marriage and the question of the mass raised constitutional issues, because coercion of the Queen would infringe her sovereign rights and was unacceptable to those who respected 'the authority'. All in all, the dissolution of the coalition of 1559–60 was clearly reflected in Knox's admission that the 'servants of God' were fighting 'a double battle', not only against 'idolatry' – the papists – but also against 'such as sometime would have been esteemed the chief pillars of the kirk' (including Lord James).

That enthusiastic Protestant James Sandilands, preceptor of Torphichen, had been despatched to France soon after the parliament of August to ask Mary to ratify its legislation, but met with a refusal. Now, in March 1561, Lord James, as official spokesman of the provisional government, went off to interview his sister, and he returned in May. The likelihood is that he indicated that Mary could count on her subjects' obedience and on freedom in the exercise of her religion provided that she did not come as the spearhead of an attempt at renewed French domination and did not take action to reverse the ecclesiastical revolution. Lord James was putting the moderates' point of view, but there were competitors. Arran was certainly in the field to represent one extreme, and no doubt there were counter offers from the religious conservatives, though we know less about them. Those who had joined the revolt on nationalist and not religious grounds must have hoped that the Queen would aim at some kind of ecclesiastical reaction, to the extent at least of tolerating the mass. They would not have welcomed any attempt to restore French influence but if that prospect could be disregarded then they might make common cause with those who had opposed the revolution. Although, after the demoralisation of 1560, expectations from Mary might take time to rally the conservatives, there were any number of grounds on which she could have formed a party to support reaction. The enthusiasts for 'the Evangel' were as yet hardly organised except in a few local congregations, and the latent sympathy and inarticulate preference for the other side might have responded to leadership. With characteristic percipience, Maitland had written in August 1560: 'Although the religion here hath in outward appearance the upper hand, and few or none that openly do profess the contrary, yet know we the hollow hearts of a great number who would be glad to see it and us overthrown and if time served would join the Queen's authority to that effect'.[2]

But while it is true that, had leadership been forthcoming, especially in the shape of lawful authority personified by a young Queen, much could have been made of the conservative element, yet Mary had little to gain from offering herself as head of a movement of uncertain strength. She could – and did – concede most of what the revolution had contended for, without forfeiting the support of conservative opinion; she would be likely to forfeit that support only in the event of her renouncing her mass and breaking off all communication with Rome. Therefore, while she could up to a point afford to offend conservatives, who were unlikely to operate against her, she had everything to gain by cultivating the reformers, conciliating them and winning their allegiance also. If it is true that Mary was invited to make for the north-east and join a reactionary movement led by Huntly, she was wise to refuse the rôle of the creator of civil war, and Huntly's past record did not inspire confidence.

The circumstances of Mary's arrival in August 1561 suggested that she had accepted the understanding which Lord James had offered. She did not come with a show of force, she brought only a modest escort and not even a bodyguard – a want which the Scots themselves had soon to supply – and although her train included three of her French uncles it did not include the two who were cardinals. Mary was not being imposed by a foreign power on reluctant subjects, she seemed to be committing herself to the loyalty of her people. As Maitland saw it, she had come with no forces 'to trust her person in our hands'.[3] Six days after landing at Leith Mary issued a proclamation forbidding meantime any 'alteration or innovation of the state of religion . . . which her majesty found public and universally standing at her majesty's arrival in this her realm'. This was tantamount to a recognition of the ecclesiastical revolution. Thus, by coming as she did and issuing that proclamation, Mary was offering what both the religious and political wings of the insurgents had contended for and was offering it without any constitutional revolution or repudiation of 'the authority'. The composition of the council, too, was far from suggesting any intention of reaction, for it consisted of Châtelherault, Huntly, Argyll, Bothwell, Erroll, Marischal, Atholl, Morton, Montrose, Glencairn, Lord James, Lord Erskine and the officials. Prelates were excluded, as were Protestant divines. Huntly's record was assuredly not that of an unequivocal papalist; Bothwell, while his loyalty to the crown and his hatred of England had made him remain faithful to Mary of Guise to the end, was a strong Protestant; nearly all the others except Montrose had been associated with the insurgents to a greater or less extent, though Atholl had voted against the legislation of 1560. By the following January other zealous Protestants were associated with the administration – Rothes, Ruthven, Lindsay, Ochiltree and Wishart of Pittarro.[4] None of the leading executive and judicial offices had changed hands in the course of the revolution, and all the existing holders continued: Huntly as Chancellor since 1546, Robert Richardson as Treasurer (1559), Villemore as Comptroller (1555), Lethington as Secretary (1558), MacGill as Clerk Register (1554), Henry Sinclair as Lord President (1558) and John Spens of Condie as Lord Advocate (1555). Neither the revolution nor Mary's return seems to have caused any dislocation.

Although Mary always refused to ratify the acts of 1560, including the one condemning the mass (which would have made her own mass illegal), her administration was conducted very much as if those acts had the force of law. In February 1562 she agreed to a scheme whereby one third of the revenues of most benefices was collected by crown officers and used partly to augment her own revenues and partly to pay stipends to the clergy of the reformed church. The fact that she was now dependent on church revenues for part of her income – and was so to an increasing extent as the years passed – must have been a strong disincentive to any attempt at a counter-revolution. Besides, the crown was able to assume many of the former papal powers in the disposition of benefices, so that crown patronage was vastly increased. Mary had a strong vested interest in the Reformation, and a simple reversal of the decision of 1560 was out of the question because it would have been financially ruinous.

Yet it is not at all certain that only a vested interest dictated Mary's conciliatory policy, because many of her actions are impossible to reconcile with rigid attachment to Roman Catholicism. She had no scruples about attending at least one Protestant baptism and several Protestant marriage ceremonies, even by the austere rites of the Scottish reformed church, and she several times expressed a favourable view of the worship of the Church of England. There were reports in 1562 that her uncle the Cardinal of Lorraine – whose liberal views caused him to be characterised by an indignant Pope as 'damned and a heretic, or to speak plainly one of the Protestants' – urged her to 'embrace the religion of England'.[5] In the spring of 1565 it was noted that she ate flesh in Lent for the first time, and this was followed by reports that she had given up her mass.[6] In 1568, when she was in England after her abdication, it was remarked that she 'doth seem, outwardly, not only to favour this form [that is, the Prayer Book] but also the chief articles of the religion of the gospel, namely justification by faith only; and she heareth the faults of papistry revealed, by preaching or otherwise, with contented ears and with gentle and weak replies'.[7] A year later she 'heard the English service with a Book of the Psalms in English [that is, an English Prayer Book] in her hand'.[8] While Mary ruled in Scotland she gave little encouragement to a papal envoy who arrived in 1562 and she did not arrange for Scottish representation at the final session of the Council of Trent, which (despite her protestations to the contrary) she could easily have done. Anyone could see how hard it was to reconcile her occasional reassurances to the Pope with her actions, which were disappointing to zealous Romanists, as she herself was well aware, for in 1563 she asked the Cardinal of Lorraine to make excuses for her if she failed in her duty towards religion. The opportunism was obvious, and she could be candid enough about it: 'Would you have me to lose France and Spain and all my friends in other places, by seeming to change my religion, and yet I am not assured that the Queen my sister will be my assured friend?'[9] Similarly, when her marriage to the Duke of Norfolk was under consideration in 1568: 'If she marries Norfolk, she loses France and Spain and all Catholic friends beyond sea: and what will she get instead?'[10] Her half-brother Lord James, by that time Earl of Moray and Regent for Mary's son and supplanter, was not likely to say anything in her favour, and he may not have been justified in doubting her sincerity: 'Her resorting to the service of the Church of England serves her turn presently, to move godly men to conceive a good opinion of her conformity. But I fear being restored to her government again . . . it should be one of the most difficult conditions to become good for that she should abandon the mass'.[11]

If Mary was no consistently faithful daughter of Rome, it is equally clear that she did not represent commitment to France. The English satellite administration of the successful revolutionaries of 1560 might have lasted had Mary not returned from France or if, on her return, she had fallen into the hands of the Hamiltons, married Young Arran and renounced her mass. Mary escaped that, and was able to pursue an independent policy. But she showed considerable enthusiasm for an understanding with Elizabeth in the interests of her own prospects in the English succession, and it was Elizabeth's fault, not Mary's, that negotiations finally broke down. Elizabeth on her side did nothing to keep Scotland in a satellite status. She could have had Mary eating out of her hand if she had conceded the Scottish Queen's right to succeed her on the English throne, but she did not do this and thereby come to terms with Mary. It is so easy to represent Mary as fighting a heroic battle to keep the Roman Catholic and francophile flag flying in the midst of a hostile people, but this is utterly at variance with the facts of the first four years or so of her personal reign.

When militant disaffection first appeared it came not from Protestants or anglophiles but from a reputedly conservative quarter. The Earl of Huntly had been a tardy and reluctant participant in the insurrection of 1559–60 and his boast that he could set up the mass again in three shires suggests that he soon wearied of the company of the Lords of the Congregation and expected Mary's return to encourage a reaction. It is, however, far from clear whether the rebellion he headed in the autumn of 1562 had much, if anything, to do with religion, and there is nothing to suggest that the Earl was setting himself up, as he might have done, as the rallying-point for the extensive, if hitherto inert, preference for the old ways. Huntly's real resentment was probably against Lord James, for Huntly had been administering the earldoms of Mar and Moray, and gifts of them in favour of Lord James were drawn up at the beginning of 1562 (though the grant of Moray was not made public until September). There was another element, in that Sir John Gordon, Huntly's third (and second surviving) son, had designs on Mary and was even believed to have plotted the seizure of her person. It may, however, be allowed that Huntly possibly disapproved of the Queen's concessions to the reformed church as well as of the anglophile policy which her government was pursuing. What happened was that Mary (who seems to have planned action against Sir John Gordon for an attack on Lord Ogilvy) reached Inverness to find that the captain of the castle, on the orders of Lord Gordon, Huntly's eldest son and heir, refused her admission. Huntly assembled a force but was defeated at Corrichie (28 October 1562) and died suddenly after his capture.

So far as the available evidence indicates, the base of support for Huntly was almost entirely familial and local. This was potentially a very great base. Huntly's family, the Gordons, were of southern origin but they had acquired lands in Angus and in both the Lowland and Highland areas of Aberdeenshire and Banffshire. The Earl had been Chancellor of the realm since 1546; he was sheriff of Aberdeen and of Inverness, and the latter sheriffship gave him nominal authority over most of the territories as far as the Pentland Firth; as bailie of the bishopric of Aberdeen he had some control over the lands of that see (where his uncle was bishop); and his cousin had succeeded to the earldom of Sutherland. Yet in his actual campaign not a single other peer took part, though Sutherland was in treasonable correspondence with him, and it was reported that he had not more than 500 men, some of whom deserted before battle was joined. This number, if correct, was a very poor showing, for much less important men than Huntly could muster two or three hundred. Among Huntly's 40 most easily identifiable supporters over half were Gordon lairds who were presumably his vassals, and 28 Gordons are named in the remission which was finally granted for the rebellion, on 26 February 1567. The other identifiable supporters were almost all lairds in Aberdeenshire and the adjacent north-eastern counties: Abercromby of Pitmedden, Baillie of Ardneily, Barclay of that ilk, Bissett of Lessendrum, Brodie of that ilk, Cheyne of Straloch, Forbes of Keithmore, Forbes of Tolquhon, Irvine of Drum, Menzies of Pitfoddellis, Douglas of Tilwhillie, Dunbar of Conzie, Dunbar of Pennik and Murray of Cobairdie. Clearly this was in no real sense a party, and the composition of such a following would rather confirm the belief that the campaign was not undertaken out of any principles, either political or religious. It is true that two or three Gordon lairds took part against Huntly and that the Forbeses were divided. There was a feud of such long standing between Lord Forbes and Huntly that Forbes undertook, along with Hays and Leslies, to fight against Huntly even if no others joined them, but the Forbeses of Keithmore and Tolquhon were on Huntly's side. Such divisions were perhaps as likely to arise from personal differences as from convictions. Apart from indications that personal motives were at work, it seems fatal to the notion that Huntly was rallying ecclesiastical conservatives that Atholl, who had contested the Confession of Faith in 1560, was Mary's lieutenant and that the Queen had the support of others who had not been on the Protestant side, like Erroll and Montrose. All in all the disaffection was so limited that it would be a somewhat lame argument to make any deductions from the names of those who were in arms on either side.

Huntly was forfeited posthumously: his sons Lord Gordon and Sir John Gordon and his cousin the Earl of Sutherland were condemned to death, and Sir John was executed. Whatever the precise significance of the rebellion,

Mary's action against it can hardly have failed to depress the Roman Catholic cause in one of its centres, and it showed clearly that a preference for Rome and the mass – though perhaps in Huntly's case not a very strong preference – was not an acceptable excuse for rebellion. At the same time, the rebellion possibly caused a measure of Protestant alarm and its suppression a measure of Protestant reassurance. It may be significant that the Protestant bond signed at Ayr (referred to earlier) was dated 4 September 1562 (by which date Mary had been a week in Aberdeen on her way to encounter Huntly), and, to judge from what was to happen three years later, at the time of Moray's rebellion, there may well have been other such bonds, in which the Queen's faithful subjects reaffirmed their Protestantism. To that extent Huntly's rebellion, or rather its defeat by the Queen, should have helped to draw Mary and the Protestants together.

Certainly it would seem that the two years and more after Corrichie represented the peak of Mary's success as a ruler. If her policy had all along been dictated by an opportunism and self-interest aimed at making her acceptable to both parties in Scotland, to both parties in England and to continental princes, then it had gone some way towards achieving its purpose, but her domestic programme seemed to be not so much equitable as weighted heavily towards the reformers. When the first parliament of her personal reign met in June 1563 it began by passing an act of oblivion to cover the period of the Protestant rebellion, reckoned generously from 6 March 1559 to 1 September 1561. Two other acts implied statutory recognition for the reformed church, one providing that the ministers should have the use of manses and glebes and another that parish churches should be repaired. Other acts, against adultery and sorcery, reflected the puritanism of the reformers, but it has to be remembered that puritanism had been similarly reflected in legislation of Mary of Guise and was not confined to Protestants, for a contemporary Pope insisted on draping nude statues and banished prostitutes from Rome. Mary several times reissued her initial proclamation to reassure the Protestants, and although she occasionally intervened to protect an individual Roman Catholic from harassment, and her own chaplains were protected, other priests, including Archbishop Hamilton (who, it was noted, had said mass at Easter 1562) were imprisoned for violating the Queen's proclamation. The whole tenor of the government's ecclesiastical policy bore the marks of an administration favourable to the Reformation. Other actions sprang not from religious or moral intent, but from a sheer desire for good government. The parliament of June 1563 renewed old legislation to restrain the export of bullion and the import of false coin, to alleviate dearth of grain and to regulate fish-traps. Other acts were aimed at curbing new methods of making salt, restraining the export of coal, regulating units of measurement, especially of capacity, and forbidding the shooting of game. The privileges of burghs were confirmed (with a guarantee that they would be consulted on foreign policy) and a commission (including some leading reformers) was appointed to review the endowments of St Andrews University.

Besides the old and oft-recurring problems with which some of that legislation was concerned, there were new problems arising from the

Reformation with which the government attempted to deal fairly and sensibly. Almost the first act of Mary's council in September 1561 had been in favour of 'poor tenants' injured when lands passed to new proprietors, and another act of council followed in December. In June 1563 parliament legislated against the removal of tenants and in December 1563 there was an act obliging new proprietors of church lands to seek crown confirmation. In that same month of December the first step was taken towards remedying the confusion into which the events of 1560 had thrown the wide jurisdiction formerly exercised by the ecclesiastical courts: in the interests of litigants, suits were to have 'the most summary process and a shorter end',[12] and a secular commissary court in Edinburgh was set up in the following year. Somewhat similarly, an element of doubt surrounding the status of notaries public, many of whom had been appointed 'by apostolic [that is, papal] authority', presumably lay behind acts of parliament of June 1563 regulating their appointment and their work in conveyancing.

Legislation for social justice, however well intentioned, could not be effective unless order prevailed throughout the land, and to this problem too Mary's government turned its attention. The age-old problem of 'putting order on the Border' was before the council at the outset, in September 1561, when provision was made for justice ayres (*anglicé* eyres) in that area. One of the acts of June 1563 was directed against the raising of bands of armed men, and an act of council of the following September was concerned with one peculiarly troublesome Highland band of armed men, the 'Clan Gregor'. Efforts were made, as they had sometimes been made by earlier governments, to quench feuds – Bothwell and Seton in 1561, Bothwell and Lord James in 1561, Hamilton and Lennox in 1564, the MacDonalds of Glen Nevis and the Camerons in 1564.

While Mary's policy must have been disappointing on purely ecclesiastical grounds to militant papalists as well as to radical Protestants, there seemed on the whole good prospects of the fulfilment of the intention of the act of oblivion that 'a common peace, union, reconciliation and quietness' should be 'perpetually observed by the whole lieges and inhabitants of this realm so that they may at their uttermost power with a uniformity of mind obey and serve her majesty in all sorts as becomes most humble and faithful subjects, to the glory of God, her Highness's contentment and common weal of their native country'.[13]

Mary's tolerant and perhaps equivocal policy went a long way to neutralise opposition. It was true that Knox preached vehemently against her mass and that Young Arran, besides making a formal protest against her initial proclamation because it protected her French servants in their private 'idolatry', refused to come to court as long as the Queen's mass persisted (though his father came, 'earnest in the Protestant religion' as he was).[14] The town council of Edinburgh issued a proclamation classifying mass-mongers with whoremongers, and when Mary went on progresses there were some local disturbances because she took her mass with her. On the other hand, three of her half-brothers, James, Robert and John, all members of the reformed church, protected her chaplain from molestation when he said mass on her first Sunday in Scotland. Many thought Knox's sermons against her mass were untimely, and his hectoring attitude probably had little support. Mary could not come to terms with him, but then neither could the Protestant Queen of England, and probably many Scottish Protestants thought as their sovereign did. Certainly the rift between Knox and Lord James became so deep that they ceased to be on speaking terms. When Knox spoke of the dwindling support he enjoyed and alluded to 'some enchantment whereby men are bewitched'[15] he was admitting the effect of Mary's charm and the fact that, as a sovereign's court at Holyrood was a novelty for all men under middle age, she had ample opportunities to win sympathy and support. A young woman with a gifted personality was in a position to reinforce, with those she met, the favourable impression made by the political wisdom of her policy.

What Mary's policies did to create, if not a following for her, at any rate favourable opinion of her, must be considered in association with the additional contribution made by her personal relationships and her place in Scottish society. Her social setting must first be seen in the light of her connections by kinship and by attachment. There can be no doubt that the Queen had the normal Scottish appreciation of the significance of blood relationship: she was indignant enough when a daughter of Lord Stewart of Ochiltree married John Knox, because this was an unsuitable match for one who was 'of the blood and name' of Stewart.[16] But, by the standard of blood relationship, Mary was remarkably isolated, at least so far as lawful kindred were concerned. The reigning line of Stewarts had all along been a tenuous one, with seldom more than one child surviving his father. Mary had, of course, no legitimate brothers or sisters, she had no lawful aunts or uncles in Scotland, no lawful first cousins in Scotland. She did not even have any lawful great-aunts or great-uncles in Scotland, and so no lawful second cousins. Only among the descendants of James II, who had lived a hundred years before, were there lawful kinsfolk of Mary in Scotland, and they existed in both the Hamilton family and the Lennox family.

Lawful kinsfolk in Scotland were, therefore, scarce indeed. Leaving aside her kinsfolk in France, on her mother's side, Mary did have an aunt and cousins in England. It is a little startling to remind ourselves that Elizabeth Tudor, Mary's first cousin once removed, was more closely related to her than any legitimate member of the royal house in the Scotland to which Mary came in 1561. But Mary's grandmother, Margaret Tudor, sister of Henry VIII, who was Elizabeth's father, had married as her second husband the 6th Earl of Angus, and their daughter, Margaret Douglas, was half-sister to James V and therefore aunt to Mary. She married the 4th Earl of Lennox, but her husband had been exiled after being forfeited for his activities on behalf of Henry VIII in 1544. Lennox did return to Scotland in 1564, but his wife, the Countess, Mary's aunt, seems even then to have remained in England; their son Henry returned in 1565 to become Mary's second husband. The Lennoxes were related through Countess Margaret to the Douglas Earls of Angus and Morton, and a sister of the 4th Earl of Lennox had been a mistress of James V and mother of Lord Adam Stewart, one of Mary's half-brothers, but possibly links through the Lennoxes meant little to the Queen, and that family came on the scene too late to do much to integrate her into Scottish society, where they themselves were almost strangers.

Mary had a more numerous kin who had not been born in lawful wedlock, the offspring mainly of James IV and James V. She had half-brothers and half-sisters in plenty. First among them was Lord James, best known as Earl of Moray. He was about ten years older than Mary, who must have known of him, very much as an elder brother, before she went to France in 1548 at the age of nearly six and again when he was in France in 1550. By the time she was widowed by the death of Francis, James had emerged as not only the eldest surviving son of James V but also as the foremost in politics, for he had been a leader of the revolution of 1559–60. When he went to France in 1561 as the spokesman of the victorious insurgents he put before Mary terms for her return which were, in substance, moderate, but if he dealt with her then, as he did shortly after her return, 'rudely, homely and bluntly'[17] their encounter cannot have been cordial. Mary may well have felt fear rather than love for this formidable and severe figure, whose ostentatious pretensions to superior virtue can hardly have made him an agreeable companion. It is true that she could sometimes appeal emotionally to their kinship: in 1566, after he had led a rebellion against her and had returned from exile in England hoping to profit by the murder of Riccio, Mary – who surely had no inkling that he had been involved in the murder plot – embraced and kissed him and exclaimed that if he had been at home he would not have allowed her to be so uncourteously handled.[18] And later, when Mary was an exile and Moray was Regent of Scotland, she seems still to have hoped that by a personal appeal she might secure a fair hearing. Moray, on his side, may well have been ready to presume on his relationship with the Queen, though probably out of calculation rather than out of human warmth. When he visited her in her captivity at Lochleven and evidently threatened her with death to induce her to ratify her abdication and his appointment as Regent, he upbraided her like 'a ghostly father',[19] which suggests an approach by someone who combined his conscious rectitude with the authority of an elder brother and a claim to the Queen's familiar attention.

Among the other half-brothers, Lord Robert, Commendator of Holyrood, and Lord John, Commendator of Coldingham, were a little younger than James and the mere fact that they lacked his pre-eminent seniority may have brought them closer to Mary. Besides, they had gone to France with her in 1548 and spent some time there. When she came back to Scotland in 1561 these high-spirited young men were much about the court and shared various amusements and recreations with the Queen. Lord John, who seems to have been particularly cultivated, was very likely Mary's favourite. She was present at Crichton in January 1562 when he married Jean Hepburn, sister of the Earl of Bothwell whom Mary herself was to marry later. John did not long survive his marriage, and when he died Mary said that 'God always took from her those persons in whom she had greatest pleasure'.[20] He left a son, Francis, presumably named after Mary's first husband and with Mary as his godmother. The Queen seems to have made much of this child, no doubt out of the affection she had felt for his father and out of grief for John's early death. There were two other half-brothers, another Robert and the Adam already mentioned who had some Lennox blood in him, but little is heard of them and, unlike Moray and the elder Robert, they are not mentioned in Mary's testamentary disposition of 1566.

Besides her half-brothers, Mary had a half-sister, Jean, who married the Earl of Argyll. She seems to have had something of the same relationship with the Queen as Lords Robert and John, and perhaps even a closer intimacy simply because she was a woman. It may have helped to draw them together that Countess Jean had unhappy relations with her husband – for which she was blamed – and Mary was sympathetic to this possibly wayward sister. Lady Jean was one of the tiny and especially intimate group who formed the supper party in the Queen's apartments on the night when Riccio was murdered.

Going a generation farther back among the illegitimate royal brood, James IV had two children who left descendants. The son, James, who like his nephew was created Earl of Moray, married into the Argyll family, so that Lady Jean's husband, as well as Lady Jean, was related to Mary. Janet, the daughter of James IV, married Lord Fleming and was the mother of Mary Fleming, one of the four Maries.

Mary Fleming was the only one of the four Maries who had a close blood relationship with the Queen, but all four shared another relationship with her that was in a sense closer than kinship. They were, of all her subjects, those whom the Queen knew best and with whom she had the warmest personal friendship. They were her childhood companions even before they accompanied her to France when she went there in her sixth year, and they seem to have remained in or about her household for the rest of her life in France and Scotland. They were, besides, involved in a set of close-knit and intricate relationships.

Mary Fleming, a grand-daughter of James V and Agnes Stewart, Countess of Bothwell (grandmother also of Mary's third husband), was the most Scottish of the four, for each of the other three – and this is highly significant – had a French mother or stepmother. However, Mary Fleming's mother, almost as if to compensate for not being French, went to France in 1548 and was for a time a mistress of Henry II. Mary Fleming's father, the 4th Lord Fleming, had been chamberlain of Scotland and warden of the east and middle marches and died when on a mission to France in 1558. Mary Fleming's brother John, 5th Lord Fleming, who succeeded his father in the title, was clearly in some favour with the Queen, who visited him at Cumbernauld five months after she arrived in Scotland and who 'made the feast'[21] when he married in May 1562. Although in holding the office of chamberlain he was merely the fourth of a continuous succession of Lords Fleming who were chamberlains, he received an unusually generous pension and in 1565 was appointed keeper of Dumbarton Castle, the strong fortress which commanded the western channel of communication with France. Mary Fleming herself married William Maitland of Lethington, Mary's Secretary of State, in 1567, after a long wooing: some thought it an odd match, because a Queen's Mary, almost by definition associated with light-hearted pleasure, seemed unfitting for the highly intellectual Secretary,

**1 George, 5th Lord Seton**

Holding a staff with the royal monogram MR in token of his office as Master of the Queen's Household

2a William Kirkcaldy of Grange

2b The Kirkcaldy Memorial in Edinburgh Castle

**3a Seal of James Hamilton, Earl of Arran and Duke of Châtelherault**

The Hamilton arms, surmounted by a ducal coronet, are encircled by the collar of the Order of St Michael, with the cockle shells which explain the usage 'The Order of the Cockle', and the badge of the Archangel. Above is the Hamilton crest, of an oak tree penetrated by a frame saw, and below is the motto 'Through'.

**3b Part of the Maitland Monument in St Mary's Church, Haddington**

On the left the effigies of John Maitland of Thirlestane and his wife and on the right those of the 1st Earl of Lauderdale and his.

**4a  Niddrie Castle**
A residence of Lord Seton

**4b  The Great Hall, Lennoxlove**
Formerly the Maitland home, Lethington, and now the residence of the Duke of Hamilton

5a  Memorial at the Battlefield of Langside

5b  Faarevejle Kirke, Denmark
Resting-place of James Hepburn, Earl of Bothwell

Traist freind we greit yow weill. We dowt nocht bot ye knaw that God of his gudenes hes put us at libertie, quhome we thank maist hartlie. Quharefore desyris yow with all possible diligence faill nocht to be heir at us in Hammyltoun with all your folkis freindis and servandis bodin in feir of weir (i.e., fully equipped for war) as ye will do us acceptable service and plessuris. Becawse we knaw your constance we neid nocht at this present to mak langer letter, bot will byd yow fair weill. Off Hammyltoun the v of May 1568. Marie R.

**6   A Summons from The Queen, 5 May 1568** *(see p. 87)*

Apud Hamyltoun xiii Maii anno etc. lxviii°

The quhilk day the quenis majeste with avise of the lordis of hir hienes counsale and nobilite hes maid and constitute hir richt traist cousing and counsalour Archibald, Erle of Ergyle, Lord Campbell and Lorne, lieutenent to hir majestie, and under hir hienes geves him power to treit and do in all thingis concerning hir hienes effaris tuicheing defence of hir hienes persoun, gude reule and ordour to be had within this hir realm and commoun wele of the samyn and liegis thairof, and to commoun with all hir unnaturall and dissobedient subjectis for bringging of thaim to hir hienes obedience and to gif thaim sik pardoun as he sall think expedient, and generally to do all thingis that hes bene gevin or grantit power to ony lieutenant of this realm be hir hienes or hir predecessouris in ony tymes bipast; and sall extend this hir hienes commissioun in honorable, ample and sure forme and geve it under hir grete sele, as be thir presentis geves him power siclike as thir presentis had past hir grete sele in forme as efferis.

MARIE R.

**7 Commission to Argyll as Mary's Lieutenant**
Prepared in some haste on the morning of the battle of Langside

5a  Memorial at the Battlefield of Langside

5b  Faarevejle Kirke, Denmark

Resting-place of James Hepburn, Earl of Bothwell

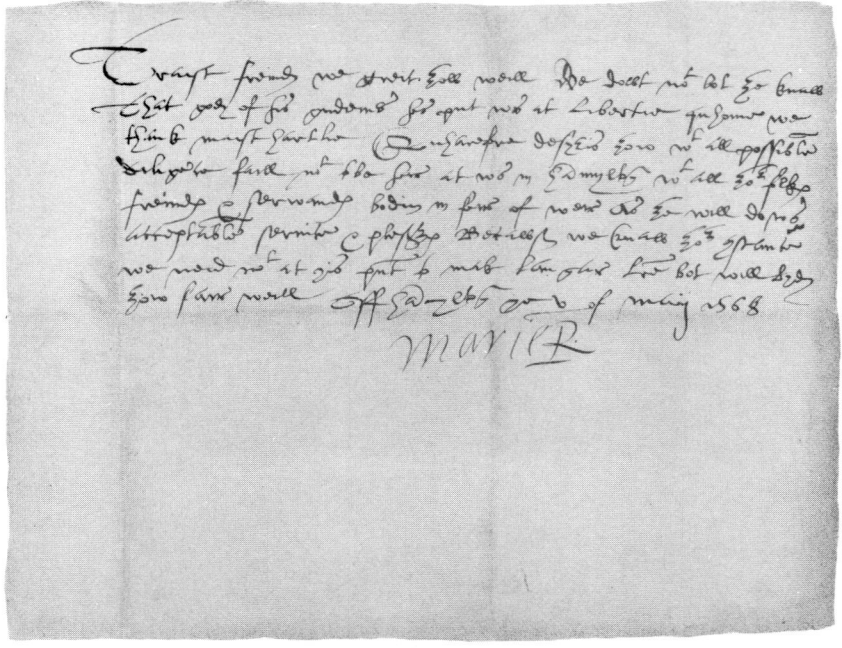

Traist freind we greit yow weill. We dowt nocht bot ye knaw that God of his gudenes hes put us at libertie, quhome we thank maist hartlie. Quharefore desyris yow with all possible diligence faill nocht to be heir at us in Hammyltoun with all your folkis freindis and servandis bodin in feir of weir (i.e., fully equipped for war) as ye will do us acceptable service and plessuris. Becawse we knaw your constance we neid nocht at this present to mak langer letter, bot will byd yow fair weill. Off Hammyltoun the v of May 1568. Marie R.

Apud Hamyltoun xiii Maii anno etc. lxviii°

The quhilk day the quenis majeste with avise of the lordis of hir hienes counsale and nobilite hes maid and constitute hir richt traist cousing and counsalour Archibald, Erle of Ergyle, Lord Campbell and Lorne, lieutenent to hir majestie, and under hir hienes geves him power to treit and do in all thingis concerning hir hienes effaris tuicheing defence of hir hienes persoun, gude reule and ordour to be had within this hir realm and commoun wele of the samyn and liegis thairof, and to commoun with all hir unnaturall and dissobedient subjectis for bringging of thaim to hir hienes obedience and to gif thaim sik pardoun as he sall think expedient, and generally to do all thingis that hes bene gevin or grantit power to ony lieutenant of this realm be hir hienes or hir predecessouris in ony tymes bipast; and sall extend this hir hienes commissioun in honorable, ample and sure forme and geve it under hir grete sele, as be thir presentis geves him power siclike as thir presentis had past hir grete sele in forme as efferis.

MARIE R.

**7 Commission to Argyll as Mary's Lieutenant**
Prepared in some haste on the morning of the battle of Langside

who was about fifteen years her senior: Kirkcaldy of Grange thought she was as meet to be the wife of Lethington 'as I am to be Pope'.[22] One sister of Mary Fleming married the Earl of Atholl in 1567, another married William, Lord Sanquhar (who died in 1550), but from the point of view of the Queen's personal friendships the more significant marriages were those of Mary Fleming's sisters to two brothers of the second Mary, Mary Livingston – Joanna to John, Master of Livingston, who fell at Pinkie, and Agnes to the 6th Lord Livingston – clearly making a very close bond indeed between the Queen's Fleming and Livingston friends.

But the Queen's association with the Livingstons had other roots. The 5th Lord Livingston had been appointed one of Mary's guardians in her childhood, in 1545, and he accompanied her to France in 1548. He died in 1553. His third wife was a Frenchwoman who herself became a lady of honour to Mary but by whom he had no issue. One of the few grants – mainly of a routine nature – which the Queen is known to have made in 1561 shortly before her return to Scotland was one to the 6th Lord Livingston, brother of her 'Mary', a week after she had made a grant to Mary Fleming. The Queen was particularly friendly with the Livingstons, whom she visited at their home, Callendar House, at least half a dozen times. True, the house, just east of Falkirk, lay on the roads which led from Edinburgh to Stirling and to Glasgow and was a convenient staging post. But that does not explain all Mary's visits. She went there in July 1565 to attend a baptism – and a Protestant baptism at that; Lord Livingston, on his side, was one of the very few Protestants to attend the baptism of Prince James, by Roman Catholic rites, in 1566. He was also one of the few peers present when Mary married Bothwell, and when she fled to England in 1568 he accompanied her. He ranks with Lord Fleming as one of Mary's most faithful friends. Mary Livingston's husband was a son of the popishly inclined Lord Sempill, described by Knox as 'an enemy to God and all godliness',[23] but the pages of the Register of the Privy Seal relax their usual austerity to note the romance twice over, once in Latin and once in the vernacular, relating that 'Mary Livingston, sister of our cousin William, Lord Livingston, faithfully and honourably served us in France and Scotland continuously from infancy, and John Sempill, son of our cousin Robert, Lord Sempill, likewise served our mother, and it has pleased God to move the hearts of John and Mary to unite in matrimony'.[24] One sister of Mary Livingston married Arthur Erskine, a son of the Lord Erskine who had been associated with Livingston among Mary's guardians in 1545. Arthur's sister, curiously enough, was the mother of the Earl of Moray, and he himself was a faithful servant of Mary, who is said to have thought him her favourite equerry. Four other sisters of Mary Livingston married lairds, two of whom – Sir Alexander Bruce of Airth and James Ogilvy of Findlater – were later to support the Queen when misfortunes fell on her, but little is known of the affiliations of the husbands of the other two – John Buchanan of that ilk and James Wetherspune, younger, of Brighous, though Buchanan would be a client of the Lennox family, which meant that after Darnley's murder he was against Mary.

Mary Beaton was a daughter of Robert Beaton of Creich. Her aunt had been a mistress of James V and mother of his daughter Jean, Mary's friend the Countess of Argyll. Her mother was a Frenchwoman and her father was in Mary's household in France.

Mary Seton's family does not seem to have been closely related to other associates of the Queen, but is interesting in its own right. The 4th Lord, Mary's father, had, like the fathers of two other Maries, found a French wife in a lady who had come to Scotland with Mary of Guise in 1538, and his sister Marion was in that Queen's household. After he died in 1550 his widow married a Frenchman and became one of Mary's ladies of honour in the 1560s. The 5th Lord Seton, Mary Seton's brother, was in France for the marriage of Mary to Francis in 1558 and was there again in 1560, 1561 and 1565. In April 1561, at Joinville, the Queen conferred pensions on three of Lord Seton's sons. He returned to Scotland with the Queen in 1561 and in October she nominated him for election as provost of Edinburgh. His family had long been closely involved with the affairs of the town and had been benefactors of the nunnery of St Catharine of Siena on its outskirts, and Seton himself had been provost previously (as a leader of a conservative faction), but the Queen's nomination in 1561 was not successful. Mary went to Seton's home, about 12 miles east of Edinburgh, for her honeymoon with Darnley, and on two or three other occasions visited the house, on a coast where, then as now, the attraction was golf. She made Lord Seton master of her household in 1563. He was conspicuous for his loyalty and was more conservative in religion than most. Mary Seton never married, and remained with her mistress to the end. Her four sisters made marriages of some significance. Marion married first the 4th Earl of Menteith and then the 10th Earl of Sutherland; Margaret married Robert Logan of Restalrig; Beatrix married George, son of Sir William Ogilvie of Dunlugus; and Helenor married the 7th Lord Somerville. As Menteith was a strong Protestant, Somerville a conservative, Sutherland of conservative leanings and Logan and Ogilvie Protestants, these brothers-in-law of Mary Seton were clearly not all of one mind in religion; Menteith later supported the King's Party against Mary, but Somerville and Sutherland were on her side.

Clearly the Maries and their families formed a close-knit group. A French connection would seem to have been significant in determining the choice of the four, and they had many bonds with the royal court. But they were at best of minor nobility, the Beatons not nobility at all, and did not link the Queen with the higher ranks of Scottish society. She was related by blood or marriage to several earls, but with none of them did she have the kind of friendship which she had with men of lower rank like the fathers of the Maries. True, the dividing line between earls and lords may not have been firmly drawn in respect of either wealth, prestige or influence, though there were earls of the first rank, like Huntly, Argyll, Crawford and Angus, who were head and shoulders above any lords, but the earls in general were absent from Mary's circle of intimates. The attitude of earls, therefore, may have been determined more by Mary's policy than by her personality, and could not be separated from politics.

Mary's place in Scottish society was very different from what it had been in French society. In France she had been a member of one large family through her mother and of another through her husband, with intimates in both family circles. In the royal family she was closest to her sister-in-law Elizabeth, her junior by two years, whose company Mary had until Elizabeth left to marry Philip of Spain in 1559; next to her came her slightly younger sister, Claude. Mary was also on good terms with her father-in-law, Henry II, and with his sister Marguerite, who did not leave France to marry the Duke of Savoy until 1559. Among the Guises Mary had six uncles, two of them dukes, one of them a marquis and two of them cardinals. There were cousins of her own age, and in the background a formidable grandmother. Mary thus lived in two families, one royal, the other ducal (though brought to royal level through her mother's marriage and her own), so that she had intimates who were her social equals. There was nothing like this in Scotland. There was then, and long continued to be, something of a ducal way of life, approaching the royal style, and in France there were dukes, with whom Mary stood more or less on terms of equality. In Scotland there were no dukes apart from the Earl of Arran with his French dukedom of Châtelherault, but his social pretensions were modest by French standards. None of Mary's intimates in Scotland could give her anything like the kind of relationships to which she had been accustomed in France. This was brought out in 1563, when within a few days her eldest uncle, the Duke of Guise, was murdered, and another uncle, the Grand Prior, died. Mary told the English ambassador at that point that she was almost destitute of friends, which suggests that she had found no friends in Scotland to take the place of those she had left in France. She can hardly have been comforted when the ambassador attempted to console her by assuring her of the love of Queen Elizabeth.[25] At a later stage Mary again confided in the ambassador, to whom she spoke 'much of France, for the honour she received there, to be wife unto a great king, and for friendship shown unto her in particular by many, for which occasions she is bound to love that nation.'[26]

It is not merely speculation that Mary's kinsfolk in France offered her affection on equal terms as no one in Scotland could do, and also that in Scotland it was friends of less than the highest rank who were closest to her heart. There is documentary evidence to that effect. In 1566, when Mary was awaiting, with anxiety, the birth of her son and wanted to provide for the disposal of her jewels and similar possessions in the event of her death, she indicated her wishes by annotating an inventory.[27] The names of the prospective beneficiaries are revealing. Out of less than 60 persons named, 14 were members of the house of Guise; not only so, but the first seven beneficiaries were a sequence of Guises and three out of the next five were Guises. Next to that family in significance were the four Maries and their kinsfolk, who also score 14, but the bequests to them were far less valuable and their names were scattered in small groups or singly throughout the list. From the Guises, who come first, Mary passed next to her illegitimate Scottish kinsfolk, about half a dozen of whom are included, and she singled out those for whom she felt particular affection, especially the women and children: her half-sister the Countess of Argyll, Moray's wife, Moray's daughter, and Francis, the orphaned son of Lord John (who received four bequests). Moray himself came later in the list, among an assortment of Scottish nobles who were perhaps included somewhat perfunctorily. Moray is designated 'mon frère' and Lord Robert, Commendator of Holyrood, is 'mon frère de St Croix'.

In Scotland no one could offer at one and the same time equal social status and familiar friendship. With those who approached most nearly to her own social level there was the complication that personal relationships could not be separated from political considerations and there may even have been a fear that by making much of men below the rank of earls – and the earls of Scotland were conscious of social cohesion and privileges – Mary would arouse jealousy. There was a risk of tension in various ways. It may well be, therefore, that Mary turned increasingly to those who were separated from her by a wider social gulf – men of little political significance individually, men who would not be prompted, even by signs of royal favour, to presume on their position.

Below the lords, then, were the lairds, those landowners who were not peers. The man in this class whom we know most about is Sir James Melville of Halhill, who in his *Memoirs* relates so much picturesque and sometimes barely credible gossip about the courts of Mary and Elizabeth. He tells us how one evening, after a serious discussion with the Queen at Stirling, 'the supper being ended, her majesty took me by the hand and went down through the park of Stirling and came up through the town, ever reasoning with me upon these purposes'.[28] It was safe enough to have such a public *tête à tête* with Melville, who was neither important nor influential politically, and his social status was too modest for anyone to imagine that he was acquiring any kind of equality with the Queen. It might have been a different matter had the Queen walked thus with, say, Huntly, Argyll or Atholl. Mary could achieve a kind of easy familiarity with a man of lairdly rank like Melville.

Another man in a similar social category was Sir Simon Preston, who was one of the commissioners whom Mary appointed in January 1561 and who was (with Lord Seton) one of her nominees for the office of provost of Edinburgh in the following October. His castle of Craigmillar lay just beyond the southern outskirts of Edinburgh, separated from the palace of Holyroodhouse by little more than the extensive royal park, and Mary visited it more than once, though her only authenticated stay of any length was in November–December 1566 and there is little to substantiate the popular impression of her close association with it. The Craigmillar family had long taken part in the affairs of the nearby burgh of Edinburgh, where one of them had been provost as early as 1434, so it was no novelty when Simon Preston was (not for the first time) appointed provost in 1565, on this occasion at the express instance of the Queen. It was perhaps more surprising that in the same year Mary made Preston keeper of the castle of Dunbar, for that was an appointment of high responsibility and one usually held by a nobleman. All the indications are that Preston was a laird in whom Mary had unusual confidence.

It might seem less in character that Mary established something approaching cordiality with John Erskine of Dun (1509–89), one of those remarkable men who, in almost any society, succeed in combining a long pedigree and considerable social status with a professional career leading to eminence in the church. As laird of Dun, where he succeeded his father and grandfather, who were both among the casualties of Flodden in 1513, he was well established in local society, for his mother was a daughter of Lord Ruthven and his first wife was a daughter of the Earl of Crawford. He seems to have had something like a prescriptive right to be provost of the nearby burgh of Montrose, an office which he held for long periods from 1541 onwards. Although educated lairds were by this time not a rarity, Erskine carried his studies farther than most, and introduced Greek, then barely known in Scotland, as a school subject in Montrose. It was a French scholar whom he brought to Montrose to teach Greek, and his second wife was a Frenchwoman. Erskine was converted to Protestantism in the early, Lutheran phase, in the 1530s, and was a signatory of the First Bond of the Lords of the Congregation in 1557, but subsequently tried to mediate between Mary of Guise and the reformers. His political standing is indicated by the fact that he was one of the eight commissioners deputed by the estates of the realm in 1558 to go to France in connection with the negotiations for Mary's marriage to Francis. A meeting of representatives of reformed congregations in December 1560, when he was present, declared him 'apt and able to minister', and he was admitted to the ministry as superintendent (an office which he himself equated with bishop) of Angus and Mearns. He had earlier had an interest in the property of the bishopric of Brechin, and one may speculate whether the superintendentship was a kind of consolation prize, when the reformers found that they could not yet appropriate the bishoprics to their own use. True, his sphere of activity extended far beyond the narrow bounds of the diocese of Brechin, but on the other hand he seems to have secured the highest stipend of any superintendent – over £700 in the Scots money of the time, equivalent today to about twice the salary of the archbishop of Canterbury – and when he went on his visitations 'my lord superintendent' was sumptuously entertained. The time was still distant when arrangements would be made for ministers of the reformed church to be members of parliament (unless they happened to be bishops), but Erskine was able to attend parliament both as a 'baron' and as provost of Montrose, and he may even have had a double vote; in the parliament of December 1567 he was one of the Lords of the Articles, the committee which prepared parliamentary legislation. This 'venerable father', as the clerks of the royal chancery designated him, was clearly impressive, and there are testimonials to his effectiveness from friends and opponents alike.

We know too little about Erskine's association with the Queen, but it was clearly a close one. His social standing was higher than that of most lairds and – as other examples show – differences about religion would be no bar to cordiality with Mary, especially as Erskine was one of the mildest of Scottish reformers. At any rate, he was about the court from time to time and turned up there rather unexpectedly on the occasion of one of Knox's stormy interviews with the Queen, when – metaphorically at least – he helped to dry her tears. 'John Erskine of Dun, a man of meek and gentle spirit, stood beside and entreated what he could to mitigate her anger, and gave unto her many pleasing words of her beauty, of her excellence and how that all the princes of Europe would be glad to see her favours'. When Knox departed, the courtly

Erskine and Mary's favourite half-brother John remained in attendance.[29] In May 1565, on the occasion of the Darnley marriage, when Mary perhaps reached the closest *rapprochement* with the reformed church, she told three of the superintendents that she would 'hear conference and disputation in the scriptures' and even hear 'public preaching', though only 'out of the mouths of such as pleased her majesty' – a pointed allusion to Knox, surely – and added that 'above all others she would gladly hear the superintendent of Angus, for he was a mild and sweet-natured man, with true honesty and uprightness'.[30] There was clearly a relationship of confidence, respect and genuine liking, though the laird of Dun was to align himself with the Erskine Earl of Mar in the King's Party when civil war started.

Mary's experience of another laird perhaps throws some light on her relations with the superintendent of Angus. Walter Lundy of that ilk was reported to have come to a decision to accept the reformed faith when he was present at the parliament of 1560: 'the old laird of Lundie confessed how long he had lived in blindness, repented thereof and embraced the Confession of Faith as his true belief'.[31] There was a sequel in March 1565, when Mary came to visit Lundy. 'At her coming to the laird of Lundie's house in Fife, who is a "grave, ancient man, white head and white beard", he knelt down to her and said, "Madame, this is your house, and the lands belonging to the same, all my goods and gear are yours. These seven boys (which are as tall men as any man hath in Scotland for so many sons, and the least 25 years of age) and myself will spend our bodies in your grace's service without your majesty's charge, and we will serve you truly: but, Madame, one humble petition I would make unto your grace in recompence of this – that your majesty will not have no mass in this house so long as it pleaseth your grace to tarry in it"'. The request was granted, and for all we know of Mary it would not cause her any difficulty to grant it.[32]

Mary had one experience of living for several months in a lairdly home, though not under the happiest auspices, when she was imprisoned at Lochleven Castle. True, the Lochleven family had a left-handed link with the royal house, for the wife of Sir Robert Douglas of Lochleven was Margaret Erskine, daughter of the 5th Lord Erskine, who had been a mistress of James V and was mother of the Earl of Moray. This lady was still alive when Mary was a captive at Lochleven, but the laird by that time was her son, Sir William. He was thus a half-brother to Moray, who had as much responsibility as anyone for Mary's captivity, but Mary seems to have had no difficulty in establishing friendly relations with the family. She was on cordial terms with young Lady Lochleven, Sir William's wife, and with a daughter and niece of the family, as well of course as with George, a younger brother of Sir William, who got into trouble for trying to arrange Mary's escape.

The attainment of social ease is a delicate and difficult matter. One can see clearly enough that Mary achieved it with princes and princesses and with dukes of royal and Guisian blood in France, whereas it would be harder to establish it with Scottish earls, some of whom may on their side have felt ill at ease with such a superior being from France. With Scottish lords it may have been simpler because there was less political involvement. Then, moving to the lairds, the relationship came to be on a totally different footing. Social assurance, straightforward with undeniable equals and hard with those who were nearly equals, became progressively simpler as one moved down the social scale, for the stage was reached when the social gulf was so wide that there could be no question of bridging it, no question of either party transgressing it. This may be one of the explanations of Mary's easy familiarity with men of servile or semi-servile status. She could unbend with men of middle rank and with servants, in a way she could not always risk doing with nobles. It may all seem a bit paradoxical. Mary had been treated with deference from her earliest years, and this had led to a certain imperiousness. Before she left France she said, so it was reported, that her subjects must be taught their duties: 'I am their queen and they call me so, but they use me not so'.[33] This prevented her from unbending much with the politically minded among her subjects, and perhaps in particular with her earls. But such restraint vanished as one went down the social scale, to a level where there was no temptation to anyone to presume. There was, however, another aspect to Mary's relations with her servants. Not the least of her qualities was a natural kindliness. It was a kindliness which, coming from a queen, was condescension, but it was so graciously and unaffectedly given their neither Mary nor her subjects thought of her attitude as condescending. Mary was a kind and considerate mistress who had no difficulty in keeping her faithful servants. At the same time, her relations with her domestics must be seen also in the light of her remark when she was living in a merchant's house in St Andrews in February 1565: 'I sent for you to be merry and to see how like a burgess wife I live with my little troop. . . . You see neither cloth of estate nor such appearance that you may think there is a queen here'.[34]

It would be easy to make too much of this, because Scotland was an egalitarian country and Scottish sovereigns had always been easy of access, while, on the other side, employment in or about the royal household seems to have been so highly prized that it was enduring and often hereditary. In 1579 the government of James VI granted a pension to Alexander Carpentyne, keeper of the royal silver, in consideration of 'his auld hairis and febilnes of body' after he had served 'King James the fyft of worthie memorie' and the King's 'derrest guiddam [Mary of Guise], father [Darnley] and mother [Mary] and his hienes self sensyne'.[35] At almost the same time, William Murray, valet in King James VI's chamber, was the son of John Murray, barber to James V. The valet is not to be confused with another William Murray, a much more prestigious 'gentleman of the chamber', who was a son of Sir William Murray of Tullibardine and whose brother Alexander was also a gentleman of the chamber. There were other Murrays in the household, and an Elizabeth Murray was the wife of Alexander Durham, who was 'argenter' to James V, Mary of Guise, Mary and James VI.[36] Yet, despite such indications that royal employment was much sought after, the conviction remains that Mary was unusually generous. A pension of 500 merks a year to George Buchanan, the elderly scholar of cosmopolitan experience who sometimes entertained the Queen by reading Livy with her after supper, was perhaps no more than his due and it represented a fair salary for a professional man. But a pension of 300 merks to Margaret Carwod, the Queen's 'familiar servitrix', given as a wedding present on 8 February 1567, was something like munificence. And the well-known promise by Mary to be present at a servant's wedding on the night Darnley was murdered testified farther to her good relations with her domestics.

There was a notable French element in Mary's entourage, and her heart may have been especially warm towards servants who came from France. The employment of Frenchmen as officials had been one of the counts against Mary of Guise, and according to the 'Concessions' by Mary and Francis in 1560 the practice was to cease. However, one of Mary of Guise's officials – Bartholomew Villemore, the Comptroller – remained in office until 1562, apparently with acceptance. And there is the interesting case of Sebastian Danelourt, who acclimatised himself sufficiently to become a burgess of Edinburgh and presumably had some professional skill, for he was appointed clerk to the commissary court of Edinburgh in September 1565, but he was described as 'a very crafty and dissimulate knave'.[37] After Mary's abdication he was evicted because his appointment had violated the 'Concessions', and it is perhaps not surprising that he fought for the Queen at Langside.

Appointments on Mary's 'French establishment' – paid for out of her revenues as Queen Dowager of France – were another matter, in which no Scottish authority could interfere, and that they were largely filled by Frenchmen is shown by a record of the state of the 'maison' or Queen's household in 1567, listing 250 names with their salaries.[38] The orthography of the French clerk causes some uncertainty about identifications: 'Madame de Letinthon' is Mary Fleming, wife of Lethington, 'Madame de Bouyn' is Mary Beaton, wife of Ogilvy of Boyne, and it is easy to recognise 'Mademoiselle de Ceton', so some other names which look French may be Scottish. Many of the employees named were clearly officials working in France and probably never present in Scotland, but several of the 16 'valets de chambre' and of other domestics, though plainly of foreign nationality, appear in Scottish records and indicate that the royal household had a distinctly continental air about it. The Frenchman Raulet preceded the Italian David Riccio (who was followed by his brother Joseph) as the Queen's secretary. There was a master of the household whom Mary had taken over from her mother – Sir John Francisco de Busso ('sieur de Bussot' in the French list), who was a knight of the order of St James of the Sword; he had been naturalised in Scotland in 1556 and married Margaret Mac-Cartnay, he received a pension of 400 merks from the bishopric of Ross in March 1566 (twice confirmed later) and he was of sufficient influence to be reckoned one of Mary's unofficial 'counsellors'.[39] Timothy Cagneoli, another Italian, who had served Mary of Guise, was an 'argentar' to the Queen. Servais de Condé, a valet of the chamber who was at one stage appointed caretaker of the palace of Holyroodhouse when the Queen was absent, was found in July 1567, after Mary's abdication, to have in his hands a quantity of silver plate which had been in the possession of the Queen's 'French officers' and which was now ordered to be handed over to be turned into coin for the use of Mary's supplanters. Among other French servitors were Eme de Saunctjean, 'furrour', Martin Picanet, apothecary, 'Angiers Marie', perfumier (probably identical with 'Angel Mary', valet of the chamber), Echiane Hawet, master cook, Firmian Aleyzart or Fremyn Alizart, cordiner (who, like Sebastian Danellourt, became a burgess of Edinburgh), and Frenchmen rewarded for less specific services were John Bewman and 'Balthasar' (who may be 'Baltazart Hully', 'maistre de garderobe' or one of the 'valletz de chambre'). 'Nicholas Hubert, dict Paris', the 'French Paris' of Bothwell's staff, was on the Queen's payroll in February 1567. The 'Bastian' whose wedding Mary attended on the night of Darnley's murder was Bastien Pages, a valet. When Mary was able to create an establishment in England, after her flight, a high proportion of her domestics were still French and several of their names can (despite difficulties over spelling) be identified with those who had previously served her in Scotland.[40]

There were Frenchmen in military posts as well. Jacques Guilliame was appointed one of the Queen's 'suddartis' or soldiers in Dunbar three weeks after she arrived in 1561, and was, unlike most Frenchmen, a deserter from Mary after her fall.[41] Nicolas Lamot was captain of 'oure soveranis culvering men on fors';[42] it is rather unlikely that he was a Scottish Lamont (a name which ignorant people now sometimes accent on the second syllable and believe to be of French origin). When a bodyguard of archers was created for the Queen in 1562 there were Frenchmen in it: Dioneise Labrose or La Broche, Nicholas Mauser, Bastiane Fulmeir, Charles La Brose, John Delamis 'called Bello' or 'Captain Bello', Corporal Jenat, John Delespinis or Delespinasse and two others who appear simply as 'Duvall' and 'La Fram'.[43]

The presence of so many Frenchmen around Mary would tend to confirm her attachment to France and French ways, but it must be seen in the whole context of the personal relationships arising in two peoples who at the time enjoyed joint nationality. Again and again in this book mention has been made of the French wives of Scottish nobles and lairds, and there were clearly some families – the Setons in particular – who must have been as much at home in France as in Scotland. It is very hard to point to a single family which had a similar relationship with England, except the Lennoxes, and English brides for Scotsmen of rank were very rare. Therefore Mary's French entourage may not have maintained any kind of barrier between her and her Scottish subjects, habituated as they were to a French connection, and it may be reckless to suggest that Mary's relations with those French menials and other employees were any more cordial than her relations with the Scots on her staff. Nor could happy relations with servants supply the kind of intimate relationships which men and women of her own social background could have given.

It is not difficult to see that Mary's kindliness led to an occasional familiarity with servants and other inferiors which some thought inappropriate or even indiscreet, but the same kindliness caused her to stand well with her subjects throughout her realm. She was possessed of great personal attraction, though it might be hard to define its many facets. When she fled to England, Englishmen who were not on political or religious grounds predisposed to favour her were nevertheless impressed by her 'eloquent tongue, stout courage and liberal heart' and 'ready wit'.[44] Her 'great wit and sugared eloquence' made her persuasive, and one observer remarked on her 'goodly personage, alluring grace, a pretty Scotch accent, and a searching wit, clouded with mildness'.[45] It emerged again and again that men who were far from being friendly to Mary on principles or policy found it hard to resist her charm when brought into close association with it. The story that Lord Ruthven, all of whose inherited and personal Protestant instincts made him hostile, had to be dismissed as one of her gaolers at Lochleven because he began to show her favour is by no means incredible. When, after her flight to England, she was denied access to Elizabeth or the possibility of making a public defence, the Englishmen who resolutely refused to give her opportunities to bring her charm into play were shrewd. There were other qualities which could be appreciated even by those who never held personal converse with her. Sir James Melville called her 'very lovesome' and even Knox conceded that her face was 'pleasant'. Her portraits do not reveal a charmer, but her personality, warm, lively and vivacious, no doubt shaped the expression of eyes and mouth in a manner no portrait could convey. Besides, she behaved as people thought a Queen should behave. She had, as she explained to Knox, been brought up in 'joyousity' in France, and few of her subjects in Scotland – though she on her side might complain of their 'gravity' – saw anything amiss in her recreations of archery, hunting, hawking and golf. She loved to wear male costume and go through the streets incognito; at a banquet to the French ambassador she and her Maries appeared dressed as men and when she took to the field with her soldiers she wore male clothing. Six feet tall like her mother, she could 'play the man', and her stature was to her advantage when she was thus attired, unlike her descendant, Charles Edward, who made such a poor showing when he was disguised as Betty Burke and found his stature embarrassing. When military operations began against Huntly in 1562, Mary showed a resolution worthy of her forefathers. Her remark that she wished she had been a man, to lie out in the fields all night, parallels Elizabeth's later speech at Tilbury: 'I know I have the body of a weak and feeble woman, but I have the heart and stomach of a king, and of a king of England too'. As she went on her frequent progresses among her subjects, from Ayrshire to Inverness and from Aberdeen to Argyll, plenty of people had a chance to see her, admire her and exlaim, 'God bless that sweet face'. There is ample testimony to the favourable impression she made, and Knox's sour complaint about 'enchantment' is a tribute to the way in which her personality, as well as her policies, contributed to make her acceptable to the great majority of her subjects.

Nor must we lose sight of the more specific appeal Mary made at times as a marriageable woman. Plenty of men fell in love with her, or professed to do so – professed, because for some the motive was nothing more, or may have been nothing more, than politics and ambition. We must in fact distinguish between men who might conceivably have married her and men who could not in their wildest dreams have thought they could do so. Leaving aside foreign suitors who never saw her, one cannot dismiss the possibility that political ambitions explain why Sir John Gordon, son of Huntly, professed to be in love with her, and later, in England, the Duke of Norfolk presumably saw the possibility of marriage to her in purely political terms. It is true that the young Earl of Arran, who had such a strong political motive for wanting to marry Mary, was passionately in love with her, to the extent that he went off his head: other men lost their lives for love of Mary, but Arran was the only one who lost his wits. When he collapsed in April 1562 there was pity for Châtelherault – 'to see the old man's tears trickling from his cheeks as it had been a child beaten'.[46] But there were others for whom politics did not enter in. The wretched Châtelard – one of those who lost their lives for love of Mary – had no political ambitions when he thrust his attentions on her. And Sir George Douglas, who fell under her spell at Lochleven, can never have thought it possible that he could marry her. If Mary could make this very powerful appeal to passion, there is here an important element which must have helped to shape her relations with most of the men she encountered, whatever their rank or political standing.

Mary's attractions, both of physique and of personality, are evident. But, however great their appeal, and however much her popularity with her subjects, or her kindness to servants, made her pleasing to others, such relationships were inevitably one-sided. Still less could politics make friends. In so far as Mary can be said to have had friendships among her Scottish contemporaries, they are attributable much more to her innate ease and assurance in social intercourse.

# 5
# THE QUEEN'S ENEMIES

*1565 July* Mary married Darnley
*August–Sept.* 'The Chaseabout Raid'
*1566 March* Murder of Riccio
*June 19* Birth of Prince James
*Dec.* Baptism of Prince James
*1567 Feb.* Murder of Darnley
*June 15* Encounter at Carberry
*July 24* Mary abdicated at Lochleven
*July 29* James VI crowned

In retrospect, the marriage of Mary to Darnley in July 1565 represents a turning-point in the reign. Until that date, Mary's personal rule had been successful, but after it crisis followed crisis and in the end came disaster. Yet it is far from clear that either crisis or disaster was inevitable. True, the marriage extinguished the prospects of an understanding with Queen Elizabeth, who professed strong disapproval, while the union of Mary with a cousin who stood next to her in the English succession (and who, some thought, had a stronger claim than Mary as he was in effect an Englishman) greatly strengthened the claim of the Scottish Queen to succeed, or possibly supplant, Elizabeth. Yet, as far as internal Scottish affairs were concerned, the marriage was not fatal to Mary's conciliatory religious policy.

It is difficult to eradicate the belief that the Lennoxes were Roman Catholics, but this is at best an over-simplification. Earl Matthew, Darnley's father, had worked for Henry VIII against the French and papalist faction in Scotland in the 1540s and had been associated with Somerset's operations, when a direct appeal was being made to Scots to join England in a stand against Rome. Later, in the minority of James VI, he was to be Regent of Scotland on terms which would not have been acceptable to anyone but a convinced Protestant. His brother Robert, Bishop of Caithness, who shared a good part of the Earl's English exile and held a prebend in the Church of England, was one of the three Scottish bishops who organised the reformed church in their dioceses. In 1564, when Lennox returned from England, he went to 'the sermon' in preference to the mass, and his brother the Bishop sometimes preached.[1] Darnley himself had professed the reformed faith in England, he absented himself from the nuptial mass at his wedding and he did not scruple to attend services conducted by John Knox in the church of St Giles. While some thought him 'indifferent' in religion, in practice he has 'always shown himself a Protestant', and when, at a later stage, he began to go to mass, it was thought worthy of remark.[2] However, the Countess of Lennox, Darnley's mother, who had that attachment to Rome which characterised more women than men both in that century and the next, seems to have done her best to groom her son as a candidate for the English throne who would be acceptable to English Roman Catholics, and at one point she brought both her husband and herself under suspicion for trafficking with papists.

As a prospective bride, Mary professed her willingness to defend 'the Catholic religion' and applied to the Pope for a dispensation for marriage to her first cousin. The ceremony was by Roman Catholic rites, though it was celebrated before the dispensation had arrived. However, Mary went out of her way to reassure Protestants, and the marriage in itself did not injure her prospects with any ecclesiastical party either in Scotland, in England or on the continent. Mary declared herself ready to hear discussions about the scriptures and even to attend public preaching, she issued a proclamation reiterating that members of the reformed church would not be molested because of their faith, and she later reissued her initial proclamation countenancing the existing religious settlement.

The major change was one that can be seen most simply in personal terms, though it was closely associated with the end of the policy of an accommodation with Elizabeth. Lord James, now Earl of Moray, had, in partnership with Maitland of Lethington, been the architect of that policy, but in its furtherance he had greatly enhanced his own position, while several possible rivals had been successively eliminated from the Queen's counsels – Young Arran by his insanity, which had caused his confinement since 1562, the 4th Earl of Huntly by his rebellion and his death at Corrichie, his son, the 5th Earl, by the effect of his father's forfeiture, and Bothwell by exile resulting from his complicity in a scheme of Arran to kidnap the Queen and from his subsequent turbulence. Moray, apart from seeing the end of his policies, saw his well-constructed position of domination undermined by the prospect of the Queen's marriage to an empty-headed fop of nineteen and the possibility that power might fall to anyone that fop might choose. He determined on action as early as March 1565, when Mary's interest in Darnley became apparent, for he then made a bond with Châtelherault and Argyll. In May he left the council and in July he and his associates asked Elizabeth for support, which she promised. They were in arms before the end of August, but resolute action by Mary frustrated them and after a series of rapidly moving operations known as 'The Chaseabout Raid' they were driven across the Border. What Moray had hoped to achieve by rebellion is far from clear. It was said at an early stage that he intended to kidnap Lennox and Darnley, and at a later stage that he intended to seize Darnley and Mary. But supposing he had been successful in capturing them, what could have followed? To have seized Darnley before the marriage might have made sense, but once the marriage had taken place the Queen and her consort could hardly be separated, and action against Darnley, no less than against Mary, was now treason. Possibly if Elizabeth had given effective help, with a view to establishing a satellite administration within Scotland, and if adequate Scottish support had been obtained, some kind of council might have been imposed on Mary, but that would have been all.

Perhaps the nebulous nature of Moray's aims had the effect of limiting the appeal he made to his fellow Scots, who did not think, as we do with hindsight, that the Darnley marriage was a turning point. Not many can have felt disposed to take up arms merely because of a change in foreign policy, namely the withdrawal from amity with England, and only those with some other grounds for dissatisfaction would have been moved by

Moray's denunciation of the marriage and of Darnley's proclamation as King. Moray could look for support in two quarters and for two motives. Firstly, he could expect the support of those who disliked Darnley's family. The anglicised Lennoxes, with their treasonable record – even though on behalf of a policy of amity with England which had triumphed in 1560 and which Moray himself so warmly supported – can hardly have been popular, and it was not only their dynastic rivals, the Hamiltons, who looked askance at the elevation of a Lennox to the position of King Consort. It was indeed reported in March 1565[3] that Lennox had a faction including not only the conservative Atholl and Caithness but the strong Protestant Ruthven and Mary's half-brother Lord Robert; but the report was by the English ambassador, who denounced the group as 'greatest enemies to all virtue' and Lord Robert in particular as 'a man full of evil', which suggests that the account had been shaped by the ostentatiously virtuous Earl of Moray. If Lennox had a party, it was not much in evidence, for it was said that when proclamation was made that the government would in future be carried on in the names of 'Henry and Mary, King and Queen of Scots', he alone cried 'God save his Grace'. Yet Moray seems to have been disappointed in his expectations of support from those who disliked Lennox, for when the rebellion took place Eglinton, Cassillis, Montrose, Ross, Livingston, Fleming and Yester, who had been numbered among Lennox's enemies,[4] were on the Queen's side.

Secondly, Moray, professing as he did to be aiming at nothing else than 'the maintenance of the true religion'[5], could hope to raise Protestants who were apprehensive about the Queen's communication with Rome and about the prospect now of an heir who would presumably be brought up as a Roman Catholic. He had the blessing of Christopher Goodman, an Englishman who thought Elizabeth's church not Protestant enough for him and had become a minister at Ayr and at St Andrews: when Moray's rebellion collapsed, Goodman went to England with the Earl, who asked the Archbishop of York to license him to preach in England, and Goodman did not return to Scotland.[6] Protestant suspicions, whether justified or not, might rally some of the reforming party to Moray's side, but he did not have the backing of more than a minority of them. The great majority were content enough with Mary's fair and equitable policy, and it is also possible that some of the more zealous may have withheld their support from Moray because, like Knox, they thought that he had been too complaisant to the Queen and too careless of the interests of the ministers. Whatever the cause, the Protestant absentees from Moray's forces were notable. He completely failed to recreate the conditions which had brought him success in 1560, for this time, without English support, he was challenging not a middle-aged dowager and French troops but a young Queen of charm and intelligence who relied on the loyalty of native Scots.

Moray's party, if it had sufficient cohesion to be called a party, was heterogeneous. To begin with, he himself lacked the customary 'following' of a Scottish magnate. He enjoyed the revenues of the wealthy priory of St Andrews and no doubt they not only enabled him to hire servants or even mercenaries but also endowed him with vassals and tenants, but the vassals and tenants of a religious house hardly stood in the same relation to their superiors and landlords as did those of a hereditary temporal magnate. His earldom of Moray had been in and out of the hands of the crown for over a century, held briefly by a son of James II (1456–7) and from 1501 to 1544 by an illegitimate son of James IV, after whose death it had for some years been administered by the Earl of Huntly; here again, therefore, as in the priory, there were no inherited loyalties on which Lord James had been able to build when he had so recently been created Earl of Moray. As to his own kin, he had half-brothers, but they showed no disposition to align themselves with him and they had in any event no ready-made followings to bring with them any more than he had. His half-sister had married the Earl of Argyll, who did join his rebellion, and his wife was a daughter of the Earl Marischal, who did not. There is no doubt that Protestant fears go some way to explain the support he did receive. His own Protestantism was not in doubt, nor was that of his principal ally, Châtelherault.[7]

The peers who joined them were Argyll, Glencairn, Rothes, Boyd, Methven and Ochiltree, all of whom had records as active Protestants. Among the lairds who were Moray's adherents were not only some who had long had reforming sympathies but some who could fairly claim to be veterans of the reforming movement: James Haliburton, provost of Dundee, who had been active in every stage of the revolution of 1559–60; Wishart of Pittarro, who had been in trouble for heresy 20 years earlier and had been associated with Knox both before and during the revolution; Kirkcaldy of Grange, who had been forfeited for his share in the murder of Cardinal Beaton; Blacader of Tulliallan, who had been with Kirkcaldy in St Andrews Castle after Beaton's murder; Dalrymple of Stair, who had opposed Arran's reactionary policy in 1544 and had been active with the 'Congregation' in its revolt in 1559–60; Lockhart of Bar, who had entertained Wishart in 1546 and destroyed images in churches long before he took part with the 'Congregation'; Monypenny of Pitmillie, who had been with Kirkcaldy and Tulliallan after the Cardinal's murder; and Wallace of Carnale, who had been one of Knox's hosts in 1556. On the other hand, of the East Lothian lairds, with their long tradition of support for the Reformation and the English alliance, Home of Spott seems to have been alone in following Moray, and in Angus, that other nursery of anglophiles and Protestants, besides Haliburton and Pittarro already mentioned there was only Durham of Grange. There were only a few Fife lairds – Lundie of that ilk, Learmonth of Balcomie, Scott of Pitgorno, Heriot of Ramorny, Seton of Parbroath and a couple of Melvilles; and there were even fewer of the godly lairds of Ayrshire – Cunningham of Cunninghamhead, Fullerton of Dreghorn and Ker of Kersland. Nor did the peers who joined Moray and Châtelherault necessarily bring all of their followings. Argyll, indeed, brought a lot of Campbell lairds, but Glencairn does not seem to have had much success in recruiting his Cunninghams, and, despite the presence of Rothes, there was a dearth of his fellow-Leslies. Contrariwise, two Douglas lairds, Drumlanrig and Hawick, as well as the devious Archibald Douglas, parson of Douglas, defied the leading Douglas, Morton, and supported Moray.

So far as the evidence goes, it suggests that Moray's mainstay was the

Hamilton interest, arrayed under Châtelherault, whose aim was not religious but dynastic: not only did the Darnley marriage represent the elevation of the heir of the rival house of Lennox, but it must have been foreseen that with Darnley as King the succession might, failing a child of Mary, pass to the Lennox family. The Hamiltons turned out in force behind the Duke: there were 37 Hamilton lairds, 120 Hamiltons of lower rank, nine non-Hamilton members of the Duke's household, 'the community of the inhabitants of the town of Hamilton', 40 'stipendiarii' (usually translated 'wagers' or paid soldiers) who were mostly Lanarkshire lairds and their kinsmen, and 76 'tenants'.[8] These made in all 300 men, a sizeable element in any Scottish rebel army and typical of what a Scottish landowner could put in the field.

In meeting Moray's challenge the duly constituted authority of a popular Queen was not dependent on persons 'without virtue' who were said to have been backing Lennox and Darnley, but made a wide appeal. It is significant that the scare over Huntly's rebellion in 1562 had led to the Ayrshire Protestant bond, and probably others like it, whereas now a rebellion on a Protestant platform stimulated bonds on behalf of the Queen; the signatories were in each case supporting the lawful government against rebels. Bonds are extant at this stage bearing the names of those who pledged themselves to the Queen in Fife, 'the west country', Nithsdale and Teviotdale; they are all under the hand of the same notary, suggesting that there was an effort of central direction and making it likely that there were similar bonds for other areas.[9] There is, besides, plenty more evidence on which to base an analysis of the loyalists. The Queen had many supporters who were every bit as much attached to the Reformation as Moray's men were. Among the peers, she had Morton, who, with Argyll and Glencairn, had committed himself in the 'First Bond' long before Moray joined the Protestant cause. Morton was 'tutor' (that is, guardian) of the young Earl of Angus, head of the Douglases, and it had been predicted that he would oppose Lennox unless Lady Lennox, Darnley's mother, renounced any claim she might have to the earldom of Angus as daughter of the 6th Earl. She made the renunciation. Other peers who supported Mary although they had been something like enthusiasts for the revolution of 1559–60 were Cathcart, Gray, Yester, Herries, Lindsay and Ruthven. Co-operating with them were many more whose attitudes to that revolution had varied from qualified support through lukewarmness to positive hostility: the Earls of Atholl, Caithness, Erroll, Cassillis, Mar, Montrose, Lennox, Crawford and Eglinton, and Lords Crichton, Fleming, Glamis, Home, Somerville, Sinclair, Sempill, Livingston, Lovat, Borthwick, Ross, Forbes, Drummond, Innermeath and Ogilvy. The Earl Marischal was absent, possibly because of ill-health, but he was represented by his son, the Commendator of Deer, whose sister, as it happened, was married to Moray. Lord Seton was away on one of his visits to France. Altogether there were 12 earls and 21 lords on Mary's side, a massive majority of the peerage.

This was not achieved without a certain amount of management, in which Mary or her advisers showed some skill. She took timely action to receive into her favour the 5th Earl of Huntly, although he had not yet been restored to the estates forfeited by his father after Corrichie, and to recall from his banishment James Hepburn, Earl of Bothwell (although, like so many other supporters of the Queen, he 'went not to mass'). It was also Mary's doing, so it was alleged, that the strong Protestant Lindsay 'shamefully left the Earl of Moray' because the Queen had played on the jealousy between him and Rothes (who was a Moray supporter) over the sheriffship of Fife. Ruthven may have been won over similarly by expectations of the office of Treasurer, though they were not fulfilled for a long time.[10] It was at this point, too (23 June 1565) that the Queen raised Lord Erskine to the earldom of Mar – or rather recognised his right to an earldom from which his ancestors had been wrongfully excluded for generations; and it was reported that she intended to elevate to earldoms her brother Lord Robert and Lords Home and Fleming. Lord Robert did get his important charter of Orkney and Shetland on 26 May, but his earldom was deferred for another 16 years.

Among lairds, a noteworthy feature is how many more of the godly lairds of Ayrshire turned out on behalf of their Queen than on the side of the rebels – Boswell of Auchinleck, Cunninghams of Caprington, Craigans, Cunninghamhead and Glengarnock, Kennedy of Bargany and Mure of Rowallan. Some of them had signed the Protestant Bond of 1562 but now signed the bond for the Queen, and the Cunninghams were rejecting the lead of their head, Glencairn, who was with Moray. Mary also had the support of an Ayrshire Campbell – Loudoun – who had been an enthusiast in 1560 but now disregarded both familial ties with Argyll and the appeal which must have been made by Moray for his support of 'the religion'. Possibly it is still more surprising that two Hamiltons – Crawford and Sanquhar – likewise pursued an independent line and ranged themselves against Châtelherault. Nearly a score of Fife lairds were with the Queen, and there were some from Renfrewshire, Lanarkshire, the south-west and the Borders. Mary could perhaps not claim as many veterans of the reforming cause as Moray could, though her friend Erskine of Dun, an active reformer since the 1540s, attempted, at the suggestion of Lord Erskine, now Earl of Mar, to mediate between Moray and his sister. Yet many of the Queen's lairdly supporters, in addition to those in Ayrshire already mentioned, had been prominent enough on the Protestant side in the crisis of 1559–60: Gordon of Lochinvar, Stewarts of Doune and Garlies, Wallace of Craigie, Carnegie of Kinnaird, Forret of that ilk, Baillie of Lamington (who would have been expected to align himself with the Hamiltons) and Jardine of Applegarth. Just as in 1560 the appeal to patriotism and religion had over-ridden family feuds, so now did the appeal of the Queen, with the result that Kers of Cessford and Ferniehirst marched with their sworn enemies Turnbull of Bedrule, Scott of Buccleuch and Rutherford of Hunthill, while the two stray Hamiltons, of Sanquhar and Crawford (who seem to have been in the habit of acting in concert), similarly marched with Wallace of Craigie. The Ker lairds were accompanied by three Ker commendators – Kelso, Jedburgh and Newbattle. Thus many men with a record of support for Protestantism found themselves in the company of conservatives like Cassillis, Eglinton, Sempill, John Wemyss of that ilk and George Moutray of Seafield. Moutray was a 'great papist' who in 1564 had ruthlessly evicted the Protestant reader of the parish of Kinghorn from his house and it was not until 1569 that he became 'a good Christian man and a favourer of the Gospel'.[11] If the party of revolution of 1560 had been something of a coalition, the Queen's party of 1565 was no less a coalition.

After the Chaseabout Raid Mary's policy underwent a change. It has been suggested that she concluded from Moray's rebellion that, as concessions to the reformers did not avert opposition, there was nothing to be gained by continuing an equivocal religious policy, and it is true that Elizabeth's opposition to the Darnley marriage and the countenance she had given to Moray's plans had shown that no desire to conciliate England need any longer influence Mary. It is as likely, however, taking into account the balance of forces at the time of the rebellion and the massive Protestant support which Mary had enjoyed, that she felt, after her triumph, that she could pursue with impunity any course which her conscience or whim dictated and that she was confident of continued loyalty even if she showed more favour to the Roman Catholic cause than she had done hitherto.

At any rate, even before the rebellion was suppressed, Mary had taken unprecedented action in Edinburgh, where, although there had been no general support for Moray, a number of extremists had been active. On 23 August 1565 she peremptorily ordered the burgh to depose its provost and accept her trusted friend Sir Simon Preston of Craigmillar in his place, and she would also have liked to insist on the dismissal of the town's chief minister, John Knox (who had recently preached so bitterly and so long when Darnley was in his congregation that the young man lost his appetite for his dinner). This might suggest that the rebellion could be used as a convenient stick to beat Protestants. Other developments indicated an idea that it was time to lean on the more conservative elements in the hope that they would be more reliable than those friends of England and of the Reformation who had joined Moray. Archbishop Hamilton was liberated after his imprisonment for saying mass, and the control of the thirds of benefices, on which ministers depended for their stipends, was taken from that 'earnest professor of the gospel', Sir John Wishart of Pittarro (who was in Moray's army), and given to Sir William Murray of Tullibardine, who was more ready to allow the crown to pillage the thirds at the ministers' expense. Besides, after being confronted with a Protestant revolt, Mary could assume the role of a suffering Catholic deserving of support from papalist powers on the continent. She therefore made an approach to Philip of Spain and sent the Bishop of Dunblane to Rome to ask for men and money, while she professed her intention to take some action in favour of 'the auld religion'.[12] Yet opportunism did not fly out of the window even now, for in December 1565 she declared that she would not adhere to Protestantism and thereby risk losing continental friends when she had 'no assurance of anything that may countervail the same' – a plain hint that she might think otherwise even now if she had a guarantee from Elizabeth.

It is far from clear that the Romanising drift apparent in Mary's policy was in itself a decisive factor in making new enemies for her, though some who had seen no reason to join Moray may now have reflected that Moray might after all have been right. For whatever reasons, we can detect the growth of a certain coolness between Mary and most of the great nobles and her increasing reliance on men of lower degree, but whether the alienation of the nobles caused her to turn to lesser men or her favour to lesser men alienated the nobles is harder to discern. Moray and his associates had already, before their rebellion, accused the Queen of turning for advice to strangers and men of base degree, to the neglect of the nobility, and this she certainly proceeded to do after the rebellion, whether or not she had done so before. In the period between the Chaseabout Raid and the following March, the peers who most frequently attended the council were Morton (who was Chancellor), Huntly, Bothwell and Atholl: Ruthven, Mar, Lennox, Crawford, Marischal and Caithness attended less often. Among all those councillors, only Atholl, Crawford and Caithness could be called religious conservatives. On the other hand, whereas councillors other than peers and officials had hardly been known before the rebellion, men now appeared who gave the council a different complexion. Alexander Gordon, Bishop of Galloway, admitted to the council on 5 November 1565 and a frequent attender thereafter, was a decided Protestant, whom Mary had earlier distrusted as 'a dangerous man', but he became a lord of session on 26 November 1565; as he was an uncle of the Earl of Huntly and (as his mother was a natural daughter of James IV) a cousin of the Queen, he was not middle-class, but he was primarily a professional man rather than an aristocrat. Gordon may have owed his elevation less to the Queen than to Huntly (for whose full restoration he had been solicitous), but there was another judge, John Leslie, who had no such connections to assist his promotion. When he first appeared on the council on 19 October he was only parson of Oyne and, far from having distinguished lineage, was a priest's bastard; but Mary soon made him Commendator of Lindores and then Bishop of Ross. Next, Mary's candidate for the Edinburgh provostship, Preston of Craigmillar, was admitted to the council along with Alexander Gordon and attended quite often. Another new councillor was yet another lawyer, James Balfour of Pittendreich; he 'once did row in the galleys' with John Knox, when they had been captured after Cardinal Beaton's murder,[13] but, appropriately in view of his early conversion to Protestantism, professed himself a Lutheran and presumably had little use for the reformed church as it had developed in Scotland. From the summer of 1565 Balfour was one of the most assiduous attenders at the council and he became Clerk Register in the spring of 1566. John Maxwell of Terregles, a laird with a Protestant record who had recently established cordial relations with the Queen, had been at the council very occasionally before but now turned up fairly often. Besides such new men of modest origins who had an official status in the council, there was activity at a less formal level by some 'crafty and vile strangers' who, it was said, 'occupy the place of native councillors and manage all weighty affairs'.[14] These low-born foreigners can be identified with some of the men who were numbered among the Queen's friends in the previous chapter – Francisco de Busso and Sebastian Danelourt – and an Englishman called Fowler who had been a servant of Lennox and Darnley. Preference for men of humble birth had helped to bring about the downfall of James III and James V, foreigners were never popular with the Scots, and it had not been forgotten that in 1560, at the time of the treaty of Edinburgh, Mary had agreed not to appoint foreigners to office. The Queen was on a dangerous course.

Meantime, of the persons involved in the Chaseabout Raid, large numbers of lesser men had received remissions, and Châtelherault had been pardoned on condition that he would go into exile for five years, but Moray, Argyll, Glencairn, Rothes, Ochiltree, Boyd and Kirkcaldy of Grange were summoned to stand trial by parliament on 14 March 1566. They had been looking for allies to bring about their restoration, and found sympathisers in Protestant lords like Morton, who had not been in the rebellion but may have been alienated by Mary's subsequent proceedings. The two groups agreed with Darnley that, in return for his undertaking to prevent action by parliament against them, they would support his claim to the crown matrimonial and the right of his family to succeed to the throne, failing issue of Mary. It was a curious alliance, for Moray's faction had raised a rebellion in protest against the elevation of the man they now proposed to elevate still more, and the presumption must be that they hoped to use Darnley as a tool to establish their own ascendancy. Moray, Ochiltree, Rothes, Kirkcaldy of Grange, Haliburton of Pitcur and Wishart of Pittarro – all strong Protestants – signed their bond to Darnley at Newcastle on 2 March 1566.[15]

One of the clauses in the bond pledged the maintenance of the reformed religion, and this must be seen against the background not only of Mary's recent actions but of a rumour that the impending parliament would grant 'liberty of conscience' – that is, to papists.[16] It was also reported that Mary was putting pressure on notables to attend mass: Cassillis, Eglinton, Caithness and Seton agreed, but Huntly, Bothwell, Fleming, Livingston and Lindsay would not.[17]

The bond to Darnley is endorsed in a contemporary hand: 'Ane band maid be my lord of Murray and certain uther noblemen with him befoir the slauchtir of Davie'. 'Davie' was Riccio, a musician who had become secretary for the Queen's French affairs and the most obnoxious of the 'crafty and vile strangers'. He seemed to be constantly about the Queen, and peers of ancient lineage were mortified when they found that their applications to Mary had to pass through the hands of a foreigner who adopted a haughty attitude not in keeping with his origins. Mary may well have been blameworthy, but only to the extent that her natural kindliness towards her dependents was in this case reinforced by a perfectly intelligible liking for the society of a congenial and entertaining servant. That anyone thought seriously that there was any impropriety, or that Riccio was the father of the child with whom Mary became pregnant in the autumn of 1565 seems rather unlikely, but there were those who were ready, for their own reasons, to encourage Darnley to doubt his wife's fidelity. At any rate, jealous nobles, Protestant agitators and a suspicious husband conspired against the Italian, who met his end on 9 March 1566. It can hardly be questioned that the murder, carried out with needless brutality in or near the presence of a Queen who was six months pregnant, was intended, at least by some of the perpetrators, to endanger the life of Mary and her unborn child and open the way to rule by a clique using Darnley as a figurehead. The ringleaders in the crime were Morton, Lindsay and Ruthven, but Moray and his associates were ready to enter Edinburgh as soon as the deed was done.

The information we have about the persons involved in the conspiracy – and it amounts to more than 120 names – suggests that there had been something of a landslide away from the Queen of many who had aided her against Moray in the previous year. It is startling to find that her Chancellor (Morton), Secretary of State (Maitland of Lethington), Clerk Register (MacGill) and Justice Clerk (Bellenden of Auchnoule) were all involved and that the Advocate and the Comptroller, if not actually in the plot, suddenly disappeared from the council at this point.

Whatever contribution may have been made by aristocratic jealousy and general xenophobia, no one who looks at the names of the conspirators can doubt that Protestant hatred of Riccio as a suspected papal agent and Protestant distrust of the policy recently pursued by the Queen played an important part in giving Darnley the support he sought for his intended *coup*. It is not surprising that Protestant zealots who had given no countenance to Moray's rebellion were now accomplices in a murder of which John Knox whole-heartedly approved. The murderers hardly needed to underline that their crime was a Protestant demonstration by adding to the slaughter of Riccio that of a Dominican friar whom Mary had been harbouring. Among the murderers or their supporters were lairds from the Lothians, Fife and elsewhere whose families had a long Protestant tradition, like John Crichton of Brunstane (with his brother Alexander), Cockburn of Ormiston, Johnstone of Elphinstone, Whitelaw of New Grange, Sandilands of Calder, Scott of Abbotshall, Lauder of Haltoun, Mure of Rowallan, Menteith of Kerse, Carmichaels of that ilk and of Meadowflat, Cunningham of Drumquhassill, Tweedie of Drumelzier, Edmonstone of that ilk and Wood of Bonnington. It was Andrew Ker of Fawdonside, signatory of the bond of April 1562 and the first Book of Discipline and frequenter of general assemblies, who held a pistol to Mary's waist. (He later married John Knox's widow, and the topics they discussed by their fireside offer a great field for speculation.) Some who had been with Moray in the previous year, like Andrew Hay, parson of Renfrew, and John Somerville of Cambusnethan, were involved again in this affair, but now they were in the company of men who had stood by the Queen in 1565, like Stewart of Doune, Murray of Balvaird, Cunningham of Cunninghamhead and Mure of Rowallan. As Morton was a leader of the plot it is not surprising that over 20 Douglases were engaged, with Carmichaels who habitually supported Morton, while Lord Lindsay brought three Lindsays and Lord Ruthven brought four Ruthvens. It is significant of familial cohesion that Hamiltons and Hepburns were conspicuous by their absence, the former because no Hamilton was likely to do anything to advance Darnley and the latter because Bothwell was, as ever, loyal to the Queen. A group of lairds from southern Perthshire – Murrays of Balvaird, Tibbermure, Touchadam and Tullibardine and the Stirlings of Keir and Ardoch – included two or three who had been active on the reforming side in 1544 and 1560, along with others who had not previously shown signs of being committed. Among the score or so of burgesses of Edinburgh known to have been involved was no less a person than Alexander Guthrie, the town clerk, a very militant Protestant.[18]

It is well known how Mary survived the physical and psychological shock of that March evening and, by detaching Darnley from the conspirators, frustrated the plotters of their wider purposes. She retained the support of most of her noble councillors except Morton and Ruthven, so that among the peers Huntly (who succeeded Morton as Chancellor), Bothwell, Crawford, Atholl, Mar, Caithness, Marischal, Cassillis and Fleming continued to attend. And, although the administration was shaken by the defection of so many officials, the Queen could still rely on some of the non-artistocratic familiars who had recently been among her advisers – Terregles, Pittendreich, Preston, John Leslie, Alexander Gordon – and one new one, David Chalmer of Ormond, another trained lawyer. She next made a startling move by offering pardons to Moray and those of his fellow-rebels who had not been pardoned already, with the result that from 29 April 1566 Moray, Glencairn, Argyll and Rothes also appeared at the council table. The note of the summer of 1566 was one of general reconciliation, for as her confinement approached Mary was anxious that there should be no strife, and on the whole her wish was respected, if only by those with whom her condition won some human sympathy. There was indeed a report in June that Argyll, Moray, Mar and Atholl led one faction in opposition to another led by Huntly and Bothwell,[19] and it is hard to believe that there can have been genuine cordiality among men who had so recently been at variance, but the fact remains that throughout the summer of 1566 and the following autumn and winter Mary was holding a large core of councillors together. She was doing so, at least to some extent, by skilful management. Whether the birth of the Prince (19 June) had done anything to strengthen her position might be debated: she had ceased to be the bulwark against a disputed succession and perhaps civil war between the supporters of the rights of Châtelherault on one hand and the supporters of Darnley's family on the other, and her removal would now mean a minority, with all the opportunities it offered to those, whether scrupulous or unscrupulous, who counted on being able to mould an infant sovereign.

It was therefore open to Mary to demonstrate her continued equitable policy in religious matters. It was true that the Prince's baptism, in December, was with Roman Catholic ceremonial, and of the regular councillors only the Earl of Atholl and the Bishop of Ross entered the chapel, along with Eglinton, Sempill and probably Seton, while Moray, Huntly and Bothwell remained outside. Nor was it merely a question of countenancing or repudiating a particular rite, for the baptism drove home the prospect of a succession of sovereigns hostile to the reformed faith. Yet men who had disagreed over the baptism continued to sit together on the council, and Mary was doing a lot to reassure Protestants once again, now by actions and not by mere words: in October 1566 there was an act ordaining that lesser benefices should go to ministers of the reformed church, in December that church received a subvention of £10,000 in cash, plus victual worth about as much, and from that point there was a series of gifts to burghs of ecclesiastical properties within their bounds. These were tangible gains, to offset the impression made by the baptism and by another surprise move – the restoration of certain jurisdiction to Archbishop Hamilton on 23 December. The restoration of powers which enabled the primate to grant divorces – a restoration soon revoked – has to be seen in relation to the wide rift which had opened between the Queen and her husband. This, as it happened, had a farther unifying effect, because some at least of Darnley's enemies were Mary's friends who wanted to release her from a union which had become intolerable. The way in which a move against Darnley could become a new focus of unity was extended when on Christmas Eve Mary pardoned the Riccio murderers, who were Darnley's bitter enemies after his desertion of them in the previous March. Thus in addition to his family's implacable foes the Hamiltons, Darnley had Morton's Douglases and Bothwell's Hepburns aligned against him.

The elimination of Darnley by his murder at Kirk o'Field on 10 February caused little grief outside his family, and even the subsequent events – the accusations of Mary and Bothwell, the trial and acquittal of Bothwell and Bothwell's abduction of the Queen – did not disrupt the council, except that Moray went abroad in March. In April Mary made a renewed bid for support on both personal and religious grounds. In a parliament attended by 10 earls, 16 lords, nine bishops and ten commendators she formally took the reformed church under her protection and passed ratifications in favour of Moray, Huntly, Crawford, Rothes, Angus, Caithness, Herries, John Sempill (son of Lord Sempill and husband of Mary Livingston), John Ogilvie of Findlater, Michael Balfour of Burleigh and George Ramsay of Dalhousie.

It has often been remarked that it was not the Darnley murder but the Bothwell marriage that was fatal to Mary. But even the Bothwell marriage, at any rate in the eyes of those who believed that she had been forced into it, was not fatal. When a confederacy was formed, on 1 May, the signatories pledged themselves to set the Queen at liberty and to defend her and the Prince; and, after the marriage had taken place, the proclaimed purpose of the confederacy was to dissolve it and so liberate Mary. This explains, quite simply, why the confederates initially had so much support: their professed objectives appealed not only to the Queen's enemies but also to the Queen's friends. Even when Mary fell into the hands of the confederates after their encounter at Carberry with the force raised by Bothwell, and, instead of being liberated, was hustled off to captivity in Lochleven Castle, the excuse at least was that she had brought this fate on herself by refusing to give up Bothwell and so accept the promised liberation. The quite limited opposition to the confederates came, presumably, from those who suspected – as some certainly did – that the real aim from the outset was to end Mary's rule and set up James as a king who could be controlled during a long minority.

The unity of the confederates was so soon disrupted, when they proceeded not only to extort Mary's abdication but to crown James, that a detailed analysis of their original strength is hardly worthwhile, but some indication can be given, particularly from the peerage. Among the party which mustered against Mary and Bothwell – or perhaps we should rather say against Bothwell – were 12 earls, ranging in opinion from the zealot Glencairn through men with clear Protestant records – Argyll, Morton, Mar and Marischal – and moderate conservatives – Atholl, Eglinton, Montrose and Caithness (who, it appears, was wavering almost from the start) – to the ultra-conservative Cassillis; Menteith, a young man who had not hitherto taken part in affairs, and Buchan, who had likewise shown little sign of activity previously, were also involved. The surprising absentee was the consistent Protestant Rothes. The remaining earls can easily be accounted for and their absence explained. Moray and Arran (Châtelherault) were out of the country when the confederacy was launched, Bothwell was with the Queen and then on the run, Huntly and apparently Crawford were pledged to the Queen because they suspected the sincerity of the confederates, Erroll was presumably uncommitted by deliberate choice. Angus was a minor; Sutherland was at the Mary-Bothwell wedding but died on 23 June 1567 and was succeeded by a minor; Lennox, though numbered among the confederates, was inconspicuous and seems to have gone to England.

The 14 lords among the confederates were, like the earls, drawn from a wide spectrum, though nearly all of them – Boyd, Ochiltree, Ruthven, Gray, Glamis, Innermeath, Lindsay, Home, Herries, St John and Sanquhar – can be put down as Protestants of one shade or another; but Drummond had played little part in affairs, Borthwick had been a conservative in 1560 and Sempill would have been characterised by contemporaries as an obstinate papist. Boyd and Herries, it should be said, seem to have been wavering from the start and soon joined Fleming, Seton, Livingston and Oliphant, who were pledged to the Queen. Officials, with the notable exception of Chancellor Huntly, were on the confederates' side – MacGill and Lethington and even Sir James Balfour, who had been one of Mary's 'new men'. The Commendators of Dunfermline, Inchcolm, Cambuskenneth, Dryburgh and Culross were also in the confederacy. Among men of lesser rank, Kirkcaldy of Grange, himself a Protestant Fife laird, claimed that 'all the whole west, Merse and Teviotdale, the most part of Fife, Angus and Mearns' were with the confederates,[20] and the detailed evidence would seem to support that claim. East Lothian, where Bothwell's influence had created a determined resistance to the revolution, the south-west (for reasons difficult to discern) and the north (where Huntly's opposition did much to shape alignment) were much less conspicuous, but the Aberdeen Forbeses (always on the other side from Huntly) were among many landowners (largely in Angus, Mearns and Perthshire) who complained that they suffered at Huntly's hands for their support of the confederates. The commissioners of burghs present at James's coronation represented Edinburgh, Montrose, Dundee, Glasgow, Stirling, Linlithgow, Ayr and Irvine. The stages by which the confederates of May–June 1567, with their professions of loyalty to the Queen, were transformed into the 'King's party' will be explained in relation to the pattern of support for the Queen.

# 6
# THE QUEEN'S PARTY 1567–73

*1567 June 15* Carberry
*July 24* Mary abdicated at Lochleven
*July 29* Coronation of James VI
*1568 May 2* Mary's escape
*May 13* Langside
*Oct.–Dec.* York-Westminster Conferences
*1570 Jan.* Murder of Moray
*July* Lennox Regent
*1571 Sept.* Death of Lennox
Mar Regent
*1572 Oct.* Death of Mar
Morton Regent
*1573 Feb.* Pacification of Perth
*May* Fall of Edinburgh Castle

A nucleus of a Marian party may be said to have existed in the summer of 1567, for even when the confederacy was at its strongest and was still not ostensibly directed against Mary, she retained a small number of devoted adherents who had been unshaken by the Bothwell marriage. There are four lists which furnish their names: those who were with Mary when she appeared before the Court of Session on 12 May to declare that in deciding to marry Bothwell she was a free agent,[1] the witnesses to the marriage contract of 14 May,[2] those present at the wedding on 15 May[3] and the privy councillors who attended meetings between 17 and 22 May.[4] Leaving out of account judges and officials who were present on some of those occasions *ex officio*, we find that Huntly (who had been Bothwell's brother-in-law but does not seem to have been aggrieved when his sister and Bothwell parted company by divorce), Crawford, Archbishop Hamilton and Bishop Leslie of Ross were in all four groups; Lord Fleming and Bishop Gordon of Galloway in three; Lords Oliphant, Boyd and Herries and Lord John Hamilton in two; Caithness, Sutherland, Seton, Livingston, Rothes, Glamis and Preston of Craigmillar in one. Two considerations must be kept in mind. First, only councillors were qualified to appear in the fourth group, and it happens that four new councillors were admitted at this stage: Archbishop Hamilton and Lord Oliphant on 16 May and Lord Boyd and Bothwell's client Thomas Hepburn, parson of Oldhamstocks (on his appointment as Master of Requests) on 17 May. Second, as the marriage ceremony was a Protestant one, conducted by Adam Bothwell, the reforming Bishop of Orkney, Lord Livingston came and Lord Seton stayed away. Rather curiously, William Chisholm, Bishop of Dunblane, a committed papalist who had been resident mainly on the continent for some time but had recently come on a visit to Scotland, did not scruple to attend the wedding. Archbishop Hamilton was there too, but his attitude was as equivocal as ever: it was not long since he had baptized Prince James by Roman Catholic rites, but in August 1567 he was 'showing himself now a conformable man both in apparel and outward orders of religion' and a year later he was 'not far' from approving of conformity with the Church of England.[5] Among others present at the wedding were the Earl of Sutherland, whose religious record was ambiguous, Lord Oliphant, who had succeeded to the title only in the previous year and had given no evidence yet of his commitment, and Lord Glamis, a firm Protestant. It is no surprise that the popishly-inclined Caithness was at Mary's side on 12 May, and Mary had acquired a devoted follower in Lord Herries, whose record had been that of an ardent reformer but who, clearly a moderate man, would in 1568 have approved of conformity with the Church of England, to which he thought the Scottish parliament would agree:[6] he was a witness to the marriage contract and was in council on 17 May.

Not many of Mary's recent councillors and associates were in the narrowly based force with which Bothwell and she confronted the lords at Carberry on 15 June. The new-wedded pair had passed their last night together, before the encounter, at Seton (where Mary had spent part of her honeymoon with Darnley), and Lord Seton marched out with them. Those other Lothian lords, Yester and Borthwick, are said also to have been in the army, but its main strength seems to have lain in Bothwell's kinsmen and neighbours whose loyalty he commanded as Lord of Hailes (near Haddington) and head of the house of Hepburn. Three Hepburn lairds – Waughton, Gilmerton and Smeaton, – two Hepburn parsons – Oldhamstocks and Prestonkirk – and an undesignated Patrick Hepburn all shared Bothwell's surname and, with Patrick Whitelaw of that ilk and William Newton of that ilk, continued to hold Dunbar Castle for him until September. Lauder of Bass, Cockburn of Ormiston – both from East Lothian – and the Berwickshire lairds of Wedderburn, Blackadder and Langton, as well as Ormiston of that ilk and Ker of the Hirsel, were probably with them at Carberry as well as in the Dunbar garrison.

The decision to march out from Dunbar and meet the challenge of the confederates in the field was clearly a mistake and although the choice is not likely to have been Mary's it was the first of three impulsive actions – the others were the decision to fight at Langside and the decision to flee to England – which were so fatal to her cause. Delay in June 1567 would have brought far more recruits to her side. Several men who were well disposed to her were perhaps undecided about joining a force led by Bothwell and could not foresee the rapidity with which Mary would surrender and be hustled away to Lochleven without their having a chance to intervene. It was reported that Huntly, Archbishop Hamilton, the Hamilton Commendators of Arbroath and Kilwinning, Lords Fleming, Ross and Boyd and Leslie, Bishop of Ross, would have been in arms for the Queen had they not been frustrated by the surrender at Carberry.[7] The Hamiltons were bound to support Mary as soon as the confederates made it clear that they intended to depose her and crown James, with Moray as Regent: while they had joined Moray in his rebellion in 1565 in opposition to Mary's marriage to a member of their rival house of Lennox, Mary was now no longer linked with the Lennox family and, besides, the Hamilton view was that if there was to be a regent the office belonged of right to Châtelherault, as heir presumptive, just as it had done in Mary's minority. Huntly, the Queen's faithful adherent in the critical days of May, not only had enormous influence in the north but also had a bond with a group of south-westerners: Lord Carlyle, Gordon of Lochinvar, MacLellan of Bombie, MacCulloch of Cardoness, the Kirkpatricks of Closeburn, Kirkmichael and Alisland. Mary would have had all this additional support if her action had been less precipitate. Besides, during a delay the disintegration of the confederates could have begun and it was from such a disintegration that much of the strength of what was to become the Queen's Party emerged. On the other hand, the disappearance of Bothwell from the scene, as a result of the encounter at Carberry, rid Mary of an embarrassment and a liability.

At any rate, the confederacy did soon break up. The actions which some of the lords took in imprisoning Mary, extorting her abdication and crowning James did not command the support of those who believed that they had taken up arms to liberate the Queen. Besides, if support were given to the crowning of James, what was to be the fate of Mary? The lords protested that if the Queen consented to her supersession by James they would not 'touch her in honour nor in life' nor 'proceed against her judicially by way of process', though otherwise they were determined to proceed against her publicly. However, an English envoy shrewdly observed that if they once went on to 'touch their sovereign in honour or credit they will never think to find any safety as long as she lives, and so not only deprive her of her estate, but also of her life'.[8] How true that 'experience hath shown that between the prisons and graves of princes the distance is very small'. Many who had been hostile enough to Bothwell and Mary were not prepared to risk bringing about their Queen's death – much as in the following century the Scots helped to bring about the downfall of Charles I but were indignant when the English beheaded him.

Consequently there were early deserters from the confederacy, such as Argyll, who aligned himself with the Hamiltons a week after Carberry; and by the end of the month it was reported that Herries, Fleming and Boyd, the Bishop of Galloway and Hamilton of Sanquhar had followed his example.[9] When we look at the signatories of the order committing Mary to Lochleven, the names of the peers present at James's coronation on 25 July and the privy councillors who witnessed Moray's acceptance of the regency on 22 August, we see the contrast to the 12 earls and 14 lords who had countenanced the initial decision to act against Bothwell and Mary – or perhaps we should rather say against Bothwell – and can plainly discern the rump of the confederacy, which was by definition also the core of the King's Party.[10] The Earls of Morton, Atholl, Glencairn and Mar, Lords Ruthven, Home, Lindsay, Sempill and Ochiltree and the Master of Montrose appear in all three lists; Menteith was the fifth earl at the coronation and Buchan made a fifth at the council of 22 August; Lords Sanquhar, Innermeath, St John and possibly Cathcart were at the coronation and Lord Borthwick at the council. At the coronation Bishop Bothwell of Orkney, who anointed the child-king, was the sole bishop, and the only commendators were Pitcairn of Dunfermline (who later became Secretary of State) and Robert Richardson of St Mary's Isle (who was Treasurer). There were a few lairds who were also officials – Murray of Tullibardine, the Comptroller, whose sister was Mar's wife, Maitland of Lethington (Secretary), Bellenden of Auchnoule (Justice-Clerk) – and four who were also provosts of burghs – Erskine of Dun (Montrose), Haliburton of Pitcur (Dundee), John Stewart of Minto (Glasgow) and John Craigingelt of that ilk (Stirling). No doubt there were many lairds who were neither officials nor provosts, but it is difficult to name any except Colville of East Wemyss, Maule of Panmure, Elphinstone of Shank and Napier of Merchiston (brother-in-law of Bishop Bothwell). There is evidence that another half-dozen lords were inclined to the Regent's side, but the rather meagre collection of names of those who were active and committed is a measure of the extent of defection from the original confederacy. It was almost a pardonable exaggeration when Mary's spokesmen rhetorically asserted that not a tenth of the nobility had taken part in the coronation of James. And, besides those who openly defected or at any rate stood aloof, there were also 'secret favourers of the Queen' among the confederates, who took the view that what Mary had surrendered under duress and without parliamentary action could not prejudice her rights. Perhaps the most significant of the group was Kirkcaldy of Grange. He was an honourable soldier to whose high character contemporaries testified: Henry II of France said 'Yonder is one of the most valiant men of our time' and a fellow Scot remarked that he was 'never cruel', but 'gentle and meek like a lamb in the house, but like a lion in the field.'[11] Kirkcaldy felt a special responsibility as it was to him that Mary had surrendered at Carberry, and he showed his continued interest in the original aims of the confederacy by taking the lead in the pursuit of Bothwell to Shetland, vowing to bring him to Edinburgh 'quick or dead' and so genuinely liberate the Queen; his only object in joining the confederates had been to 'restore my native country to liberty and honour' after Bothwell's treasonable deeds.[12]

Yet, however many well-wishers Mary might have, the fact was that she was under lock and key in Lochleven Castle, and it was not clear what course was open to her friends. Their initial actions proved abortive. On 10 September 1567 Gavin Hamilton, Commendator of Kilwinning, the Earl of Atholl and Lords Livingston and Boyd protested that the Queen should be set at liberty and that the coronation of James should not prejudice the rights of the Hamiltons. Two days later the Hamiltons and their allies proclaimed their aims to be the liberation of the Queen and the pursuit of Darnley's murderers and nominated their own regency – Lord John (until Châtelherault should return from France), Argyll and Huntly, who were to act in the name of James (but as Prince, not as King). They intended to levy forces, to which it was expected that Argyll would contribute 5000 men, the Hamiltons, Huntly, Crawford and Herries each 1000.[13] Gavin Hamilton was sent to fetch the Duke home and by 2 October Châtelherault was reported to be at Dieppe, but even had he then proceeded to Scotland it would have been too late, for the proposed resistance to the confederates rapidly crumbled. Already on 15 September most of those who had recently proclaimed their intention of resisting – Huntly, Argyll, Kilwinning, Herries and Boyd – suddenly offered their allegiance to the King.[14] They were scattered before they mustered their proposed forces; Bothwell's followers surrendered Dunbar; and Huntly's allies in the south-west renounced their bond to him in October. A parliament held by Moray in December was attended by 12 earls, including Huntly and Crawford who had been so loyal to Mary in May, as well as Argyll who had defected from the confederates in June; 15 lords (not, however, including the conspicuous Marians Livingston, Seton, Boyd and Fleming); four bishops, including Gordon of Galloway, who had been on Mary's council to the end; 14 commendators; and representatives of the unusually high number of 28 burghs. Even Fleming and Livingston, who were not at the parliament, subsequently appeared on Moray's council, along with Huntly and Bishop Gordon. It looked at this stage as if Moray was going to consolidate his position and little was going to come of the Marian cause.

Then came Mary's escape, on 2 May 1568. She was at liberty for only 11 days before her defeat at Langside, but in that brief space there rallied to her a force of between 5000 and 6000 men. No doubt some arrangements had been made to receive her should the escape attempt succeed: George Douglas, brother of the laird of Lochleven, who had tried to free her earlier, was there to welcome her at the lochside and Lord Seton met her with 30 horsemen some two miles away. Yet no one could have counted on success, and it is inconceivable that substantial numbers of men were standing by, ready armed. There must have been both remarkable rapidity in sending out summonses and alacrity in obeying them.

In her flight, Mary crossed the Firth of Forth to South Queensferry, where she was met by Lord Claud Hamilton, whose family had property at Abercorn and Kinneil, not far away, and who must have had warning that an escape was being attempted. The first halt was a few miles to the south-west, at Niddrie Castle near Winchburgh, which belonged to Seton. He would presumably at once send out messages to East Lothian, where his own influence chiefly lay, and to other parts of the south-east, from which men were able to set out in time to join the Queen before the 13th. But after only a couple of hours at Niddrie Mary pushed on (joined on the way by Herries) to Hamilton, which she reached on the 3rd and where she remained until the morning of the engagement at Langside, ten miles away. From Hamilton hasty messages went out[15] and were able to reach at least the centre and south-west of the country in time to bring men in from those areas. The French ambassador, who presumably had some experience of what mustering an army involved, remarked that he 'never did see so many men so suddenly convened'.[16] The history of those 11 days from 2 to 13 May is not the least instructive in Mary's whole career. No doubt the year that had elapsed since Carberry had done something to allow the pitiable tale of her misfortunes to eclipse the memory of the ineptitude and folly, if not crime, of which she had been guilty, and no doubt there were many who found that they could not work with Moray and craved a return to political power under different auspices, but it will become abundantly clear as the tale of her party unfolds that there is no single of simple explanation of the massive support she was able to rally.

The Queen's supporters – perhaps we should rather say sponsors – at Hamilton decided to make for the rock-fortress of Dumbarton, held by the friendly Lord Fleming. This was sound enough strategy, for had they reached Dumbarton they would have had security until they received the reinforcements which could confidently be expected from the north. Moray happened to be in the vicinity, at Glasgow, but the countryside was not well disposed to him and his force was far smaller than Mary's. It was therefore hoped to catch him at a disadvantage and consolidate the Queen's position, and the Hamiltons, who were for the time being dominant in Mary's counsels, calculated that a swift victory, before they were outnumbered by others, would ensure their continued ascendancy. Had Mary reached Dumbarton or in some other way kept her forces intact until they were reinforced, Moray could have been swept away in another Chaseabout Raid. As it was, Moray outmanoeuvred the Queen's army and won an easy victory, in a battle which should never have been fought. After Langside, impetuosity again prevailed. There had been few casualties and Mary's forces would have rallied again in increased numbers to continue the war with vigour. But she was in terror for her life and made a precipitate flight to the south-west and then across the Solway into England. Once more, as after the sudden imprisonment at Lochleven, her followers were left somewhat at a loss.

Moray made some headway. In June, the month after Langside, he toured Clydesdale, Galloway, Nithsdale, Annandale and Tweeddale, capturing castles and receiving submissions, but the lasting impression his expedition made was limited. The parliament he held in July-August was attended by only four earls (Morton, Glencairn, Mar and Menteith), nine lords (Lindsay, Sempill, Ochiltree, Cathcart, St John, Home, Glamis, Innermeath and Borthwick), two bishops and nine commendators. He was experimenting in 'management', for the Queen's supporters were threatened with forfeiture, there was a promise of pardon to those who laid down their arms and there are indications of an attempt to exploit crown patronage. Earlier, Moray had apparently used the priory of Pittenweem and the office of Lord President to detach Balfour of Pittendreich from the Queen; Lord Sempill, who as a Roman Catholic seems an improbable adherent of Moray, was won over by the escheat of the Commendator of Paisley and a promise of the office of commendator should forfeiture follow; and there was a report that Fleming would have surrendered Dumbarton if Moray had given him an abbey he asked for[17] – obviously Whithorn, where the Flemings had something like hereditary rights. It had been promised to Lord Fleming in 1565 but went instead (in September 1568) to Lord Robert Stewart, the youngest of James V's bastards and the only one of them who had not already been provided for in some way.

But during and after the sitting of Moray's parliament the Queen's men were very active. In August Huntly was said to be in the field in Fife and Angus with an army estimated at from 2000 to 5000 men, Argyll and Fleming were preparing to besiege Glasgow with 1500. In the last months of the year, when Moray was away in England to take part in the investigations into the charges and counter-charges between Mary and him, it was reported that 'Huntly reigns in the north' and 'the Hepburns in East Lothian lie in garrisons', while Lord Claud recovered Hamilton Castle from

Lord Sempill, and some of his kinsmen, as well as Fleming and Herries, were capturing houses and taking prisoners, including that 'honest and true gentleman' Ker of Fawdonside.[18]

No one could have foreseen, or even thought possible, Mary's lifelong detention in England, but the uncertainty which prevailed during the investigations had induced irresolution and indecision in Scotland. While the formal outcome, announced at Hampton Court on 10 January 1570, was inconclusive, Moray came back with a measure of recognition from England and a subsidy in his pocket. There was no immediate improvement in his position, for in February he had not added a single earl or lord to those who had supported him in 1567 and even in March he complained that his enemies were very active. However, in April between 60 and 70 Marians submitted to him, on 14 May Huntly made a solemn submission, including a promise to compensate those he had injured, and in June it was reported that 'the state grows to obedience and quietness'.[19]

Yet those who had followed the proceedings in England could see that they had not been wholly to Mary's disadvantage. At the worst, it was evident that there had been those on both sides who did not wish to push the matter to extremities. Maitland of Lethington, though on Moray's side, was said to have wanted to have the question settled 'in dulce manner'; Herries, on Mary's side, was said to 'labour for a reconciliation without odious accusations'; and both Herries and Mary's other commissioner, John Leslie, Bishop of Ross, lacked complete conviction about her innocence and would have welcomed a compromise. Yet the presentation of her case had seemed formidable. One of the English noblemen who were present remarked that 'her proofs will fall out best, as is thought', and it cannot have been unnoticed that the supposedly damning evidence against Mary – the Casket Letters and the Book of Articles – were produced only after her commissioners had withdrawn and were no longer there to challenge them.[20] Besides, no one could have thought that Mary received fair or equitable treatment, at any rate after the early stages at York. The principal injustice lay in the refusal to allow her to appear in person, as Moray was allowed to do, and in the decision of Elizabeth to receive Moray but not to come face to face with Mary. The point is that Mary's case, which impressed those in England who heard it presented, was cogent enough to make an influential party in Scotland fight for it when the opportunity came.

It came when Moray was murdered at Linlithgow in January 1570 by James Hamilton of Bothwellhauch with the connivance of Archbishop Hamilton. His death made difficulties for the King's Party. Anxious for English support, they in effect invited Elizabeth to choose a new Regent, and her selection was Darnley's father, Lennox, who was appointed lieutenant of the kingdom in June and Regent in July. His record as a one-time agent of Henry VIII did not commend him to patriots, he was even more repugnant than Moray had been to the rival house of Hamilton, and his determination to avenge the murder of his son was a threat to the many who were under suspicion.

There was therefore an accession of strength to the Marians, and more serious civil war began. The government had to conduct operations against

Huntly in the north, Argyll in the west and the Hamiltons in the centre and south-west. On English mediation a truce for six months was arranged in September, but war was resumed when it expired. The capture of Dumbarton Castle for the King in April 1571 reduced the possibility that the Queen's Party would receive French help through that channel. From that point, although Huntly was still in power in the north-east and the Hamiltons in control of Clydesdale, interest focused on Edinburgh, where Kirkcaldy of Grange, now on Mary's side, held the castle and dominated the town. When Lennox was killed (4 September 1571), he was succeeded by Mar, and real power passed to Morton, though the latter did not become Regent until November 1572, following Mar's death in October. Morton, in view of the anglophile and Protestant tradition of the Angus Douglases whom he led, deserved English support if anyone in Scotland did, and he had been negotiating for it in England in the spring of 1571. For a time Elizabeth toyed with the idea of handing Mary over to Mar, but after his death English policy was directed towards securing the King's Party without any reference to what was to become of Mary. Defections from the Queen's Party enabled the Regent's forces to reoccupy the town of Edinburgh in the autumn of 1572, but English help was necessary to reduce the castle, where the Scottish artillery train was housed, and it fell on 28 May 1573.

That brief sketch of events suggests that, in view of the vicissitudes and varying intensity of six years or so of intermittent strife, the composition of the Queen's Party must have changed from time to time. Its members did not all have identical motives, yet its objective was always the restoration of Mary to at least titular sovereignty, and any study of it must take into consideration all who *at one time or another* gave their support to Mary's claims and repudiated the authority of the Regents. There is no scarcity of evidence. In the first place we have the Bond drawn up at Hamilton on 8 May 1568, when the Queen's supporters came flocking to her side after the escape from Lochleven; to this bond nine earls, nine bishops, 17 lords, 14 commendators and about 90 lairds put their names.[21] Secondly there is the Dumbarton Bond of 12 September 1568, drawn up after Mary had gone to England and it was evident that investigations were going to be made into her alleged crimes, but to which only slightly fewer notables put their names – seven earls, 12 lords, eight bishops and nine commendators.[22] There is also, at an intermediate date, a letter to Elizabeth on Mary's behalf in July 1568, signed by eight earls and 12 lords.[23] Far more names are disclosed in the *Register of the Privy Seal*, which records those who were escheated or forfeited for their support of the Queen and those who subsequently received remissions for their activities against the government of the Regents, and there are also lists in the *Acts of Parliament* and the *Register of the Privy Council* of men who likewise found themselves on the losing side. Adding a number of stray references, analysis can be based on some 700 names (leaving aside the townsfolk of Edinburgh, of whom Dr Michael Lynch has made a special study in *Edinburgh and the Reformation*).

In 1567 there were about 19 earls on what may be called the active list, though that includes Sutherland and Menteith, who were still under 20, and Montrose, who was nearly 80. Of the 19, 11 or 12 can be put down as committed Marians – the same number who had initially supported the confederacy against Mary, but of those 12 only five had gone on to support the deposition of Mary and attend the coronation of James. There is a comparable contrast between the 17 lords who signed the Hamilton Bond and the eight who were at the coronation. Among the bishops there was something very close to unanimity for the Queen. Of the commendators, 14 signed the Hamilton Bond and nine the Dumbarton Bond (including four who had not been at Hamilton): this means that Mary had the support of more than half the commendators.

Outstanding on the Queen's side were the Hamiltons, who were as emphatically for her now as they had been for Moray at the time of the Chaseabout Raid, and their motives were again dynastic. While a Hamilton was heir presumptive to Mary, it was not so clear that a Hamilton was heir presumptive to James, for James's father, Darnley, had been King, and this raised the question whether the succession to James, if he died without issue, should pass to Darnley's family, the Lennoxes. This was seriously discussed by constitutional lawyers at the time. Another matter that was seriously argued was the right to the regency. While some lawyers thought that the regency belonged of right to the heir presumptive, others thought that council or parliament had freedom to choose a regent. The Hamiltons (as already mentioned) argued that, if Mary were deposed and a regency necessary, it should go to the head of the Hamiltons as heir presumptive, and there was little hope that they would be reconciled to a regency in the hands of Moray or his successors.

The head of the house of Hamilton was the Duke of Châtelherault. Though pardoned in January 1566 for his part in Moray's rebellion in the previous year, he was in exile in France until the end of 1567 and then in England until February 1569, but Mary had appointed him as Governor on her behalf on 12 July 1568, very soon after her arrival in England, and he was the figurehead of the Queen's Party. Even with him, leadership was weak, and it was perhaps not much better without him. His eldest son, 'Young Arran', erstwhile suitor of Mary, was insane, and the next surviving son, Lord John, showed few of the qualities of leadership. The Hamilton interest seems to have been guided mainly by two astute ecclesiastics – John, Archbishop of St Andrews, the Duke's half-brother, and Gavin, Commendator of Kilwinning and coadjutor of St Andrews. The cadet branches of the family turned out to support their heads: 46 Hamilton lairds and another 26 Hamiltons of lesser rank are traceable among the Queen's Men. They were remarkably unanimous, for no Hamilton was active on the other side. Along with bearers of the Hamilton name were a number of men with other names who had been 'wagers' of Châtelherault in 1565.

While it was generally agreed that a Hamilton was heir to Mary, if not to James, the exact state of the succession was far from straightforward. Châtelherault's imbecile eldest son could have become king only under the direction of curators; and, while ambitious men no doubt thought of this as an opportunity, there was no precedent for curators to a sovereign, and it was more likely that the wretched Arran would be passed over. His next brother, Gavin, was already dead; Lord John, the effective heir, though at least 25, was not yet married, nor were his younger brothers, David and Claud. The succession might therefore be open to those related to the Hamiltons through a female line, and it is no accident that four of the peers prominent in the Queen's Party – Fleming, Eglinton, Huntly and Argyll – were so related. In general, marriage connections (often contracted somewhat artificially in the vain hope of ending feuds) were far less influential in sixteenth century Scottish politics than blood relationships were, for brothers-in-law, fathers-in-law and sons-in-law often belonged to different parties. But in this instance it was different. One of Châtelherault's daughters, Barbara, had married the 4th Lord Fleming (d. 1558) and had by him a daughter. The 5th Lord Fleming, who was a Queen's Man, was a brother of Barbara's husband and therefore uncle to a possible future queen. The next daughter of Châtelherault, Jean, had married the Earl of Eglinton, and although their marital difficulties had helped to put Eglinton on the other side from Châtelherault in 1560, a divorce had removed this source of friction and Eglinton was in the Queen's Party. Then came Anne, wife of the 5th Earl of Huntly, one of Mary's strongest supporters and the father of two sons who might have their prospects. Going a generation farther back, Châtelherault's sister Helen had married the 4th Earl of Argyll, and this helped to bring their son, the 5th Earl, into the Hamilton connection.

To suggest that all those peers were in the Marian party simply because of their reversionary rights to the royal succession is not a novelty, for it was reported in 1567 that the Hamiltons, Argyll and Huntly were all for Mary on the ground that if they opposed her and she were nevertheless restored no one stood to lose more than those who were nearest to the crown, and it was remarked later that 'the Hamiltons, Argyll and Huntly, being of alliance in blood, will ever be adverse to the King'.[24] The Hamiltons themselves – even though one of their cards was a possible marriage of Mary to Lord John – coolly calculated that it might be best of all for their prospects if Mary were to be put to death: 'for she being taken away, they account but the little king, who may die, between them and *home*'.[25] (Shakespeare puts that same metaphor into the mouth of Richard, Duke of Gloucester, the future Richard III, in *Henry VI part 3*, Act III scene 2: 'And yet I know not how to get a crown, For many lives stand between me and *home*'.) If that is how people reckoned their chances, there can be little doubt that aspirations extended beyond the prospective lives of Mary and James. At the same time, links with the Hamiltons were not the whole reason why those four peers were on Mary's side. Fleming was a straightforward case, already numbered among 'The Queen's Friends'. Eglinton probably had religious grounds for favouring Mary; he attended mass in 1561, in 1562 he was said to have mass daily, he was present at James's baptism and in 1572 mass was reputed to be said at the place from which he took his title. Huntly, who inherited the feud with Moray which lay behind his father's rebellion in 1562, was one of those who had been faithful to Mary in May and June 1567. He had attended Moray's council in December 1567 but joined Mary on her escape and, after briefly submitting to Moray in 1569, became Mary's lieutenant in 1570. So far as Argyll was concerned, his desire for a divorce was opposed by Moray, his wife's half-brother and acknowledged head of James V's illegitimate brood:

besides, Argyll had a brother who, like Lord John Hamilton, was a possible consort for Mary. Argyll was one of many who combined consistent attachment to the Reformation with what had been on the whole a cordial relationship with the Queen. He had been active with the Congregation in 1559–60, he had attended at least one general assembly, he had not countenanced the Prince's Roman Catholic baptism and when he got his divorce he married a daughter of the ultra-Protestant Glencairn. But the Queen, his wife's half-sister, addressed him as 'your right good sister and best friend for ever' and, despite his participation in Moray's rebellion in 1565, Mary forgave him so completely that at the time of James's birth orders were given that he was to have accommodation next to the Queen's. He joined Mary on her escape from Lochleven and was her lieutenant at Langside, where he had a fainting fit.

Earls who were not within the Hamilton nexus had various reasons for supporting Mary, and with some of them religion was probably a motive, even although they can hardly have been confident that a restored Mary would do more for 'the old religion' than she had done before her abdication. Gilbert Kennedy, 4th Earl of Cassillis, had shown more attachment to the mass than most, though he had not been unshaken, perhaps especially when he married a daughter of the Protestant Lord Glamis in 1566. It is not certain that he raised his voice against the anti-papal legislation passed by the parliament of 1560; he was reported in 1561 (on Mary's return) to have been at 'the preaching' on Sunday and at the mass on Monday and to have 'repented his conduct' – though in what particular does not appear.[26] It had been said of his father, the 3rd Earl (who had been on the English side in the 1540s and had offered to assassinate Cardinal Beaton) that he was 'a very greedy man and cared not how he got land'.[27] The 4th Earl seems to have inherited his father's failings, for his religious professions did not endow him with either humanity or respect for the property rights of others. He is best known for his exploit in roasting the Commendator of Crosraguel in Dunure Castle to make him part with abbey lands. It is hardly surprising that Cassillis had refused to subscribe the Book of Discipline, which proposed to put most of the ecclesiastical wealth at the disposal of the reformed church. He had supported Mary against Moray in 1565.

David, 10th Earl of Crawford, can be reckoned to have given some support to the Protestant revolution, because, whether or not he disapproved of the anti-papal legislation which he saw pass through parliament in 1560, he did approve of the proposal that Young Arran should marry Elizabeth. Yet his religious inclinations seem to have been conservative, whether or not because of the influence of his wife, a daughter of Cardinal Beaton, and their son continued the ecclesiastical conservatism of the family. Crawford had supported Mary against Moray in 1565.

John Stewart, 4th Earl of Atholl, seemed more clearly cast than even Cassillis and Crawford for the part of a Queen's Man, at any rate on the assumption that religious motives counted. He had opposed the Protestant legislation of 1560, though he approved of the Arran-Elizabeth marriage scheme, he had attended mass thereafter and was described as 'très grand catholique'. Dunkeld, a town under his patronage, was one of the places where mass was reported to be said in October 1572. Atholl had been in Mary's innermost circle after the Darnley marriage and had been her lieutenant against Moray in the Chaseabout Raid. Yet in 1567 he not only, like so many other men of diverse view, joined the confederates, but advised Mary to abdicate and attended James's coronation. In 1568 he did not sign either the Hamilton or the Dumbarton Bond and he showed extreme reluctance to come out on the Queen's side. Atholl's first wife was a sister of the 5th Earl of Huntly and his second a daughter of the 3rd Lord Fleming, but those links with the Marian party, like his religion, may have counted for less than his animosity against Argyll, probably arising from conflicting territorial ambitions, which had possibly helped to put him on the opposite side from Argyll in 1560 and 1565. Nor was Atholl entirely at ease with his other territorial neighbour, Huntly, though the latter was his brother-in-law. Atholl's second wife was a sister of Lethington's wife and it may have been the influence of this brother-in-law which prevailed on the Earl to join him in his switch of allegiance to Mary's party in 1569. At any rate, for a time the Protestant Argyll and Huntly, on the Queen's side, confronted the Catholic Atholl on the King's.

William Graham, 2nd Earl of Montrose, had supported Cardinal Beaton against Arran in 1543 and had subsequently opposed Lennox and the English party. He stayed away from the parliament of 1560 and attended Mary's first mass, he was described in 1563 as a supporter of the Romanist cause, and he favoured the Darnley marriage. In 1567 he supported the confederates in their original design of separating Mary from Bothwell, but he dissented from Mary's deposition and imprisonment and he signed the Hamilton Bond. By this time a very old man, he did not fight at Langside and died in 1571. His wife was a daughter of the 3rd Earl Marischal, and their son, who was killed at Pinkie in 1547, married a daughter of Malcolm, 3rd Lord Fleming, leaving a posthumous son, who succeeded to the earldom. This young man took the opposite side from his grandfather, for he was at James's coronation, fought in Moray's army at Langside and continued to support the regents.

George Sinclair, 4th Earl of Caithness, though he had not been very active in affairs, can be put down as another man of conservative inclinations, for he agreed to go to mass in 1566 and Knox described him as a papist. He seems to have stood aside from the critical events of 1567, and in 1568 he did not sign either of the Marian bonds. Yet he was even then unquestionably a Marian sympathiser, who wrote to Elizabeth on the Queen's behalf in July 1568.

The earldom of Sutherland had passed by marriage only in 1535 to a younger son of the 2nd Earl of Huntly. John Gordon, 10th Earl, who had been forfeited for his involvement with his cousin Huntly in the Corrichie affair in 1562, died in June 1567, the month of crisis, and was succeeded by his son Alexander, aged about 15. Whatever his views, this youth could hardly have done other than follow Huntly, whom he would regard as the head of his house, into Mary's camp, but he had another link in that he had been married, more or less by force, to a daughter of the Earl of Caithness, whose ward he was, and he was in no position to resist pressure from his father-in-law.

George Hay, 7th Earl of Erroll, had no very clear record one way or another and was not involved in 1567, but he signed the Hamilton Bond and fought for Mary at Langside in 1568. His son and heir, the Master of Erroll, was in the King's Party in 1568-9.

Cassillis, Crawford, Atholl, Montrose, Eglinton and possibly Caithness were all men who might have been expected, from their religious views, to support Mary, and Huntly's record of political and personal loyalty, though he did not share the Queen's religion, would have made it inconceivable that he should not join her in 1568. Sutherland's behaviour, equally, was predictable, but one cannot say as much of Erroll. Argyll's support for Mary was, like Huntly's, explicable, but owed nothing to his religious views, and this is even more true of Andrew Leslie, 5th Earl of Rothes, whose family had been heavily involved with the English and Protestant cause: his father had been acquitted and two of his brothers forfeited for the murder of Cardinal Beaton. He himself had been a full participant in the revolution of 1560. In September 1561, when the Queen spent a night in his house, some plate and other articles went missing,[28] so the visit can hardly have endeared Mary's entourage to him. At any rate, he supported Moray in 1565 and approved of the Riccio murder. He ultimately (though only in 1573) married a daughter of Lord Ruthven, whose house was as strongly Protestant as his own. Yet Rothes signed both the Hamilton and Dumbarton Bonds and was a consistent member of the Queen's Party thereafter. It is conceivable that his allegiance to Mary owed something to his feud with that other Fife landowner Lord Lindsay, a bigoted supporter of James, just as Atholl's presence on the King's side may have owed something to his feud with Argyll. Mary had given judgment in his favour against the claims to the earldom of his forfeited elder brother William, but we can rule out any question of gratitude, because the Queen's decision had been given in January 1565 and Rothes supported Moray later that year.

It is not possible to analyse the lords on the same scale as the earls, if only because there is as a rule less information available, but enough can be found to demonstrate that they, too, had mixed antecedents, outlooks and motives. This time there is a distinct group, consisting of some of the nobles, below the rank of earls, with whom, as was suggested in Chapter 4, Mary established especially friendly relations – Fleming, Livingston and Seton. Fleming has already been mentioned in this chapter because of his connection with the Hamiltons, but that was only one element which may have helped to determine his alignment. One of his sisters was one of the Queen's Maries and wife of Secretary Maitland, a second was married to that Queen's Man Lord Livingston. The 3rd Lord Fleming had been captured at Solway Moss in 1542 and had agreed to further an alliance with Henry VIII's England; he had fought in 1544 against Arran after the latter abandoned his flirtation with reform, but next year he founded the collegiate church of Biggar, where intercession was to be made for the souls of James V and Cardinal Beaton, and in 1547 he was killed at Pinkie in an army no doubt largely moved by patriotism but under the banner of the Church. His eldest son, the 4th Lord, had presumably been regarded as unreliable when Mary of Guise selected him for 'brain-washing' in 1550, and his brother, the 5th Lord, who succeeded in 1558, refused to go to mass. Fleming signed the Hamilton and Dumbarton bonds and held Dumbarton Castle for Mary until its fall, when he escaped to France, to return and meet his death in the fighting which took place between Queen's Men and King's Men at Edinburgh in 1572.

Livingston, Fleming's brother-in-law and brother of another of the Queen's Maries, was, as explained in Chapter 4, in some ways even closer to the Queen than Fleming was. He was present at Mary's marriage to Bothwell and tried to secure her release from Lochleven. When she did escape he signed the Hamilton and Dumbarton Bonds, fought in the Queen's army at Langside, attended Mary in England and then spent some time at the French court. He did not acknowledge James until 1574. His wife, after accompanying him to England, returned to Scotland, where she was imprisoned for two months for intriguing on Mary's behalf. Their son also fought for Mary and was captured when Dumbarton Castle fell in 1571. Livingston was, like Fleming, a Protestant and refused to attend mass.

George, 5th Lord Seton, a brother (or rather half-brother) of the Queen's Mary Seton, was like Livingston one of Mary's intimates but, as explained in Chapter 4, even more gallicised and, unlike Fleming and Livingston, was conservative in religion. He agreed to go to mass in 1566, and according to Knox was a man 'without God, without honesty and often times without reason'. He seems to have played a major rôle in preparing for Mary's escape from Lochleven, was ready to join her and conducted her to his castle of Niddrie before she went on to Hamilton. He signed the two Marian bonds, was captured at Langside, but was released and was then active on Mary's behalf in France between 1569 and 1571. He did not submit to James's government until 1573, he was in Paris again in 1577, and in 1579 was confined on suspicion of holding communication with the exiled Archbishop Beaton. He maintained the continental connection by sending one of his sons to Spain and another to Rome for their education.

Besides those three lords who had long been numbered among Mary's intimates, there were two – Herries and Boyd – who had not been so close to her earlier but joined the group closest to her in her adversity. John Maxwell, Lord Herries, was the second son of Robert, Lord Maxwell, and succeeded to the Herries title by marrying the heiress of the 3rd Lord. He had been a friend of Knox and a very active reformer who not only supported the Arran-Elizabeth match but signed the Book of Discipline. In 1565 he had tried to mediate between the Queen and those who opposed her marriage to Darnley, but when the crisis came he took Mary's side and entertained Mary and Darnley at Lochmaben. He was a devoted partisan of Mary from 1568 to 1571 and was one of her spokesmen at the investigations in England. Robert, 5th Lord Boyd, whose name appeared third on the Hamilton and Dumbarton Bonds, after those of Herries and Fleming and before that of Seton, had been in earlier years even more detached from Mary than Herries had been. He had succeeded his father in 1558, and in 1559–60 had taken part in every act of 'the Congregation', apparently with a zeal hardly equalled except by that other Ayrshire nobleman the Earl of Glencairn. He joined other Protestants in supporting Moray in 1565 and was on Moray's council when he became Regent in 1567. Yet on Mary's escape in 1568 he lost no time in declaring for her, and after she fled to England he was one of her most trusted and devoted agents. He appeared as one of her commissioners in the investigation of Moray's charges against her, was involved in a plot to free her from her English prison and negotiated on her behalf with the Duke of Norfolk as well as with the Spanish governor of the Netherlands. In Scotland he was accused of taking part in the murder of Moray, but he attempted reconciliation in Mary's interest and tried to persuade Elizabeth to come to terms with her. He was said to be 'constantly at the Queen's obedience' until August 1571, when he agreed to serve the King. His son and heir and two of his cousins were with him at Langside. It is just possible that Boyd's more favourable attitude to Mary in the later 1560s had been affected by his relations with the Earl of Eglinton and his Montgomeries. The two families had been at feud since 1484, when the Master of Eglinton murdered the 2nd Lord Boyd; in 1530 it was agreed that the future 5th Lord Boyd should marry a daughter of Eglinton, but this failed to secure peace, for in 1547 the 4th Lord Boyd murdered Montgomery of Lainshaw. Terms were arrived at again in 1561 and the feud can be said to have ended by 1563. This made it possible, or at any rate easier, for Boyd to appear in the same party as Eglinton, to whom he had been opposed in 1560, 1565 and 1567.

Among the other Marian lords, Borthwick, Ross and Somerville had a record of religious conservatism and attachment to the Queen. William, 7th Lord Borthwick, belonged to a family with a loyal tradition, and he was related by marriage to both Lord Seton and the Earl of Crawford. His predecessor had supported Arran in his conservative policy in 1544, he fought against the English at Ancrum in 1545 and held the castle of Hailes against the English in 1547; the English thought him 'unconstant' – that is, to their cause. In 1559 he was one of the last nobles to remain faithful to Mary of Guise and although he approved of the treaty of Berwick, by which Elizabeth agreed to aid the Scottish insurgents in 1560, and the Arran-Elizabeth match, he dissented from the Protestant legislation of 1560. Mary visited him at Borthwick in January 1562 and August 1563. The 7th Lord succeeded in March 1566; Mary and Bothwell were received in his castle of Borthwick in June 1567, and in 1568 he signed the Hamilton Bond. James, 4th Lord Ross, was described as 'neutral' in 1560, which probably emphasises that he was not an enthusiast for the Protestant cause, and he was later regarded as a Roman Catholic. He supported Mary against the rebellion under Moray in 1565, and Mary visited him more than once at Melville, in Midlothian, a property which he held through marriage, although the lands of Halkheid or Hawkhead, from which he took his territorial designation, were in Renfrewshire. He signed the Hamilton Bond, was captured by Moray at Langside and thereafter seems to have been a somewhat ineffective supporter of the Queen. James, 5th Lord Somerville, seems to have supported the political rather than the religious aims of the insurgents of 1559–60, for he signed the bond at Leith, the treaty of Berwick and the petition in favour of the Arran-Elizabeth marriage, but dissented from the anti-papal legislation. He supported Mary in 1565, signed the Marian bonds of 1568 and fought for the Queen at Langside. After he died in

1569 his son Hugh, who was described as a papist, was at first active in the Queen's Party but moved away from it in the course of 1571, to earn the designation 'neutral'.

Another Marian who may have had popish leanings was Michael, 4th Lord Carlyle, for he had mass in December 1560. But he had been on the English side in the 1540s and had been summoned for treason in 1548. He came to terms with Moray, as others did, in October 1567, but was a Marian in 1568, when he signed the Hamilton Bond though not the Dumbarton Bond. The Oliphants, too, had a conservative tradition. Laurence, 3rd Lord, had been captured at Solway but had not signed the secret articles in favour of Henry VIII, and when he was released in 1543 he was reckoned one of the least pliable to England. He did not sit in the parliament of 1560 and he died in 1566. Laurence, 4th Lord, who succeeded his father, joined Mary on her escape from Lochleven and was appointed one of her lieutenants in January 1569. He soon submitted to Moray, but after Moray's murder rejoined the Queen's Party though he was not very active. He was counted a Roman Catholic.

None of the remaining Marian lords showed anything like zeal for Roman Catholicism, and some of them were almost as clearly Protestant as Livingston, Herries and Boyd. William, 6th Lord Crichton of Sanquhar, was a son of a daughter of Malcolm, 3rd Lord Fleming. He did not take much part in the rebellion of 1559–60, but subscribed the Book of Discipline and died in 1561. The 7th Lord, his brother, supported Mary and Darnley in 1565 but was with the confederates at Carberry and at the coronation of James. Yet in 1568 he signed both the Marian bonds. He can be presumed to have had Protestant sympathies, and it is hardly significant that his son, who succeeded him as a minor on his death in 1569, was later described as a papist. William, 5th Lord Hay of Yester, had been active in the Protestant revolution, even to the extent of subscribing the Book of Discipline, yet he signed the Marian bonds in 1568, fought at Langside and was active in the Queen's Party in 1570 and 1571. James, 5th Lord Ogilvy of Airlie, had been in arms with 'the Congregation' in 1560, but signed both Marian bonds in 1568, though like some others he acknowledged Moray in 1569 and does not seem subsequently to have rejoined Mary's party. Alexander, 5th Lord Home, by contrast, was a late convert to the Queen's side. After supporting the revolution of 1560 and disapproving of Mary's mass, he joined the confederates, took part in James's coronation and at Langside commanded troops for Moray, who made him sheriff of Berwick and bailie of Lauderdale. But he then sat at Mary's parliament and joined Kirkcaldy in Edinburgh Castle, to be imprisoned on its fall. Of the remaining signatories of the Marian bonds, Maxwell (John, 8th Lord), who was related to Herries, had just come on the scene as a young man, Drummond (David, 2nd Lord) took no prominent part in affairs and Elphinstone (Robert, 3rd Lord) seems to have been below standard mentally; William, 4th Lord Sinclair, signed the Hamilton Bond but is not otherwise notable and died in 1570.

While it is very plain that many quite zealous Protestants, as well as others who were not so enthusiastic about religion, supported Mary, it may well be thought that few Roman Catholics would support the Regents, but Atholl was one earl who did so for a considerable time and there was one lord who remained consistently on the King's side – Robert, 3rd Lord Sempill. His religious conservatism had made him a victim of that militant Protestant, the Earl of Arran, and a grudge against the Hamiltons (whose base at Paisley was close to his headquarters) may have done something to determine his attitude in 1568. The line he took proved profitable, at least on paper, because Moray gave him the escheats of several Hamiltons and the prospect of possession of the abbey of Paisley.

The bishops, it has been mentioned, were almost solidly for the Queen, but there was no unanimity in their motives. John, Archbishop of St Andrews, and James, Bishop of Argyll, were Hamiltons, half-brothers of Châtelherault, whom they inevitably followed. William, Bishop of Aberdeen, and Alexander, Bishop of Galloway, were both Gordons, one a great-uncle and the other an uncle of that leading Marian the 5th Earl of Huntly. Hamiltons and Gordons alike were not in agreement ecclesiastically, for John Hamilton and William Gordon were both broadly conservative, though neither was wholly intransigent, whereas James Hamilton and Alexander Gordon had become committed Protestants, yet all four were together in the Queen's Party. Bishop Patrick Hepburn of Moray was the great-uncle of Mary's third husband and was naturally found in a party which had much Hepburn backing; he was unsympathetic, but not hostile, to the reformed church. The young Alexander, Bishop of Brechin, was Protestant and a Campbell, and, though not closely related to the Earl of Argyll, may have been influenced by him. It is even more likely that that active Protestant John Carswell, Bishop of The Isles, who was a client of the Argyll family, was under orders to support Mary, though, to be fair, he may have had a sense of gratitude to the Queen who had given him his bishopric. The only bishops who may have been inclined to the Queen primarily by religious convictions were Robert Crichton of Dunkeld, a respectable figure and a fairly consistent, though not wholly unyielding, conservative, and John Leslie of Ross, who finished up on the continent as a Roman Catholic bishop but at an earlier stage had been described as 'almost a Protestant';[29] yet both of them had their family affiliations with the Queen's side, for the Crichtons generally were for Mary, and Leslie looked to the Earl of Rothes, a Queen's Man, as head of his house. The only two Scottish bishops who were completely committed to the papal cause – Beaton of Glasgow and Chisholm of Dunblane – were out of the country. It may be added that only two bishops were on the King's side, and their positions too are instructive. Robert Stewart of Caithness was a keen Protestant, but the telling fact was that as brother of the Earl of Lennox, uncle of Darnley and great-uncle of the little King, he was bound to stand for the Lennox interest against the Hamiltons and against a Queen who – so propaganda at least asserted – had been responsible for the murder of the heir of Lennox. Adam Bothwell of Orkney was the thirteenth bishop. His family affiliations were essentially middle-class and indeed, with the exception of the priest's bastard John Leslie, he had the least distinguished lineage of any of the hierarchy. Kinship might have put him on either side, for he was related to Balfours and Melvilles, and indeed less directly to Kirkcaldy of Grange, who were Queen's Men, but also to Napiers and

Bellendens who were not. However, after officiating at the marriage of Mary to the Earl of Bothwell he crowned James VI and supported the King's party. Surely a striking illustration of how convictions about the rights and wrongs of sovereignty, and possibly also the claims of kinship, counted for more than religious attachment is found in the attitudes of Gordon of Galloway and Bothwell of Orkney: each had been consecrated before 1560, each had joined the reformers and organised the reformed church in his diocese, each had become a judge of the court of session, yet now they were on opposite sides.

Mary had less proportionate support among the commendators than she had among the bishops. These men were the heads of Scotland's abbeys and priories, managing, enjoying and sometimes squandering their ancient properties; for a generation and more it had been rare for a Scottish religious house to have a genuine abbot or prior who was a member of the monastic order to which the house belonged, and while some of the commendators were indeed clerics of a kind, the great majority were laymen, and when it came to choosing sides they acted as other laymen acted. Eighteen commendators put their names to either the Hamilton or the Dumbarton Bond or both, and one or two others were in the Marian party under another guise: the Commendator of Scone was Patrick Hepburn, Bishop of Moray, the Commendator of Tongland was Alexander Gordon, Bishop of Galloway, and the Commendator of Iona was John Carswell, Bishop of the Isles. Of the 18, three were Hamiltons, for John and Claud, sons of Châtelherault, held Arbroath and Paisley, and Gavin held Kilwinning. Edward, Commendator of Dundrennan, was a Maxwell, Alexander, Commendator of Pluscardin, was a son of Lord Seton, James, Commendator of Inchaffray, was a Drummond, John, Commendator of Soulseat, was a Johnstone, John and Patrick, successively Commendators of Lindores, were Leslies; it is reasonable to believe that all of them aligned themselves with the heads of their families – Lords Maxwell, Seton and Drummond, the laird of Johnstone and the Earl of Rothes. The Campbell Commendator of Ardchattan on Loch Etive would similarly follow the Earl of Argyll; it might be going too far to suggest that a Campbell so remote from the family's headquarters on Loch Awe as Thomas Campbell, Commendator of Holywood in Galloway, likewise followed Argyll, but he was a brother of Campbell of Loudoun, in Ayrshire, who was also a Marian. It is more difficult to explain the Stewarts; James Stewart, Commendator of Inchcolm, a son of the Marian Stewart of Doune, was in due course to marry a daughter of the Earl of Moray, and Alan Stewart, Commendator of Crosraguel, was the 'half-roasted abbot' who was tormented by Cassillis in August 1570 to make him convey lands but is not known to have been tortured to make him join Cassillis in the Queen's Party. The position of Thomas Hay, Commendator of Glenluce, may be explained not by any connection with Lord Hay of Yester but by the influence of Cassillis, this time acting in a more kindly mood to protect the house of Glenluce – for a consideration. At Jedburgh, Andrew Home seems to have anticipated Lord Home in his allegiance to Mary, for Lord Home was still on Moray's side when the Commendator signed the Marian bonds. Walter Reid, Commendator of Kinloss, signed the Dumbarton Bond, but did not long remain in the Queen's Party, for Huntly, as Mary's lieutenant, declared him forfeited in 1569; Nicholas Ross, Commendator of Fearn, may well have been influenced by the considerable support of Mary in Easter Ross, which will be examined later. The one Commendator who signed neither of the Marian bonds but subsequently supported the Queen's cause was John Maitland, who had recently acquired Coldingham and who followed the example of his brother, Secretary Lethington. The one instance in which religion was probably the leading motive in putting a commendator on Mary's side was that of Gilbert Brown, Commendator of New Abbey, who was constantly in trouble for saying mass. There is no evidence to show the allegiance of the Commendator of Balmerino, John Hay, or the Commendator of Coupar, Leonard Leslie, who might have been expected to align themselves with other Hays and Leslies, or about George Durie at Dunfermline, a religious conservative who might have been expected to support the Queen, and about some others. The Erskine Commendators of Cambuskenneth and Dryburgh were, with the Erskine Earl of Mar, on the King's side, as were Alexander Colville at Culross and presumably Robert Keith at Deer, of the family of the Earl Marischal.

The hundreds of lesser men who are known to have been in the Queen's Party obviously cannot be investigated individually like the notables, but analysis is helped by the fact that most of them fall into groups which reflect the character of Scottish society. Their territorial distribution is itself relatively easy to set down, but that distribution is clearly related to the allegiance or attachment of most of them to some magnate whose following they composed. There is a danger that our evidence, based though it is on several hundreds of names, may involve a certain distortion, since the majority of the known Marians are recorded because of their presence in the Queen's army at Langside. Other activities on Mary's behalf, let alone favourable attitudes to her cause, are less often recorded, because the offence which alone laid a culprit undeniably open to prosecution was that of confronting the King's army in the field. Not only was the battle fought near Glasgow, but the call to muster for the conflict had been made chiefly from Hamilton, and the few days between Mary's escape and the engagement allowed little time for summonses to reach remote areas, for men to be called together and for them to reach the Queen's camp. No doubt mounted messengers could have arrived in Aberdeen or Inverness in a couple of days if changes of horses were available, but the better part of another week would pass before men living mainly in scattered rural communities could be notified, leave their homes, be gathered together and marched off on foot to reach the Glasgow area. It may be doubted, indeed, if many troops from north of Perth could have arrived in time for the battle. Yet these simple facts of geography and communications are not the whole story, because, as will emerge, the number of recruits who came from Fife and from the area round Stirling was relatively small and almost negligible compared to the numbers which came not only from nearby Lanarkshire, Renfrewshire and Ayrshire, but also from East Lothian, most of which was more distant than Fife and all of it more distant than Stirling.

It is logical to begin a topographical analysis with the areas nearest to the scene of the military operations of 1568. Hamilton, where Mary had her headquarters, is in Lanarkshire, and Langside, the scene of the battle, was close to the Lanarkshire-Renfrewshire border. It is hardly surprising, therefore, that our lists yield 75 names from Lanarkshire and about 40 from Renfrewshire, though these are not startlingly high figures compared with those of some other sheriffdoms. Half the recruits from Lanarkshire were Hamiltons and others were tenants of Hamiltons: Dalyell of that ilk headed a contingent of a dozen, seven of them bearing his own name; the 12 Baillies, headed by Baillie of Lamington and mostly from Lanarkshire, were in the main dependents of Hamiltons and had been in Châtelherault's following in 1565; others who had been followers of Châtelherault were Roberton of Ernock, Weir of Blackwood and Lockhart of Cleghorn – the last from a family which was divided, because while Kirkwood, Lee and Wicketshaw were, like Cleghorn, for Mary, Bar was for the King. Another leading Marian, Lord Fleming, who had his properties at Biggar in Lanarkshire and at Cumbernauld near Glasgow, was followed by half-a-dozen Flemings and had at least one dependent in Renfrewshire, Fleming of Boghall, who was in the garrison which, under Lord Fleming, held Dumbarton Castle for the Queen. James, 5th Lord Somerville, and Hugh, who succeeded him in 1569, were both for Mary, and were followed by Alexander Somerville of Tarbrax, who was a client of Archbishop Hamilton, and James Somerville, younger, of Cambusnethan, who had been designated a dependent of Châtelherault. The younger Carmichael of that ilk was in the Queen's Party at Langside, but his father, who was attached to the Douglases, favoured the King and the Regents. Gilbert Cameron in Birkinshaw, James Cairncross of Allanshaw, John Bannatyne of Corehous and five Knelands were other Lanarkshire recruits for the Queen.

The influence of the Hamiltons spilled over into Renfrewshire, where they dominated Paisley through their commendatorship of the abbey, so that sheriffdom yielded another three Hamiltons. There were also from Renfrewshire half a dozen or more of the 29 Crawfords, who came mainly from Ayrshire. There was no single dominating figure in Renfrewshire. One of the most important was Lord Cathcart (whose lands straddled Renfrewshire and Lanarkshire) and he was a King's Man, but that did not prevent Alan Cathcart of Drumsowane from supporting the Queen. Similarly, Lord Sempill was for the King, but other Sempills for the Queen. Maxwell of Nether Pollok was for the Queen, and thus in the same camp as Lord Maxwell, who was his superior although his own property was far away in Dumfriesshire and the blood relationship between the two was very remote, but Nether Pollok himself had hardly to stir from his own ground to be on the battlefield of Langside. This sheriffdom showed a good deal of cohesion among small groups of Marians – three Houstons, five Shaws, two Wallaces, three Whitefords and two Woods, John Cochrane of that ilk and his son. Other Queen's Men were John Stewart of Cardonald and Hugh Ralston of that ilk.

Adjoining Renfrewshire and Lanarkshire to the south and west lay the large sheriffdom of Ayr, one of the most productive recruiting grounds for the Queen, with no less than 114 names in our lists. There were four influential noblemen – Cunningham, Earl of Glencairn, Montgomery, Earl of Eglinton, Kennedy, Earl of Cassillis, and Lord Boyd of Kilmarnock – and the sheriffdom was divided into three bailiaries – Cunningham, Kyle and Carrick (running from north to south) – to which the spheres of influence of the three earls roughly corresponded. Glencairn, consistently a zealous Protestant, was for the King, but Cassillis, Eglinton and Boyd were all for Mary. Loyalties among their followers seem, however, to have been seriously divided in every case save that of Boyd, who was at the head of eight lairds of his own name and another score of Boyds of lower rank. Despite Glencairn's stand for the King, six Cunninghams, headed by John of Drumquhassill, were among the Marian defenders of Dumbarton, while Cunninghamhead and Caprington followed the Earl. Four Kennedy lairds – Barclannoquhan, Bargany, Culzean and Girvanmains – joined Cassillis in Mary's camp, but three did not long remain in it, which hardly seems impressive considering the repute of the Cassillis family as 'Kings of Carrick':

> 'Twixt Wigtown and the toun of Ayr,
> Portpatrick and the Cruives of Cree,
> No man needs think for to bide there
> Unless he court with Kennedie.

On the other side were the Kennedys of Bennane, Lambie and Dalquhirran. Seven Montgomeries (mostly of little importance) joined Eglinton. The other Queen's Men in Ayrshire included over 20 lairds, more than half of them Crawfords, and that name (which, as already mentioned, was strong in Renfrewshire too) contributed another half-dozen of lower rank. There were probably few areas where religious differences were sharper than they were in Ayrshire, for, despite the conservatism of Cassillis and Eglinton, Protestantism was deeply rooted among the lairds. This, however, did not turn them into recruits for the King, any more than it turned Lord Boyd into one, and several of the Queen's supporters had a clear record of adherence to the reformed faith: John Boswell of Auchinleck and Sir Alexander Dunbar of Cumnock had signed the Protestant bond at Leith in April 1560; John Mure of Rowallan had sat in the parliament of 1560 and had signed the Ayrshire Protestant bond in 1562, and he was not hindered from joining the Queen (with three other Mures) by his feud with the Boyds; John Fergushill of that ilk had signed the 1562 bond. Other Ayrshire Marians were David Barclay of Ladyland, his brother Barclay of Perceton and three other Barclays, Kelso of Kelsoland and Boyle of Kelburn, who later on had a bond with Lord Boyd. Two of the Ayrshire Marians deserve special mention – Campbell of Loudoun and Kennedy of Bargany. Loudoun had been a firm Protestant who acted with Glencairn in 1559, he was at feud with Cassillis, he was related through his mother to Darnley, and when he had supported Mary in 1565 had been supporting Darnley's wife and not Darnley's alleged murderer. Yet he turned up to fight for Mary at Langside. Possibly he was influenced by Argyll, who was the head of his name, and in those days when men habitually travelled by sea Argyll was not as remote from Ayrshire as it is today, but another Protestant Ayrshire Campbell, Kinyeancleuch, was for the King and attended James's coronation. Thomas Kennedy of Bargany, whose father had signed the Book of Discipline, was 'from the beginning on the side of religion' but signed the bond for support of Mary against Moray in 1565 and was a member of the Queen's Party in 1568–9. Described as 'wise and courteous, and therewith stout and passing kind',[30] he rescued the Commendator of Crosraguel after he had been half-roasted by Cassillis. He was connected by marriage with both the conservative Eglinton and the Protestant Ochiltree, and he had feuds with Cassillis and Boyd, but as a Marian he was aligned with Eglinton, Cassillis and Boyd.

Moving east from the heartland of the Queen's Party we come to West Lothian, a small sheriffdom containing important Hamilton estates and Lord Seton's castle at Niddrie, and bordering on Lord Livingston's headquarters at Callendar. Over a score of Marians are recorded, half of them Hamilton lairds and their followers, three or four Livingston lairds, one Seton follower, and Robert Moubray of Barnbougle.

In Midlothian it was mainly lairds rather than nobles who counted. Perhaps the only influential peers were the Earl of Bothwell, who was Lord of Crichton, and his neighbour Lord Borthwick, from the top of whose great tower it is still possible to see Crichton Castle in the next valley; Sir John Hislop in Crichton was in the Queen's Party and there were four Borthwicks – Michael of Craigingelt, John of Raschaw, Thomas of Castellaw and William of Watterstoun. The Queen's Man in Midlothian whose following has left most trace in the records was Sir William Sinclair of Roslin, a score of whose clients, mostly small men in Roslin and the parish of Pentland, are named, and with them we can reckon Thomas Warnour of Auchendinny, west of Roslin. Sir William had sat in the parliament of 1560 and possibly there had been an early 'cell' of Protestantism on his lands, for the provost of the Sinclair family's collegiate church – Rosslyn Chapel – had been found to be a heretic in 1540. In addition, there was one Hamilton, Thomas of Priestfield, the father of a famous son, Thomas, Earl of Haddington, who was to serve Mary's son so well as Lord Advocate, Lord President and Secretary of State. Beyond that, there was a scatter of lairds – Cant of St Giles Grange and Sir Archibald Napier of Merchiston, both on the southern outskirts of Edinburgh; Sir James Forrester of Corstorphine, to the west of Edinburgh, who, with his brother Henry, had helped to plot Mary's escape; George Wilkie, a tenant in Saughtonhall, and his son, who were neighbours of Forrester; George Touris of Inverleith, on the north side of Edinburgh; and George Ramsay of Dalhousie, whose lands lay close to those of Crichton and Borthwick. Forrester and Touris had signed the Protestant bond of April 1560, but nothing is certain about the religion of the others. Whether Cuthbert Ramsay, parson of Crichton, was a Queen's Man primarily because he was a Ramsay or because the lord of Crichton was his patron remains in doubt. Robert Blackie in the Mill of Heriot was not very far from Borthwick and Crichton.

East Lothian, from which we have about 70 names, is particularly interesting. The main influence here was that of the Hepburn Earl of Bothwell, now in his capacity as Lord of Hailes. There were in the Queen's Party nearly a dozen Hepburn lairds – Bolton, Fortune, Gilmerton, Kingston, Kirklandhill, Luffness, Smeaton, Stevenson, Waughton, Whitecastle and Whitsome – and some other Hepburns, including Thomas, parson of Oldhamstocks. Several of them were believed to have had a hand, with Bothwell, in Darnley's murder. In addition to men who bore the surname Hepburn there must have been many more who had 'borne a good mind' to the house of Hepburn because they could say, like John Knox, 'my great-grandfather, grandfather and father have served under your lordship's predecessors, and some of them have died under their standards'.[31] A second influence was that of Lord Seton, whose properties lay at the western fringe of the sheriffdom, where the early sixteenth-century collegiate church of Seton and the much later Seton House still represent the kernel of the estate. Twenty-seven of Seton's followers are named among the Queen's Men. The Maitland home at Lethington near Haddington was still the property of the aged and blind Sir Richard (born 1496), a scholarly lawyer and litterateur who perhaps signified his affiliation to the Seton family by compiling a *History of the House of Seton*. His own views were conservative – Knox described him as 'ever civil, albeit not persuaded in religion' – and it was appropriate that his distinguished sons William (Secretary of State) and John (a future Chancellor), although they became Protestants, found their way into the Queen's Party. Lord Hay, although he took his territorial title from Yester in this sheriffdom, was mainly important in Peeblesshire, but two prebendaries of his collegiate church – another building still to be seen, in the grounds of Yester House near Gifford – were in the Queen's Party; one of them was a Hay, and both owed their appointments to Lord Hay as patron. There were two Hamiltons – Innerwick and Samuelston. When we add to these the other lairds who are named – Broun of Colstoun, Carkettles of Fingland and Markle, Cockburn of Langton, Congilton of that ilk, Heriot of Trabroun, Lauders of Bass and Popill, Newton of that ilk, Wauchopes of Cakemuir and Stottandcleuch and Whitelaw of that ilk – two points emerge. One is that this sheriffdom was preponderantly for the Queen and the other is that the list of Marians reads in the main like a list of men who had long adhered to the pro-English and reforming side. There was Douglas influence from the Angus fortress of Tantallon, but it seems to have done nothing to outweigh the predominance of the Queen's Party in East Lothian.

In the area which can be called central Lowland Scotland, lying west of Lothian and Fife, there seem to have been relatively few Marians. Possibly the most important single influence was that of the Erskine family, whose head, the Earl of Mar, was a leader of the King's Party and became Regent in 1571. He had his seat at Alloa, and his family held the nearby abbeys of Cambuskenneth and Inchmahome (on the Lake of Menteith). Mar was keeper of Stirling Castle, in the centre of the area, which was the residence of the young King and must have been regarded as a stronghold of his party; it was so effectively held that when the Marians under Kirkcaldy of Grange raided it in 1571 they were repulsed. These facts may explain why the Queen's Party made a poor showing here. However, one Erskine (Little Sauchy) deviated from the family line to support Mary, and a canon of Cambuskenneth, Robert Mackeson, defied his Erskine commendator and left the cloister to fight at Langside. The attitude of the old Earl of Montrose, a Graham, probably carried David Graham of Fintray and John Graham in

Saltcoats (Stirlingshire) to the Queen's side. The Bruces of Airth and Clackmannan, close though the latter was to the Erskine seat of Alloa, supported the Queen, and no doubt they had their local followers, like Patrick Williamson in Airth. Besides, Sir James Stewart of Doune (whose son, curiously enough, was to marry a daughter of the Regent Moray and become 'The Bonnie Earl o' Moray') and William Stewart of Dunduff stood by the Queen as many Stewarts did. The Murrays and Drummonds of southern Perthshire did not play a noteworthy part: Murray of Tullibardine (whose sister was married to Mar) was on the King's side and probably carried Pardewis (his brother), Touchadam and Tibbermore with him, and Lord Drummond, though himself a Queen's Man, did not bring a detachment of Drummonds with him. Stirling of Keir, however, was a Marian. John Blacader of Tulliallan, who should perhaps be associated with his neighbours to the east, in Fife, had been in St Andrews Castle with the Cardinal's murderers in 1546, but in 1568 he signed the Hamilton Bond and fought for the Queen. It is difficult to see any influence of the Earl of Argyll, though he had his lowland fortress at Castle Campbell, near Dollar.

Fife, like Midlothian on the opposite side of the Firth of Forth, was a sheriffdom where lairds rather than lords counted. The leading noble (and hereditary sheriff) was Lord Lindsay of Byres, whose Fife properties were centred in the eastern part of the sheriffdom, and he was an energetic King's Man. It is hard to see much of an explicable pattern among the lairds. Outstanding among Mary's supporters were the Balfours, who were essentially a Fife family because the place from which they took their name is there and up to 20 lairds of the name at one time held lands in the sheriffdom. Eight of them were in the Queen's Party, but the reasons for this are not clear. The conspicuously devious, but highly intelligent, Sir James Balfour of Pittendreich, who had joined the murderers of Cardinal Beaton and suffered in the galleys with John Knox, had been close to Mary in 1565-6 and had held Edinburgh Castle for her and Bothwell until he was detached by Moray, but he rejoined the Queen's Party after Moray's death. His brother Gilbert, who acquired Westray in Orkney in 1560, had been Mary's master of the household and was an active Marian. The 'loyal Melvilles', as they have been called, had an interesting record. Sir John Melville of Raith had been suspected of heresy before the end of James V's reign and his activities in the English interest in the 1540s led to his execution for treason. He does not seem to have been personally involved in the Cardinal's murder, but several of his kinsmen were, like other Fife lairds. With the exception of Sir Robert, of Murdocairnie, third son of Sir John, they had not taken a very conspicuous part in the events of 1559-60, but their Protestantism seems never to have been in any doubt, and one of them had been with Moray in 1565. In the crisis of 1568 and the following years, Sir Robert and his brothers – James, of Halhill, Captain David, of Newmill, Andrew, of Garvock, and Walter – were Marians. The Beatons, who held lands mainly in Fife and Angus, were descended from Norman Bethunes and had nothing to do with the West Highland Macbeths who borrowed their name; they were represented on Mary's side by Creich (brother of the Queen's Mary Beaton) and Westerhall.

George Douglas, brother of the laird of Lochleven in nearby Kinross-shire, defied family allegiance – for the Douglases were almost solidly, with Morton, for the King – and, captivated by Mary during her imprisonment at Lochleven, was in the party which conducted her away on her escape and fought for her at Langside. There were some nests of support for Mary on the southern shores of Fife. The 4th Lord Sinclair had property there, centred on Ravenscraig Castle, and he signed the Hamilton Bond, though he died in 1570, apparently without being strongly committed. This may explain the appearance among the Marians of James Young in Dysart and Henry Balmanno in Auchtertool. The commendator of Inchcolm was a Marian, and this may likewise explain the appearance of William Clerk in Couston, at Aberdour on the mainland opposite the island of Inchcolm. Kirkcaldy of Grange himself, whose estate lay near Kinghorn, was another coastal laird with a Protestant record, and his wife was a sister of the loyal Melville brothers. Forbes of Rires – far from the Forbes country in the north-east, where the Forbeses were for the King – David Spence of Wormiston (with his son James), Alexander Pitblado of that ilk, James Sandilands of St Monans and George Durie, brother of the laird of Durie, represent something of a scatter through the sheriffdom. Scott of Balwearie, whose home was less than three miles from the Sinclair Castle of Ravenscraig and who had mass in December 1560, may have been a Marian chiefly because of his religion; the same may be true of the Duries, and Sir John Wemyss of that ilk had shown conservative leanings, but on the whole Mary's supporters in Fife were Protestants.

The areas so far examined are roughly those from which men could without insuperable difficulty have reached Langside in time for the battle. Moving farther afield, to areas where the evidence for Marian activity is mainly related to later operations, the Borders deserve first place – that is, the sheriffdoms of Berwick, Roxburgh, Selkirk and Peebles, which yield over 70 names. The largest group is one that was attached to Sir Thomas Ker of Ferniehirst. His father, Sir John, had been very active both as an English adherent in the 1540s and as a Protestant in 1559–60, and Sir Thomas, who succeeded in 1562, married a daughter of Kirkcaldy of Grange. Like many more with Protestant backgrounds he supported Mary and Darnley in the Chaseabout Raid. He was in time to join the Queen at Hamilton before Langside and subsequently took a very active part in Marian operations, as a member of the detachment (under Kirkcaldy) which attacked Stirling in 1571 and as a member of Kirkcaldy's garrison of Edinburgh Castle. Over twenty individuals, mostly rather small men centred around Blainslie near Lauder, are recorded as being in action with Sir Thomas, and no doubt his leadership and influence accounted for a good many more of the Borderers who appear as Marians. The Kers, however, were divided: Sir Andrew, of Cessford, who was at feud with Ferniehirst, stood by the Regents and he had the company of that godly man Fawdonside who had threatened Mary on the night of Riccio's murder. On the other hand, the Kers of Carchester (or Kerchester) and Cavers sided with Ferniehirst. There may have been some Hepburn influence in this area as well as in East Lothian, for the Earl of Bothwell had been warden of all three marches and bailie of Lauderdale.

Certainly one Berwickshire Hepburn – Sir Alexander, of Whitsome – aligned himself with the East Lothian Hepburns, just as three Border Hamiltons – from Sprouston, Nesbit and Tweedside – likewise took the family line. Cockburn of Skirling, too, was a Marian like other Cockburns, and he appeared as one of Mary's commissioners at the enquiry in England. Lord Home, the most important man in Berwickshire, was a late recruit to the Queen's Party, but remained firm to the end as one of the garrison of Edinburgh Castle. Most of the Homes did not follow him in his change of allegiance, but Ferdinando Home of Brumehouse, George Home of Spott (in East Lothian) and John Home, provost of the Homes' collegiate church of Dunglass, were Marians. The third great Border family, alongside Kers and Homes, were the Scotts. They were persistently at feud with the Kers (despite intermarriages arranged from time to time in an effort to secure peace), but in circumstances when the Kers were themselves divided Scotts could and did side with the Queen and still find it possible to cross swords with some Kers. Sir Walter Scott of Branxholm and Buccleuch, who had succeeded his grandfather in 1552 when the latter was killed by Kers, was a son-in-law of John Beaton of Creich and a kinsman of the Queen's Mary Beaton. The Queen had appointed him captain of Newark Castle in May 1565 and his loyalty to her after 1568 caused him to suffer at the hands of the English invading force of 1570, which blew up Branxholm Castle. He took part in the raid on Stirling by the Queen's Party in 1571. About a dozen other Scotts followed Buccleuch into Mary's service. Lord Hay of Yester must have had considerable influence as sheriff of Peebles, but the only local Hay identifiable as a Marian was Hay of Tallo, who had been an associate of Bothwell on the night of Darnley's murder, along with Ormiston of that ilk (Roxburghshire). There were two Cranstons – Morriston and Thirlestanemains. Beyond men who were connected with leading families, Borderers among Mary's supporters had a number of familiar names – Ainslie, Auchincraw, Brownfield, Bryden, Darling, Hoppringle, Redpath, Trotter and Tweedie. Many of the Borderers had been collaborators with the English in the 1540s, both Lord Home and Ker of Ferniehirst (the elder) had been on the reforming side in 1560, and there is little to suggest that many of them were conservatives in religion.

From 'the Borders', which are strictly the eastern Borders, we move to the south-west – Dumfriesshire (which included the western end of the Border), the stewartry of Kirkcudbright and the sheriffdom of Wigtown. Dumfriesshire produced a substantial number of Queen's Men, thanks largely to the leadership of Edward, 7th Lord Crichton of Sanquhar, and John Maxwell, Lord Herries, though here again we cannot ignore the possible influence of the Earl of Bothwell, who had been Lord of Liddesdale with its great castle of Hermitage. Both Crichton and Herries, we have seen, were something like converts to the Queen's cause and may have been especially zealous. Herries is likely to have been more significant than his nephew John, 8th Lord Maxwell, who had been born only in 1553. The latter's grandfather, the 5th Lord, had introduced the act for the vernacular scriptures in 1543 and for a time acted in the English interest, but was not consistent. He died in 1546, his son, the 6th Lord, in 1552 and his eldest grandson, the 7th Lord, in 1555. Both the 5th and 6th Lords married Douglases, and that represented an influence antipathetic to Mary, but when the 8th Lord grew to manhood he became something of a Roman Catholic leader. Our lists give at least three Crichton lairds from this area, and three Maxwell lairds. Sir Charles Murray of Cockpool was an ally of Maxwell. John Johnstone of that ilk, still under age in 1569, belonged to a family which had varied relations with the Maxwells, but he had a Hamilton mother and this may have helped to put him on Mary's side. Like others he submitted to Moray in 1569 but immediately after Moray's murder he joined the Queen's Party and brought with him three other Johnstones, two of them lairds. Sir John Gordon of Lochinvar (Kirkcudbrightshire), a son-in-law of Herries, had, like him, been active with 'the Congregation' in 1560 but was now a Marian and was nominated one of Mary's commissioners in England in 1568. Among isolated Marians in the district was Kirkpatrick of Closeburn; nothing is known of his previous record, but two other Kirkpatricks had been strong collaborators in the 1540s. Other Marians were Thomas MacLellan of Bombie, Alexander Stewart, tutor of Castlemilk, and Thomas Mackbrair, a burgess of Dumfries who was surely related to the well-known Protestant John Mackbrair, a canon of Glenluce who was imprisoned for heresy in 1550, served in the Church of England in 1552–4 and 1559–84 and between 1554 and 1559 was an exile in Frankfort and other places in Germany. Over the whole of this area there is little indication that popery had much to do with support for the Queen, because most of the known affiliations were Protestant. The more remote areas of the far south-west yield the names of John Brown of Carsluith, John Brown in Land, John MacDowell in Airis, Uthred MacDowell of Garthland and Gilbert Mackilwraith in Trolorg.

Returning to the east and moving north of Fife, across the Tay, we find deep divisions in Angus and Mearns and the adjoining eastern fringe of Perthshire – an area where, of course, the Reformation had taken early roots. John Lyon, Lord Glamis, was for the King, and no Lyons appear on the Queen's side. Also in the King's Party was Thomas Maule of Panmure, who had succeeded his father in 1560; he was 'ane godlie persone gevin to redine of the scripture' and married his son and heir to a daughter of John Erskine of Dun, that influential Protestant laird, provost of Montrose and superintendent, who, despite his cordial relations with Mary, supported her son. The Lords Ruthven had a consistent record as Protestants and anglophiles, and William, 4th Lord, who had succeeded in 1566, was a strong King's Man. His neighbours Hay of Melginch and Blair of Balthiok took the same line. Patrick, 4th Lord Gray, who had a long record as a collaborator with the English and a promoter of the Reformation, was a confederate in 1567. This, however, did not prevent one of his sons and two of his grandsons from joining the Queen's Party. There they found some of their neighbours. David Lindsay, 10th Earl of Crawford, had given some support to the Protestant revolution but seems to have had conservative inclinations, and he brought at least one Lindsay laird from this area – Evelick – into the Queen's Party. Lord Ogilvy of Airlie, who had, like most Ogilvies, been active with the Congregation in 1560, seems to have carried several Ogilvies into the

Queen's Party, and John Ogilvy of Inverkeilor and his son, John Ogilvy of Balgro, were especially active, though Ogilvy of Inverarity was for the King. The Lords Oliphant were neighbours of the Ruthvens and at feud with them: the 3rd Lord had given no countenance to the Reformation, and the 4th Lord, who had succeeded in 1566 and was a member (though not a very active one) of the Queen's Party, apparently had Roman Catholic sympathies. Ramsay of Bamff, on the Angus-Perthshire border, like Ramsays elsewhere had shown Protestant inclinations and was a Marian. North of Angus, in the small sheriffdom of Kincardine or Mearns, there was William Rait of Hallgreen. Sir Robert Carnegy of Kinnaird, an important laird in Angus, had joined the reformers in 1560, possibly with some reluctance, and his son, who succeeded in 1566, was another Marian who was not consistently active, though he suffered for his attitude when his castle was handed over to those King's Men Lord Glamis and Haliburton of Pitcur. It should be mentioned that one burgess from the Protestant stronghold of Dundee, whose name appears as James 'Wedder' but must have been a member of the well-known Dundonian Wedderburns, was in the Queen's Party. This part of the country was more than once the scene of serious military operations, for Huntly from time to time swept into it from his base farther north and was joined by local men, who were subsequently accused of taking part with him against the King's subjects at Kinclaven and in 'the hauchis of Mekill Lour' in 1568, of assisting in 'erecting' the Queen's authority in April 1570 and in fortifying and holding the castle and the famous round tower of the cathedral ('pyramidis lie *stepill*') in August 1570.[32]

In Aberdeenshire and other sheriffdoms beyond the Dee lay the territories of the Gordons, headed by George Gordon, 5th Earl of Huntly, 'the Cock of the North'. This ancient ascendancy was recalled in the aberration of those who planned the reorganisation of local government in 1974–5 and thought it appropriate to designate part of Aberdeenshire 'Gordon', although the real place Gordon is in Berwickshire, from which the family came. Huntly had been superseded as Chancellor by Morton in November 1567 and ordered to surrender the seals; he certainly surrendered at least some of them, but the prestige of his recent office may have made it especially easy for him to carry on an administration in the Queen's name in his own territory. It may be assumed that most of the Gordon lairds would follow the 5th Earl in 1568, as more than a score of them are known to have followed his father to Corrichie in 1562 (though the 4th Earl was then fighting against the Queen and not for her). This time only six – Carnburrow, Auchindoir, Creich, Geicht, Haddo, Lesmoir – happen to be mentioned, but in view of the way the Earl was lording it in the area it is plain that most of his vassals must have been on the same side. The Aberdeen Leslies seem in the main to have been in the habit of acting with Huntly, though it must be remembered that the head of their name was the Earl of Rothes, who was himself a Marian. John Leslie of Parkhill, for example, was associated with Huntly in demanding the surrender by Thomas Menzies of Pitfoddels of a house in Aberdeen that was held on behalf of the King, and two or three other Aberdeenshire Leslies are named as Marians, but Leslie of Balquhan was in the King's Party. The

Cheynes appear likewise to have been dependents of Huntly, and five of them are named as Marians – Arnage, Cruvie, Esslemont, Fortre and Straloch. The odd thing is that a couple of those Cheynes fought at Langside, which they could hardly have done unless they chanced to be somewhere in the south of the country when Mary escaped, and were thus able to hasten and join her force in time. The Barclays were also attached to Huntly: Barclay of that ilk had been with the 4th Earl at Corrichie and was with the 5th Earl now, and Barclay of Towy was also in the Queen's Party, with Cullairnie and Mathers. The Abercrombies, though of Fife origin, were now mainly in Aberdeenshire and were followers of Huntly: two of them – Pitmedden and Pittelpie – had supported the 4th Earl at Corrichie and they supported his son now, with Abercromby of that ilk. Other Aberdeenshire men who appear as Marians were a Fraser, a Leith (of Harthill), a Meldrum, a Menzies, a Rowan (burgess of Aberdeen), a Turing and Udny of that ilk. The chief interest against the Queen in the area was that of the Forbeses, who had a feud with Huntly against which the crown had taken action in 1546. At a later date (1578) William, Lord Forbes, John, Master of Forbes, Duncan Forbes of Monymusk, John Forbes of Aberiatrie and their 'kin, friends, and dependers' explained that they had been the 'kindly' or hereditary possessors of certain lands which Cardinal Beaton had let, over their heads, to Huntly and other Gordons.[33] But the feud was older than that, for in 1537 the Master of Forbes was accused of treason by Huntly and executed. That victim's brother was the 7th Lord Forbes, and his son, the future 8th Lord, signed the Protestant bond at Leith in April 1560 (as Huntly did) and continued the feud with the Gordons, despite marrying a daughter of the 4th Earl of Huntly. In the course of the fighting between Queen's Men and King's Men he was captured by Adam Gordon of Auchindoun in December 1571 and sent as a prisoner to Spynie Castle, the residence of Bishop Patrick Hepburn of Moray, uncle of the Earl of Bothwell, Mary's husband. The Bishop was an aged, syphilitic reprobate whose natural son caused such scandal by his relations with the wife of the captive Master of Forbes that her husband subsequently divorced her. Curiously enough, and it is a commentary on the absurdity of looking too much to religious motives to explain party affiliations at this stage, two of Lord Forbes's sons became Capuchin friars. Forbes of Pitsligo and Forbes of Balfour were, like Lord Forbes, in the King's Party and several Forbeses were killed in the action in which the Master of Forbes was captured. Bannerman of Wattertoun was an associate of the Forbeses, and a few other Aberdeenshire lairds were also in the King's Party. Generally speaking there was probably a good deal of religious conservatism in the area and although Huntly himself was not a Roman Catholic Old Aberdeen was one of the places where mass was reported to be said in October 1572.

Gordon influence extended not only up the river valleys from the Moray Firth, but also north of that Firth into Easter Ross and beyond. In October 1568 an expedition organised by Huntly, as Mary's lieutenant in 'the north pairtis of this realme', captured the royal castle of Dingwall from Moray's supporters, and the Earl of Sutherland was himself a Gordon, Huntly's cousin. But the main agent in rallying northerners to the Queen's cause seems to have been another Gordon, the resolute Adam of Auchindoun, whose own home was near Mortlach in the highlands of Banffshire. In November 1571 he led a substantial force which routed an army led by the Master of Forbes, hereditary foe of the Gordons and now lieutenant for the King. The scene of the battle was 'the Craibstane', on the outskirts of Aberdeen (indeed within the bounds of the present city), but many of Adam's army had come from remote areas. A remission lists the names of over 100, mostly relatively obscure men who are not easy to identify, but those who can be identified were inhabitants of Easter Ross and Sutherland, over 20 of them from Dornoch, seat of the Bishop of Caithness (which included Sutherland), a town dominated by the Earls of Sutherland. From other sources we learn that the provost, magistrates and people of Elgin, the cathedral city of Moray, were also with Adam Gordon, and we find the names of more than twenty lairds in the sheriffdoms of Banff, Elgin, Nairn and Ross, some of them very influential men: John Grant of Freuchie, Lachlan Mackintosh of Dunachton, James Innes of Drainie, Robert Innes of Innermarkie, Walter Kinnaird of Culbin, Robert Munro of Foulis, Alexander Ogilvy of Boyne, James Ogilvy of Findlater, Alexander Ross of Balnagown, Hucheon Ross of Kilravock, Alexander Sutherland of Duffus and Walter Urquhart, sheriff of Cromarty. As usual, there was cohesion among bearers of the same surname, for there were more than a score of Murrays, who were more common in Ross and Sutherland than in the province of Moray where their ancestors presumably originated. Taking these particulars in relation to the total number of Marians who were in one way or another officially recorded, this area – admittedly vast in extent – was clearly an important recruiting ground for the Queen's Party. Huntly, as Mary's lieutenant carrying on an administration in her name, had royal patronage at his disposal, and gave the abbey of Kinloss, forfeited by Walter Reid, to John Grant of Freuchie.

Farther north and farther west significant information is scanty, and in those days the central and north-west Highlands were hardly sufficiently integrated into the life of the nation to care much whether the throne was occupied by a king or a queen, for they were not likely to obey either. There were, however, two notables who belonged to the Queen's Party for a time – Y Mackay of Far on the north coast, straddling the modern Caithness and Sutherland, ancestor of Lord Reay, and Colin Mackenzie of Kintail, in Wester Ross, ancestor of the Earls of Seaforth. It has already been noted that even in Argyll, despite the influence there of the Earl, there is little evidence of much activity by Queen's Men other than Campbell of Ardkinglas, but this may have been simply because Argyll had no local King's Men to contend with, in the way Huntly had in the north-east. It must have been essentially a personal gesture when Patrick Bellenden of Stennes published one of Mary's proclamations in Orkney, though he may well have had the support of some local lairds.

To assess the significance of the foregoing analysis of the Queen's Party along territorial and familial lines two qualifications must be kept in mind. For one thing, while we know that the 500 or so men recorded as having fought for the Queen at Langside represented about a tenth of her army, it is impossible to say what the proportion is between the total names we have and the total number of Marians, and the evidence is certainly uneven in its geographical spread. The other qualification is that the chances of men of some note and social standing being recorded are greater than of those of lower rank: probably between a third and a half of the names we have are those of lairds or other figures of social consequence. Each of those lairds would undoubtedly have his following, but in what numbers we can too seldom say. Dalyell of that ilk had a following of ten, Hamilton of Livingston one of seven, and Lord Seton had 27 followers (who happen to be named). Occasionally we have stray names of 'servitors' – three of Archbishop Hamilton, one of Lethington, one of Cairncross of Colmslie, one of Crawford of Kilbirnie, one of Kelso of Kelsoland and one each of the Lauders of Bass and of Popill. Thus it may be that not many of the hundreds or thousands of individuals who supported the Queen but who are not named were in a position to make up their own minds. There is one startling example of independence of thought – Alexander Gibson, a servitor of Lord Ruthven, was on the opposite side from his master.

Besides 'servitors', habituated to service with a noble or landed family in return for food and lodging and not much more, there were some who were paid to enlist. These were the 'wagers' or hired men, among whom one hears of Peter Bairdy and John Mayne on the Queen's side, but there seem to have been more on the King's. Moray ordained 'certain companies and bands of men of war to be taken up' and Captain David Murray (brother of Tibbermure) raised a company of soldiers whose wages he himself paid.[34] In a special category were the royal gunners in Edinburgh Castle, including John Chisholm, captain of the royal artillery, who rejected the Regents' claim that they should adhere to the King and instead took part with Kirkcaldy when he held the castle for Mary. Them apart, it is unlikely that the rank and file of Mary's 'wagers' were professional soldiers, but the many 'captains' who appear on both sides may have served in continental armies. Some of the Marian captains had obvious family affiliations: Captain Patrick Fleming was a 'servant' of Lord Fleming; Captain David Melville was one of the loyal brothers and joined his brother-in-law, Kirkcaldy, in Edinburgh Castle; Captain James Cunningham was brother of Drumquhassill, who held Dumbarton for the Queen; Captains Hugh Lauder, Robert Lauder and David Wemyss also had kinsmen in the Queen's party. Captain James Moffat had no known affiliations, nor had Captains Alexander and John Coutts, though the latter pair may have belonged to a military family, for Alan Coutts, who was said to have supported the King in 'the lait civile trublis', was appointed a colonel in 1581. There is some indication how troops were organised: Captain James Bruce had John Hamilton in Kilbowie as his lieutenant and John Robertson in Braidwodsyde as his ensign; Captain Thomas Kerr had James Arbuthnott as his lieutenant and Thomas Dawling as his ensign; and Captain Gilbert Wauchope had Matthew Aikman as his lieutenant and Corporal Jennet as his ensign.[35]

From professional soldiers we move to the normally peaceful townsmen. Among the lists of men present at Langside there are very few burgesses, and only one or two more appear in later operations: one from Glasgow and two from Kilmarnock (all of them Boyds), one from Ayr (a Crawford), one from Brechin (a Cockburn) and one each from Lanark, Dumfries, Jedburgh, St Andrews, Dundee and Aberdeen. It may be that the burgesses generally were not fighting men. But in Edinburgh, although only three burgesses are named as having been in Mary's army at Langside, one of them a Frenchman and another one of the Queen's own servitors, about 70 were named later in remissions as accessories to Kirkcaldy of Grange in the castle, a list of those who were summoned to underlie the law for supporting the Queen contains nearly 200 names, and there is other evidence, so that a total of 470 can be reached.[36] We do know that Kirkcaldy was able to put considerable pressure on the burgesses, and we know that he had to get supplies for his garrison. We can guess, too, that the merchants and craftsmen of the town were not averse from selling their goods and services in a ready market, without regard to politics. It certainly appears that Kirkcaldy was doing himself fairly well: he had supplies from three apothecaries, three candlemakers, six maltmen, four bakers, nine tailors and clothiers, two goldsmiths, two shoemakers, three skinners, two smiths and a great many more, including the printer Thomas Bassandyne who was soon to produce the first Bible printed in Scotland. It does not escape notice that some of the burgesses, like some of the captains, shared surnames with the Queen's noble or lairdly supporters – Borthwick, Cranston, Crichton, Fleming, Hamilton, Heriot, Melville, Lauder, Nisbet, Ramsay, Touris, Wallace and Wauchope – and may therefore have been Marians out of family loyalty. But even so the information about Edinburgh is startling. It is apt to be thought that the aristocratic support of Mary's party was counterbalanced by middle-class support for the Regents, but this may have been too facile a generalisation. It is interesting, too, that George Hacket, who, as Conservator of Scottish Privileges in Flanders, represented mercantile interests, was a Marian.

If the degree of support which the Queen received from some burgesses is a partial corrective to the view that her party was predominantly an aristocratic one, it would nevertheless seem that on the whole, if she had birth and breeding on her side, her adversaries had a greater share of professional experience. Even the clergy – apart from the bishops and those bogus clergy the commendators, who were mainly aristocratic and followed the majority of the nobles into Mary's camp – do not figure much in the Queen's Party. Of less than 20 names which come to light, there were three Hamiltons, one Hepburn, one Campbell and one Home, who presumably went with lay members of their families, though it is odd to find two Douglases, who should have been with Morton. Besides – though again we have to remember that men of higher standing were apt to be over-represented in the evidence – the great majority of the clergy who supported the Queen were dignitaries, either of collegiate churches (which were in effect proprietary in noble or landed families) or of cathedrals.[37] George Weir, a monk of Melrose, was escheated for his part in the murder of the Regent Lennox, there was one vicar who was a reader or assistant minister in the reformed church and there was one minister, Thomas Hepburn, parson of Oldhamstocks, an associate of Bothwell. Perhaps not many ministers, or for that matter priests, were likely to take part in military operations on either side.

The other professional men who counted were lawyers and officials. It was noticeable that when the investigations into Mary's case took place in England in 1568, Moray was able to produce a galaxy of talent – a group of lawyers and councillors like Bishop Bothwell of Orkney, Robert Pitcairn, Commendator of Dunfermline, and Henry Balnaves of Halhill, besides George Buchanan, the scholar and historian, Maitland of Lethington, the Secretary, and MacGill of Rankeillor Nether, the Clerk Register. On the other side, none of Mary's supporters could be described as much more than competent – Bishop Leslie of Ross, Gavin Hamilton, Commendator of Kilwinning, Robert Crichton of Eliok, former Lord Advocate, and Thomas MacCalyean of Cliftonhall (who were all professional lawyers); and there were minor figures like John Muschet, commissary clerk of Dunblane, John Moscrop, an advocate, James Harlaw, a solicitor, a couple of macers, a notary, and Adam MacCulloch, Marchmont Herald. Mary later gained two notable recruits in Maitland of Lethington and Sir James Balfour of Pittendreich, former Clerk Register, who was won over by Moray in 1567 but later abandoned the King's cause. Lethington's brother, John Maitland, also joined the Queen's Party, but at this stage had not yet revealed the ability which was later to make him King James's Secretary of State and Chancellor. No doubt lawyers, like others, were moved partly by familial associations – Crichton and Balfour notably.

It was perhaps partly because the King's Party had good lawyers that it produced effective propaganda, giving the impression that it was not merely officially committed to Protestantism but that it was *the* Protestant party, arrayed against a party of papists. This grossly over-simplified view was reflected in a remark of the English Bishop Parkhurst in 1573 that 'the godly Scots' had taken Edinburgh Castle and turned out 'the papists'.[38] Had Mary been depending solely on practising Roman Catholics, or even on men of Roman Catholic sympathies, she would have made a poor showing, and the Queen's Men were made up mainly of those who, if not all enthusiasts for the reformation – as many of them certainly were – at least found the reformed church acceptable. A Scottish prelate was more perceptive than Parkhurst, for John Spottiswoode remarked, in somewhat naive terms, 'Albeit that all the papists within the realm of Scotland had joined with her, the danger had not been great. . . . But alas! . . . to see the hands of such as were esteemed the principal within the flock to arm themselves against God.'[39] They would of course have denied that they were arming themselves against God, or even against the reformed church as it was organised in Scotland. In July 1567, when the general assembly met in Edinburgh, where Moray conducted his government, apologies came from Argyll, Lord John and Lord Boyd, who explained that although they were members of the reformed church it was not safe for them to attend. It would have been hard to show that the policy of the Regents could in practice be any more favourable to Protestants than the legislation of Mary's parliament of April 1567 had been. It was not only that Mary's policy – whether it be characterised as tolerant, equivocal or opportunist – had been favourable to the reformed church, it was not only that her cause had the legal appeal of duly constituted authority, but Protestants, who knew their Bible, were familiar with those verses in Romans xiii which have so often tortured the minds of Christians contemplating revolt: 'Let every soul be subject unto the higher powers; for there is no power but of God: the powers that be are ordained of God. Whosoever therefore resisteth the power resisteth the ordinance of God'. The revolutionaries of 1560 had tried to get round the dilemma by protesting, perhaps somewhat disingenuously, that they did not intend anything against 'the authority'. That solution might salve their consciences when confronting a French Dowager ruling in the name of an absent sovereign, but it was not so tenable in face of the person of a native Queen regnant, duly crowned and anointed.

If the Queen's Party was not a Roman Catholic party, neither was it essentially a pro-French party. It is true that Mary's cause was advocated by the exiled Archbishop Beaton of Glasgow, who had taken up residence in France because he could not come to terms with the reformed church, but her supporters in Scotland included old friends of the cause of Anglo-Scottish amity. After all, Châtelherault, whom Mary appointed as Governor on her behalf, had been the figurehead of the insurgents who had received English help in 1560, and among her supporters latterly was Maitland of Lethington, who had always aimed at Anglo-Scottish co-operation and, after he left the King's Party, viewed Mary's restoration in that context. It is not as surprising as her critics have sometimes thought that Elizabeth showed neither haste nor enthusiasm for helping the Regents. When, in 1568 and 1569, she was seriously considering Mary's restoration, it was in the context of an Anglo-Scottish understanding based on religious conformity, and the proposal for Mary's marriage to Norfolk must also be seen in that context, for Norfolk, though associated with the English Roman Catholic party, was not himself a recusant. Mary's personal links with France actually helped in prompting Elizabeth to consider her restoration under English auspices, with a view to preventing France from intervening in Scotland on Mary's behalf. As late as 1570 Mary's restoration was still at least a possibility, and it was not until 1571 that Elizabeth permitted the publication of matter which seriously incriminated her cousin. It was only then that Mary stood publicly indicted as a murderess. The reaction of English parliamentarians, at any rate, was plain: Mary had 'heaped up together all the sins of the licentious sons of David, adulteries, murders, conspiracies, treasons and blasphemies against God'.[40] The massacre of St Bartholomew's Eve (August 1572) intensified feeling against Mary, in England at least, and in September and October Elizabeth contemplated handing her over to the Scottish government, but after the death of Mar and the accession of Morton to the regency (November 1572) Elizabeth directed her policy towards a settlement in Scotland without reference to Mary at all. But it was a short-term intervention, like that of 1560. After the English troops had done their job of capturing Edinburgh Castle they withdrew, leaving control of Scotland to the Earl of Morton, a consistent supporter of the Reformation and the English alliance, but allowing him an independence which a mere satellite would not have had.

# 7
## CONCILIATION

*1570 Jan.* Murder of Moray
*July* Lennox Regent
*1571 April* Capture of Dumbarton Castle
*Sept.* Death of Lennox
Mar Regent
*1572 Oct.* Death of Mar
Morton Regent
*1573 Feb.* Pacification of Perth
*May* Fall of Edinburgh Castle
*1578 March* End of Morton's regency

The history of the years since 1560, if not indeed since the 1540s, suggests that few Scots were steadily committed to a consistent party or faction and that many of them can almost be described as volatile. There were those who supported the Protestant revolution with Moray in 1560 but five years later supported Mary in suppressing a rebellion by Moray, those who supported Moray's rebellion against Mary in 1565 but three years later upheld the rights of the now deposed Queen against Moray's regency, those who helped to overthrow Mary in 1567 but only a year later rose in arms on her behalf, and those who rebelled with an Earl of Huntly against Mary in 1562 but six years later joined an Earl of Huntly in her defence. Religion, foreign policy, opposition to arbitrary rule, a belief in the constitutional rights of either a *de facto* or a *de jure* sovereign, need not be disregarded as bases for unwavering convictions, but these convictions could find expression in different loyalties as circumstances changed. This meant that the formation of coalitions was relatively easy: the rebellion of 1560, Mary's stand against Moray in 1565, the confederacy of 1567 and the Queen's Party itself all represented coalitions among men of differing views, and all but the last were successful. But it is almost in the nature of coalitions to be short-lived, and all of those broke down. In particular, the confederacy of 1567 dissolved, leaving Moray in a perilous position: he had failed again, as he had failed in 1565, to re-create the circumstances of 1560, for there was far less unity behind him in Scotland and he did not win English support for his party. But the volatility of so many Scots not only facilitated the formation of coalitions. A coalition, by definition, involved some conciliation, and the volatility meant that conciliation between Queen's Friends and Queen's Enemies, between Queen's Party and King's Party, was not likely to present insuperable difficulties.

Almost paradoxically, there had been a phase of conciliation before the most serious part of the civil war ever began. In the early months of 1569, after Elizabeth declined to restore Mary and instead gave Moray a measure of recognition, many of the Queen's supporters were so discouraged that they acknowledged the Regent's government. There were negotiations with Châtelherault (who as already mentioned had arrived back in Scotland, by way of England, in February), Cassillis, Herries, Argyll and Huntly, and there were punitive expeditions, especially in the north-east and in the Borders (where some English military assistance was obtained). The upshot was that although Moray did not receive satisfaction from Châtelherault and Herries (who were imprisoned for a time), and perhaps Argyll, a convention which he held in July was attended by ten earls, two heirs to earldoms, 15 lords, one heir to a lordship, five bishops and seven commendators: Earls of Moray, Morton, Huntly, Atholl, Crawford, Mar, Cassillis, Glencairn, Buchan, Menteith; Masters of Marischal and Graham; Lords Home, Lindsay, Ruthven, Oliphant, Glamis, Gray, Ogilvy, Semple, Innermeath, Ochiltree, Lovat, Maxwell, Borthwick, Cathcart, Saltoun; Master of Sinclair; Bishops of Galloway, Caithness, Orkney, Brechin, The Isles; Commendators of Coldingham, Pittenweem, Dunfermline, Balmerino, Culross, Kinloss, St Mary's Isle. This was a big change from the five earls and eight lords who had been present at James's coronation and more like the 12 earls and 14 lords who had been among the confederates when they first rose against Mary and Bothwell in 1567. The peers, it will be observed, included Huntly, Crawford, Cassillis, Boyd, Oliphant, Ogilvy and Maxwell, who had signed both the Hamilton and Dumbarton Bonds in Mary's favour and would readily be labelled 'Marians', as well as others who had shown less unqualified allegiance.

It would have been too much to expect unanimity in such a heterogeneous gathering. When a proposal was brought forward by Lord Boyd to press for Mary's divorce (which could have been expected to facilitate her restoration), nine members were for it and 40 against. It would, however, be wrong to see the presence of 'Marians' in this convention as merely a move to divert policy in the interests of their own cause, for the proposal was, after all, in accordance with the original professed aim of the confederacy to separate Mary and Bothwell, and the division was not along existing party lines. Huntly and his uncle the Bishop of Galloway, both Marians, supported Boyd's motion, but were associated with Atholl, Gray and others who had not been Marians, while Crawford, Cassillis and Maxwell, though they had supported Mary, voted in the negative. Nor were all the Marians present, for Châtelherault, Argyll, Herries and Fleming were not there. It should be added that the ten burgesses present were all against the proposal and that Secretary Maitland and the Comptroller were for it, while the Clerk Register, the Justice Clerk and the Advocate were all against it – a remarkable division in Moray's administration. It is rather revealing that at this stage men of different views, who had been in conflict, were prepared to meet round a table and argue a case instead of resorting to arms.

Moray's death in January 1570, however, and the five months' vacancy in the regency which followed, gave new hope to the Queen's Party and left the *de facto* government without a focus. Desertion was immediate, for of the numerous Marians who had been at Moray's convention in the previous summer only one – Cassillis – attended his funeral and was present at the council on 14 March which affirmed that the regency should continue. The Hamiltons – who, of course, had been responsible for Moray's murder and must have been jubilant – assembled in Glasgow on 20 February with 140 horse and 80 harquebusiers, most of the former Marians renewed their support of the Queen, and her party received new recruits as well. Home left the King's Party, but the most important accession was Maitland of Lethington, the Secretary. With his brother John he had been in the minority at the July Convention and had subsequently been tried for complicity in Darnley's murder and committed to the charge of Kirkcaldy of Grange, in Edinburgh Castle. He now persuaded Grange to declare for the Queen and make that fortress, which housed the regalia and the royal artillery train, a Marian stronghold. His apologia explained that in 1567 at Carberry he and his fellow insurgents had had two aims, the punishment of Bothwell for the murder of Darnley and the dissolution of his marriage to the Queen. He had personally guaranteed Mary 'as thankful obedience as ever she had' if she would abandon Bothwell, which she refused to do, wherefore she had been taken to Lochleven in order to 'sequestrate her body' from Bothwell. The confederates then found that 'the Lord Huntly and many others rose up against us, so that they were the greater party than we. So that we, finding no other way to preserve us from inconveniences, the ... setting up of the King's authority was but a fetch or shift to save us from great inconveniences; not that ever we meaned that the same should stand or continue'. He admitted that he now felt he 'did very evil and ungodly' in the setting up of the King's authority, for 'he can never justly be King as long as his mother lives'.[1]

On Maitland's premiss that the erection of James had been a temporary expedient, the end of Moray's regency was a time for reconsideration, and it was probably owing to the skill of such an enthusiast for Anglo-Scottish amity that the restoration of Mary, in joint sovereignty with her son, was at this stage under very serious consideration by the English government. All in all, there was plenty to encourage the Marians and it is not surprising that, according to a report in June, 'The Earls of Eglinton and Cassillis, Lord Boyd and others are in their own countries and remain constantly at the Queen's obedience and cause all courts and other things to be set forward in her name', while Huntly 'has been diligent in the north in causing the Queen's Majesty to have universal obedience there'.[2] Mary had been proclaimed at Brechin and Forfar by Ogilvy, Home, Balfour and George Gordon, and there is proof that Huntly, as Mary's 'lufetennent', was conducting an administration in her name with all due legal forms and was suppressing 'pretended' jurisdictions.[3] With such resurgence of the Marian party, it was at this point that the King's Party probably reached its nadir: of the earls, only Morton, Mar, Glencairn and Buchan could be relied on, with the heir to the earldom of Montrose (the Master of Graham); and of the lords only Ruthven, Lindsay, Glamis, Ochiltree, Cathcart, Methven, Saltoun and Sempill. Mary's party, by contrast, could muster about 12 earls and 14 lords, and a contemporary commented in April 1570, 'the son's party daily decays, the mother's party daily increases'.[4]

It did not improve matters for the King's Party when Matthew, Earl of Lennox, Darnley's father and the King's grandfather, was appointed Regent in June. He did not seem cast for the role of either focus or conciliator.[5] It was to his disadvantage that after residing in England for 20 years following his forfeiture in Scotland in 1544, he was regarded as an English subject: 'Think ye', asked Lethington, 'that my Lord of Lennox, being an Englishman sworn, can be lawful regent of this realm?'[6] Besides, at 55 and in indifferent health, Lennox was past his prime. Only five earls and nine lords took part in his formal 'election and constitution'.[7] He may have attracted some Stewarts, like Garlies; and Johnstone of that ilk, likewise in the south-west, submitted to him. There were also some successful military operations, with a certain amount of English help. Brechin, which had been the scene of a good deal of fighting, was captured, as were Doune Castle and some Maxwell strongholds in the south-west (in August 1570); Paisley was taken from the Hamiltons in February 1571 and Dumbarton Castle fell to the Regent's forces in April 1571. According to an accusation against Lennox, he seems to have shown little disposition towards conciliation, and rather engaged in somewhat brutal assertions of power. When he despoiled Hamilton lands in Lanarkshire and West Lothian he took away cattle from the poor tenants, and in East Lothian he did much the same at the Maitland home of Lethington, making free with the possessions of the aged and blind Sir Richard, the father of William. Lord Seton's properties at Niddrie and Seton also suffered. On the lands of Lord Fleming Lennox's forces destroyed not only the deer but also the rare 'white kye and bulls' which, it was said, 'have been kept these many years in the forest of Cumbernauld; and the like were not maintained in any other parts of the isle of Albion, as is well known'. The sixteenth-century conservationist deplored the fact that these unique creatures were used 'for Lennox's banquets in Edinburgh'.[8] (Oddly enough, a similar herd of this ancient breed, long kept at Hamilton, is now at Lennoxlove, which was once Lethington, the home of the Maitlands, and is at present the home of the Duke of Hamilton.)

Not all of these exploits had lasting results, for it was said that as soon as the Regent's back was turned Huntly was again out in force in Angus, and it was during Lennox's regency that the Queen's Party was, if not at its strongest in numbers, at any rate at its most ostentatious, especially as Kirkcaldy of Grange dominated Edinburgh from the castle. Among those conspicuous on the scene were Châtelherault, Lords John and Claud, Huntly, Argyll, Home, Herries, Maxwell and Boyd; several important lairds – Gordon of Lochinvar, Balfour of Pittendreich, Maitland of Lethington, Ker of Ferniehirst and Scott of Buccleuch, as well as many Hamiltons; two commendators – Gavin Hamilton of Kilwinning and John Maitland of Coldingham, Lethington's brother. As Morton held his own castle of Dalkeith, and the King's Party was established in Leith, there was a lot of military movement: '70 spears'; '200 or 220 horse'; 'six score of hagbutters'; '400 horsemen and 300 footmen, all hagbutters except 30 or thereby of pikemen'; '600 men of horse and foot'; 'Lord Herries with his Annandale men'.[9] The Queen's followers took possession of the tolbooth or town-house of Edinburgh and also of the great church of St Giles. The latter was a military objective, as all churches were apt to be in those days when few other structures offered platforms for fire from artillery and small arms, and the Marians cut holes in the roof so that they could if necessary annoy worshippers inside. But so far were they from being hostile to reformed worship that they used it as a church themselves. John Knox, with his usual prudential regard for his own safety, decided for the third time in his career that Edinburgh was too dangerous for him, and departed for St Andrews on 5 May after bitter recriminations with his old associate Kirkcaldy. In his absence his pulpit was usually occupied by his colleague John Craig, and at least twice the Duke, Lord Claud, Huntly and 'the rest' – that is, the other Marian lords – went to hear him preach; on the first occasion they swept out of the church after the sermon, but on the second they remained for 'the prayer' – that is, the great intercession after the sermon which, in the order then used in Scotland as in the English Prayer Book, was a Prayer for the Whole Estate of Christ's Church. Their hesitation about listening to Craig's prayer on their first visit may have arisen from a fear that he would pray for King James, whereas they had ordained that prayers should instead be made for Queen Mary. On 17 June the pulpit was occupied not by Craig but by the reforming Bishop of Galloway, Alexander Gordon, who preached on 'charity' and argued that Mary's moral shortcomings did not disqualify her as a ruler: 'Sanct David was a sinner, and so is she; Sanct David was an adulterer, and so is she; Sanct David committed murder in slaying Uriah for his wife, and so did she; but what is this to the matter? The more wicked she be, her subjects should pray for her to bring her to the spirit of repentance. . . . I pray all faithful subjects to pray for their lawful magistrate, if it be the Queen. It is the Queen, as I doubt not. . . . No inferior subject has power to deprive or depose their lawful magistrate.'[10] The bishop – assuming he has been correctly reported – had been reading Romans xiii as well as 2 Samuel xi, and was unshaken by the revelations about Mary which caused such a revulsion against her in the English House of Commons.

In that same month of June a Marian parliament was attended by Châtelherault, Huntly, Home, Maxwell, Somerville, Herries, Gavin and Claud Hamilton, the Bishops of Dunkeld and Galloway, proxies for the Bishops of Moray and Aberdeen, and the Commendators of Holywood, New Abbey, Coldingham and Pittenweem.[11] It was held in the tolbooth of Edinburgh, the usual meeting-place of parliaments, and adorned with the regalia, brought down from the castle. By contrast to this splendour, the Regent had been able to hold his parliament, on 14 May, only without the precious 'Honours' or regalia and only in the nearby Canongate, where the members had to go to and fro on their hands and knees to dodge fire from Kirkcaldy's guns in the castle, so that the gathering was called 'the creeping parliament'. The confident frame of mind of Mary's Party emerged when they were confronted by commissioners from the general assembly who went to the castle in an effort to 'pacify the troubles of the country'. The delegation had a singularly prestigious leader in John Winram. Under the old dispensation he had been – and still was – subprior of the Augustinian house at St Andrews which was the chapter for the primatial see, and as the office of prior was held by a layman the subprior was vicar general during a vacancy in the archbishopric. Under the new dispensation Winram had become the lord superintendent of Fife, which qualified him for the designation *Episcopus Fifanorum* or Bishop of the People of Fife, and he still went to parliament as 'Prior of Portmoak'. Maitland of Lethington, unimpressed, said to Winram:

'The principal of the nobility of Scotland are here, to whom they that are in the Canongate are far inferior in rank.'[12] He had made much the same comment a few weeks earlier to William Cecil: 'It is a mystery to me that so many noblemen who would be glad to do the Queen of England service should be neglected for the pleasure of a few inferior to them in degree, forces and all other things.'[13] (Incidentally, one would like to know what Knox, in his bolthole at St Andrews, said to Winram when the latter courageously set out for Edinburgh.)

Yet the 'creeping parliament' had taken significant – if rather token – action in declaring the forfeiture of some of the Marians: Archbishop Hamilton (who was not personally much injured thereby, as he had been hanged after he had been taken at Dumbarton Castle), Gavin Hamilton, Commendator of Kilwinning (who was not much injured by the sentence either as he happened to be killed a few days later) and the three Maitland brothers, William, John and Thomas. It is noticeable that no peers were forfeited at this stage. However, another parliament was held by the Regent at Stirling at the end of August, and this time it aimed at higher game: Châtelherault, Lord John, Huntly, his brother Adam, the Bishops of Dunkeld, Aberdeen, Moray, Ross and Galloway, as well as a score of lairds, including seven Balfours and four Melvilles.[14] An important change had taken place between those two parliaments of May and August. The three Ayrshire peers – Cassillis, Eglinton and Boyd – with Argyll and apparently Yester, gave their allegiance to the King, possibly because, unlike the Bishop of Galloway, they had been impressed by disclosures about Mary's delinquencies and were not prepared to risk the penalties of forfeiture. In September Lennox was killed when Kirkcaldy of Grange made a surprise attack on Stirling in the hope of rounding up the leaders of the King's Party before they dispersed after their parliament. Perhaps Kirkcaldy was thinking of revenge, perhaps of demonstrating that Stirling was no more secure than the Canongate, but he may have calculated that the nobles who had recently joined Lennox would not fight against their recent comrades or that if they were captured they would return to the Queen's cause. On the night of the attack Eglinton was actually taken prisoner by his old friends, but when they had to withdraw he was freed. Kirkcaldy did not achieve his aim, but in the confusion Lennox was killed.

The Earl of Mar, who succeeded Lennox and held office from September 1571 to October 1572, was perhaps more likely to enjoy some success as a conciliator. He had never been a strong party man, he seems to have been generally respected, he was mild in temper and it was said that his death after only a year in office was due to the fact that he loved peace and could not have it. It seems that more nobles now came over from the Queen's Party. When Mar was elected as Regent, the 12 earls present included Argyll (who had tried to mediate in May), Crawford, Cassillis, Eglinton, Montrose, Caithness and Sutherland, who had been Queen's Men, as well as the stalwarts of the King's Party – Morton, Mar, Glencairn and Buchan. The 16-year-old Earl of Angus, a Douglas and a ward of his uncle Morton, made his first appearance. Among the seven lords was Boyd (who had tried to mediate in the previous April), in the company of his recent foes Ruthven,

Glamis, Sempill, Cathcart, Ochiltree and Methven. Among the lairds were Cunningham of Drumquhassill, who had held Dumbarton for Mary, and Kennedy of Bargany, who had once been a Marian. No bishop had yet come over from Mary's side, for the only bishop present, except that committed and veteran King's Man Adam Bothwell of Orkney, was the wretched John Douglas, the aged rector of St Andrews University, who had just been nominated to the primatial see by the government but not yet approved by the church and found himself in an unhappy situation: 'The superintendent of Fife inhibited the rector of St Andrews to vote as one of the kirk, till he should be admitted by the kirk, under the pain of excommunication: Morton commanded him to vote (as bishop of St Andrews) under the pain of treason.'[15] It appears that he voted. Nor had commendators abandoned the Queen, for the 'Commendator of Arbroath' who was at the parliament was not Lord John Hamilton but George Douglas, an illegitimate son of the 6th Earl of Angus, who had persistently claimed Arbroath and went down in history as 'the Postulate'. It was no accident that in both St Andrews and Arbroath a Hamilton was succeeded by a Douglas, the head of whose house was the Earl of Morton. The inauguration of the new Regent was marked by a remission to over 80 Marians, largely Boyds and Crawfords.

When the convention proceeded to nominate a privy council, the erstwhile strong Marians Argyll, Crawford, Eglinton, Cassillis and Boyd were all included. Then this convention, itself quite representative, proceeded to issue an 'Admonition' to Kirkcaldy and the other defenders of Edinburgh Castle. Some of them, it was remarked, had been 'as earnest as any other' to promote the King's authority, or even 'the chief instruments of his promotion', and 'the greatest part' of them had sworn obedience to him. The King was now 'the rising star' and the Marians were told that they would not have been able to hold out as long as they had 'if the King's house and munition were not at your devotion'. An appeal was made to them to surrender before there was further bloodshed and inevitable defeat.[16] This appeal had little effect, and the evidence of the recorded remissions does not suggest that many more individuals came to the King's side during the remainder of Mar's regency, though Lord Somerville seems to have done so, Lovat was won over by appointment as chamberlain of the bishopric of Moray, and two Highland chiefs – Donald Gormsoun in Skye and Lachlan Macintosh of Dunnachton – both received pensions of 1000 merks, one from the bishopric of Aberdeen, the other from that of Moray, for assisting the Regent's government, in February 1572. Maxwell and Herries were reported, perhaps wrongly, to have submitted in February 1572, and, besides those who had actually committed themselves to the King, Atholl, Rothes, Elphinstone, Ross and Carlyle were now reckoned 'neutral'.[17] Fleming was in France, Seton in Flanders. All in all, it was now a somewhat emaciated Queen's Party.

Yet there was still a lot of Marian activity, and not only in the Edinburgh area, where forces seem to have been not unevenly matched. It was at this stage that Gordon of Auchindoun, Huntly's brother, defeated Forbes, the King's lieutenant in the north, first at Tullyangus and then at the Craibstane, where he captured Forbes. A rival administration, in Huntly's name, was still carried on in the north-east, and the ministers there who refused to pray for Mary were summoned to underlie the law for violating the acts of the Queen's parliament. Hume Brown's account states mildly, 'The country to the north of the Forth was for some months at the discretion of the party of the Queen', but the contemporary Richard Bannatyne said more bluntly that Adam Gordon 'plays King Herod in the north', presumably because he was massacring the innocents.[18] Herries and Lochinvar were in arms in the south-west, and in the Borders Ferniehirst tried to take Jedburgh but was repulsed by Ruthven. The people of Edinburgh were still quiet, under Kirkcaldy's surveillance from the castle, and in May 1572 'used all the pleasures which were wont to be used in the said month of May, viz. Robin Hood and Little John'.[19] A truce was agreed on 1 August, for two months, later extended to the end of the year.

When Mar died in October, the next Regent was Morton, who had long been leader of the King's Party in all but name. He did not have as promising a record as a potential conciliator or appeaser as Mar had had, because, unlike him, he was a strong party man on the side of England and the Reformation. He started with the support which had gathered round the government during the two preceding regencies, and the convention in November 1572 which elected him (in preference to Glencairn) was fairly representative. Though only seven earls were present, their backgrounds are revealing. Archibald Douglas, 8th Earl of Angus, was only about 17 and was just beginning a career as a constant ally of his uncle Morton and the inheritor of Morton's Protestant and anglophile opinions, and this Douglas attitude was likewise taken by the Earl of Buchan, who was the son of Sir Robert Douglas of Lochleven and had recently acquired the title by marriage to the heiress. The 3rd Earl of Montrose, who had succeeded his father in 1571, had, as Master of Graham, been constantly on the Regents' side. The only earl of longer standing who could show a consistent record was Glencairn, always a committed Protestant and a strong anti-Marian. Crawford and Cassillis, by contrast, had recently abandoned Mary's cause for that of the King. Eglinton and Argyll, who had likewise changed sides, were not at the convention but soon sat in the council and obviously approved of the new Regent, who relinquished the office of Chancellor to Argyll; while Erroll, who had been for a time a Marian, if not a very militant one, joined the council later. Among the lords too it was evident that the King's Party had gained ground, because those who had adhered to it when it was at its nadir now found, seated alongside them, Lords Boyd, Maxwell, Sinclair, Borthwick and Somerville and the Master of Herries, who had all been Marians, as well as Sandilands of Calder, now Lord Torphichen, whose record is less clear. Certain lords who were absent from the convention were also known to be favourable to the King – Forbes, Saltoun and Gray, who had always been on that side, and Oliphant, who had not latterly been active in the Queen's interest. Bishops were still reluctant to accept the regency, and the faithful Adam Bothwell was accompanied only by John Douglas of St Andrews (who was less likely than ever to withhold his obedience from Morton now that the latter was Regent) and Robert Stewart of Caithness, the King's great-uncle. The turnout of commendators was more impressive:

## Conciliation

Robert Pitcairn of Dunfermline was there as Secretary of State, with Robert Richardson of St Mary's Isle (although he was no longer Treasurer), George Douglas of Arbroath, the Erskine Commendator of Dryburgh, Mark Ker of Newbattle, Walter Reid of Kinloss, Alexander Home, appointed to Coldingham in place of the Marian John Maitland, and Alan Stewart of Crosraguel, again in proximity to his tormentor Cassillis. Twenty-eight lairds are listed by name, *cum multis aliis*; while the great majority of those named had clear records as King's Men, there were among them John Cunningham of Drumquhassill, James Forrester of Corstorphine, Robert Lauder, younger, of Bass, Robert Munro of Foulis and Lachlan Mackintosh of Dunachton, who had all been active as Marians. That Morton, at the beginning of his regency, had the support of men with such varied records suggests that he made a promising start.

His government did not take long to enter into negotiations with the remaining Marians, who were showing signs of dividing among themselves, for before the year was out Châtelherault, his sons, Huntly and Seton had left Edinburgh Castle. It may be that opinion had been affected by the Massacre of St Bartholomew's Eve in August, a shock to Protestant feeling which caused a revulsion against anyone like Mary who had been connected with the French royal family. The Scottish government certainly decided to take a more rigorous line against papists at home, for a convention in January 1573 passed an act of conformity ordering all holders of benefices to subscribe the reformed Confession of Faith on pain of deprivation, and an act against attempts to give effect to papal bulls obtained by Mary. On 23 February, by the Pacification of Perth, an undertaking to accept the King's authority and support the reformed church was given by Châtelherault, his sons, 22 Hamilton lairds, Huntly, Bishop Gordon of Galloway, Gordon of Auchindoun, Barclay of that ilk, Muirhead of Lauchop, two Baillies (dependents of Hamiltons), James Glen of the Bar and William, his son, for themselves and on behalf of their 'kin, friends, servants and partakers'. If the signatories had suffered forfeiture they were now to recover their property. It was almost characteristic of the Scottish way of life that the plenipotentiaries of the King's Party with whom those Marian leaders reached agreement included their erstwhile colleagues Argyll and Boyd.

These heavy defections from the Queen's Party enabled the Regent to reoccupy the town of Edinburgh, but English help was necessary to reduce the castle. When it fell, at the end of May 1573, there was little vengeance. It seems that the only executions were those of Sir William Kirkcaldy of Grange, his brother James, James Mossman, a goldsmith who had helped to finance the garrison (and who owned the house falsely believed to have been that of John Knox the reformer), James Cockie, Mossman's brother-in-law and also a goldsmith, and Thomas Mitchell, another burgess of Edinburgh. Lethington escaped execution by dying shortly after his capture, and his brother John was confined for a time, as were Lord Home, Sir Robert Melville and Bishop Crichton of Dunkeld. With those few exceptions, the Castilians were permitted to leave (though without their arms) and depart whither they pleased, and there was a special proclamation to protect from molestation or annoyance the 'ladies, gentilwemen and uther wemen' who had been in the castle.[20] The war had included one or two brutal episodes, notably the burning by Adam Gordon of Auchindoun in November 1571 of the castle of Towie, a seat of a Forbes family in the valley of the River Don and not far from Kildrummy. The laird was absent when the Gordons descended, and his lady, a Campbell, fired upon the leader of a party sent to demand her surrender, which so provoked Auchindoun that he put the place and its defenders to the flames. Despite such an incident, the operations between Queen's Men and King's Men ended in a remarkably civil manner, and behaviour at this point contrasts favourably with some of the sanguinary doings of the covenanters in the middle of the following century.

Morton, while perhaps not cast for the role of a conciliator, was not vindictive. It is early in 1573 that the remissions to Marians become for the first time numerous, and they go on in considerable numbers throughout that year and the next, with a trickle continuing thereafter. Of course the concentration of remissions from early 1573 and on into 1574 is not necessarily a proof of Morton's leniency, because the cessation of the military operations was obviously the point at which Marians would seek to come to terms with the administration by craving pardon for past offences, but even so it seems likely that if Morton had been more severe the remissions might well have been fewer. The years of Morton's rule certainly represented a sharp contrast to what had gone before, and it was no idle phraseology that was contained in a kind of official testimonial at the end of his regency in 1578: he 'pacified the seditions and civil war by which the realm was miserably afflicted, wherethrough our sovereign's lieges enjoyed a reasonable quietness and rest during the time of his regiment'.[21]

The Queen's Party as it had fought against successive Regents came to an end with the Pacification of Perth and the surrender of Edinburgh Castle. Apart from direct defections to the other side, Lord Crichton had died in 1569 and had been succeeded by a minor, and Lord Fleming had been killed in a skirmish in 1572. Atholl, although he was not at Morton's convention in November 1572 and was not comprehended in the Pacification, came into the Regent's allegiance later and was at a convention in 1575. Some Marians had gone to France. Lord Seton, who must have been nearly as much at home in France as in Scotland, was there in 1569, 1570, 1571 and 1577; Livingston was there in 1572–3; and both afterwards submitted to Morton. Thomas Maitland, one of Lethington's brothers, accompanied Seton to France and died in Italy in 1572. Lord Ogilvy was in France in 1571–2 and Sir James Balfour of Pittendreich went there in 1572. After the fall of Edinburgh Castle Sir Thomas Ker of Ferniehirst and Adam Gordon of Auchindoun left Scotland for France.

The earlier visitors to France had gone with some expectations of French help, the later ones probably rather in despair, but there is a possibility that Balfour, Ker and Gordon may have been *émigrés* on the classic model, hoping that some turn in events would enable them to return one day in triumph. That latter group rank among those whom it was difficult if not impossible to reconcile to Morton's rule. There were not many such irreconcilables. Lord Home was released from prison in 1575 but died shortly thereafter. John Maitland, Lethington's brother, was imprisoned until early in 1575, when he was permitted to suffer no more than a kind of house-arrest with his cousin, Lord Somerville, and was not a completely free man until Morton fell from power. Melville of Murdocairny, somewhat similarly, was released in 1574 but not restored to his property until 1579. Robert Crichton, Bishop of Dunkeld, was also released after a term of imprisonment. Some others about whom we know less may have proved hard to reconcile to Morton, for they were not admitted to 'pacification' until after the end of his regency. Others, though they had submitted earlier, showed occasional signs of being restive. Gordon of Auchindoun and his brother Huntly were under suspicion of treason in 1574 and the latter was imprisoned for a time; Lords Maxwell and Ogilvy were imprisoned in 1576 and released after Morton's fall; John Sempill of Bultries, who may, unlike Lord Sempill, have been a Marian, was forfeited in 1577 for plotting to murder Morton, and was rehabilitated after the regency came to an end. Others, like Gordon of Lochinvar, who emerged as enemies of Morton when he fell from power in 1580, may all along have been unreconciled. These stray pieces of evidence may suggest that the Marian cause, though now hardly militant, was not extinct in men's minds and hearts.

Early in Morton's regency it was already beginning to look as if there was taking shape under him something like the kind of coalition which, experience had shown, was the key to success in governing Scotland, and with the passage of time this became still more evident. A convention in March 1575 included 12 earls, 17 lords, three heirs to peerages, seven bishops and 15 commendators. The increase in the number of bishops was not entirely the result of conciliation and of the capitulation of former Marians, though Gordon of Galloway was there (for the last time, as he died later in the year); the episcopal ranks had been recruited through the appointment by the government to sees (vacant by death or forfeiture) of men who would act as overseers within the reformed church. The first such appointment, already mentioned, had been of a Douglas – John, to St Andrews – and another Douglas was George, the erstwhile 'Postulate of Arbroath', who became Bishop of Moray. They were not the only Douglases who benefited from Morton's patronage. The Regent elevated his nephew, the Earl of Angus, to the sheriffship of Berwick, the lieutenancy of all three marches, the bailiary of Lauderdale, the stewardship of Fife and the captaincy of Falkland Palace. Douglas of Parkhead became keeper of Edinburgh Castle and provost of the burgh; Douglas of Mains was chamberlain of the lordship of Linlithgow and captain of Blackness Castle; John Douglas was captain of Tantallon Castle. Carmichael of that ilk, who had married a half-sister of Morton, was keeper of Liddesdale, had many gifts of escheat and a pension from the archbishopric of St Andrews. Morton's natural sons were well provided for, though they did not hold significant offices. The impression one forms is that Morton was not to any significant extent using crown patronage even to confirm in their allegiance Marians who had come into the King's allegiance in 1572 and 1573, far less to win over those who were less disposed to be reconciled. The only office of the first importance which went to a Marian was that of Chancellor, which the 5th Earl of Argyll held briefly before his death in the autumn of 1573 and was then held for nearly five years by the consistent King's Man Glamis until after Morton's regency had ended. When the treasurership fell vacant in 1571 it went to Ruthven, who like Glamis was a consistent King's Man. Lord Boyd indeed was Collector General until July 1578 and a James Boyd was Collector Depute, and when these facts are viewed in the same context as the appointment of another James Boyd to the archbishopric of Glasgow, it would seem that the Boyds were specially favoured: but if Lord Boyd thought that the collectorship would be lucrative he can hardly have been encouraged by the experience of one of his predecessors, Wishart of Pittarro, who, as late as 1582, had still not received payment of the £4000 or so which he had 'superexpended' when he demitted office in 1565. No other bishopric was used as Glasgow was, for the Hepburn appointed to Ross does not seem to have been a client of one of the many Hepburns who had supported Mary, and Dunblane went to a Graham, nominated no doubt by the new Earl of Montrose, a King's Man. Some offices which, though not politically important, were probably lucrative, went to ex-Marians: Cunningham of Drumquhassill, although it was not until 1579 that he got a formal remission (along with several other Cunninghams who with him had held Dumbarton for Mary) had been in favour before that and was made bailie of the earldom of Lennox in 1576; and Munro of Foulis was appointed bailie of Ross and Ardmannoch in 1577. On the other hand, Lord Maxwell, whose family had almost a hereditary right to a Border wardenship, was appointed Warden of the West Marches in 1573, some months after he had come over to the King, but was superseded in 1577 by Morton's kinsman the Earl of Angus and did not recover the office until after the end of Morton's regency. It would seem that with some exceptions the Marians, even though pardoned, were kept rather in the background, while Morton devoted a lot of patronage to his kinsmen and clients.

Yet it was no resurgence of the Marian cause, or even the frustration of unreconciled Marians, which brought about the end of Morton's regency. This seems to have arisen mainly from personal differences. Morton made enemies by carrying things with a high hand and disregarding the animosities he might stir up. An early instance of this related to the 5th Earl of Argyll. He was of course an ex-Marian, in whose favour Morton resigned the office of chancellor, but the desirability of keeping on good terms with him did not stand in the way of Morton's insistence that the Countess of Argyll, who was the widow of the Regent Moray, should give up certain crown jewels which her first husband had appropriated. Argyll, as it happened, died in 1574, but Morton soon antagonised his brother and successor, Colin, the 6th Earl. In February 1576 Argyll claimed that his powers as Justice General (an office which he held heritably) invalidated a commission which had conferred on the Earl of Atholl certain powers over his own territories. There was a good deal of violence between the followers of the two Earls, and Argyll moved against Atholl with some force. Atholl, disgruntled, seems to have entered into a league with Lords Ruthven and Lindsay in the summer of 1577 whose object was defined as 'the maintenance of the King',[22] which of course does not mean the support of James against his mother but the furtherance of his rights against his Regent. In October

1577 Argyll was reconciled to Atholl and his faction and the league 'in defence of the King' was extended to include 'some personages of the house of Mar' – the family responsible for the care of James.[23]

In the spring of 1578 the King was approaching the age of 12 – the age at which his grandfather had been formally 'erected' as head of the administration – and on 4 March Atholl and Argyll, admitted to the royal presence at Stirling, asked James to summon the nobility to pronounce on certain differences between them and the Regent. Morton sent a message that he must either have power to punish those who challenged his authority or else be relieved of his office, and his opponents persuaded James to accept the latter alternative. It may well have been to Morton's disadvantage that he had done nothing to ingratiate himself with the young King; indeed, he spent most of his time in Edinburgh and at his own castle of Dalkeith, and had rarely if at all visited James in his seclusion at Stirling. A council was formed to carry on the government in the King's name and the regency came to an end. The membership of a convention which met at Stirling at this juncture to give effect to the coup shows clearly the extent to which support came from men who for one reason or another had been antagonised by Morton.

The list may be headed by Argyll and Atholl, whose attitude has been mentioned; when Lord Glamis, who had been Morton's choice as Chancellor, was murdered a few days after the coup Atholl was appointed to succeed him. The Earl of Montrose, who had tried to mediate between Argyll and Atholl and had perhaps helped to form their faction, had his own quarrel with the Regent over a charter by Andrew Graham, who had been appointed Bishop of Dunblane presumably on Montrose's nomination. The young Earl of Mar was at this stage under the sway of his uncle, the Master, who had become guardian of the King in succession to the Regent Mar and had given his support to the disaffected lords, possibly because he felt that he, like the King, had been neglected by Morton. Lord Maxwell, as we saw, had lost his wardenship of the West Marches and believed himself entitled to a third of the earldom of Morton. Mark Ker, Commendator of Newbattle, was affected by a dispute between Morton and his nephew, Ker of Cessford. Others who were present in the convention were the natural associates of some of those malcontents: the Erskine Commendator of Cambuskenneth naturally acted with the Master of Mar, effective head of his house, Herries was Maxwell's uncle, and Lord Innermeath, a Stewart, may have been influenced by the Stewart Earl of Atholl, though he was something of a dependent of Ruthven,[24] the Treasurer, who remained in office. Yet the issue was not clear-cut between a pro-Morton and an anti-Morton faction, for the Douglas Earl of Angus and the Douglas Bishop of Moray were present at the convention which in effect deposed Morton. Neither was there any sign that Marian sympathies had any relevance. It is true that former Marians like Eglinton, Caithness, Ogilvie, Somerville and the Commendator of Inchcolm were present, but they were balanced by such consistent King's Men as Ruthven, Cathcart, Glamis, Lindsay, Menteith and the Bishop of Orkney. A document ratifying Morton's resignation was signed by a similarly wide-ranging group of ten earls, eight lords, four bishops and eight commendators;[25] and a council was nominated consisting of Argyll, Atholl, Montrose, Caithness, Lindsay, Herries, Erskine of Gogar, the Commendators of Deer (a Keith) and Newbattle (a Ker) and the Bishop of Caithness, among whom antipathy to Morton was far more important than any ideology.[26]

Morton's restoration to authority (though not to the office of Regent) likewise came about without any appeal to principle or to former party affiliations. The young Earl of Mar simply decided that he and not his uncle the Master should have the guardianship of the King, and when he successfully asserted himself Morton joined him. A convention met in June, attended by nine earls, 11 lords, eight bishops and eight commendators, and agreed that Morton should have 'first place in council'. The only earls present now who had been absent in March were Glencairn, son of a King's Man, and Rothes, a Queen's Man, while Erroll and Crawford, successors of Marians, and Menteith, a King's Man, were now absent. The changes in the composition of the lords were the addition of Oliphant and Seton, of the Queen's Party, Ochiltree, a King's Man, and the rather neutral Sinclair. Volatility could hardly have been plainer, and there was obviously no question either of King's Men coming back or of Queen's Men going out when Morton returned to power. It had been said in May that Angus, Mar, Glencairn and Rothes were pro-Morton, while Argyll, Atholl, Montrose and Caithness were against him, and in June there was still no sound consensus. A new council, of variegated composition, was nominated on 25 July – Morton, Argyll, March (otherwise the Bishop of Caithness), Eglinton, Glencairn, Rothes, Buchan, Boyd and Cathcart, with the Commendators of Dryburgh and Cambuskenneth – but less than a week later Argyll, Atholl, Montrose and others in effect proclaimed themselves the government and denounced Morton for seizing the King.[27] Both sides took to arms and possibly it was only the fact that they were well matched that prevented bloodshed. A compromise was reached, and Morton's influence gradually prevailed, to continue to the end of 1580, while Atholl, who had been perhaps his main adversary, died in April 1579.

Yet Morton did not have complete control of policy, and one of the pieces of evidence which suggests this is that in 1578 and 1579, after the formal end of the regency, a considerable number of former Marians, who would never have been reconciled as long as Morton held office, were admitted to the 'Pacification'. In July 1578 Lord Home, Cranston of Moriston, Maitland of Auchingassill (a cousin of Lethington), Hepburn of Whitsom, Thomas Hepburn, parson of Oldhamstocks, and Captain Robert Lauder were so admitted. Then in October 1579 parliament took striking action. The meeting was well attended and suggests a degree of unity. The Earls of Morton, Angus, Argyll, Atholl, Lennox, Erroll, Mar, Montrose, Eglinton, Rothes and Buchan, Lords Ruthven, Lindsay, Seton, Oliphant, Somerville, Herries, Cathcart, Innermeath, Ogilvy, Forbes, Ochiltree, Saltoun and Sinclair, all sat together, nearly half of them from families which had been on Mary's side. There were six bishops, five of them of the new variety instituted in 1572, but the sixth was that veteran Bothwell of Orkney. There were no less than 17 commendators, including some whose names seldom appear in parliamentary sederunts, like Deer, Whithorn, Balmerino, Soulseat, Pluscardin and Blantyre; two or three of them were men whom Morton had appointed to replace forfeited Marians. There were representatives of the unusually high number of 33 burghs. The council which was nominated consisted of Morton, Lennox, Montrose, Rothes, Eglinton, Buchan, Lindsay, Boyd, Ochiltree, Cathcart, Herries, Dryburgh, Deer, Newbattle, Inchcolm, Culross, Erskine of Dun and Haliburton of Dundee, with the officials. This parliament, whose wide-ranging composition almost suggests a three-line whip, extended the Pacification to Lord Fleming (the successor of Mary's Fleming), Rothes, Crichton of Drylaw, the heirs of Patrick Whitelaw of that ilk, Henry Echlene of Pettadro, Patrick Hepburn of Kirklandhill, Henry Hepburn of Fortune, Lord Somerville, Robert Melville of Murdocairny, David Melville (brother of John Melville of Raith) and James Spence of Wormiston – some of them former men of great influence in the Marian party. But the same parliament which took this significant step of conciliation also proceeded to a measure which could hardly have been foreseen, namely the forfeiture of Lords John and Claud Hamilton, a batch of Hamilton lairds – James of Wodhouslie (or Bothwellhauch), Gavin of Roploch, Robert of Dalserf, David of Monktonmains, John of Shawtoun, Andrew of Heleis, Robert of Lethame, John of Kilbuy – and some Hamilton dependents – James Muirhead of Lauchop, Robert Balfour, brother of Pittendreich, Alexander Baillie of Littilgill, younger, and his brother. The Hamiltons had been inconspicuous since their admission to the Pacification of Perth in 1573; while the titular Earl of Arran was now the deranged onetime suitor of Queen Mary, Lord John, his next brother, was head of the house but had taken no great part in affairs. Lords John and Claud had signed a bond of friendship with Morton in March 1575.[28] It is not immediately obvious why the administration decided to strike against them at this time. It did, however, happen that while the Pacification had exempted the Hamiltons from the penalties of their disaffection to the King's government, it did not cover their guilt in the murders of Moray and Lennox, and, on the ground that the King was now ruling in his own person, their forfeiture was decreed.[29] Taking the forfeiture of the Hamiltons in conjunction with the admission in 1578–9 of so many former Marians to the Pacification, it is hard to avoide the conclusion that the Queen's Party was at this point in effect extinguished.

The temporary elimination of the Hamiltons, whose interests had done so much to shape the course of events in 1560, 1565 and 1567–8, was soon followed by the permanent elimination of Morton himself. He finally lost power at the end of 1580, when he was arrested on the charge of having taken part in the murder of Darnley, and he was executed in the following June. He had remained on the stage longer than most of the men who had played leading parts in the revolutions of 1560 and 1567 and in the civil war: Fleming died in 1572, Crawford and the 5th Earl of Argyll in 1573, Erroll in 1574, Châtelherault, Glencairn, Home and probably Sempill in 1575, Huntly and Cassillis in 1576, Glamis in 1578 and James Hepburn, Earl of Bothwell (in his Danish prison) in the same year, Atholl in 1579 and Buchan in 1580.

# 8
# CONSERVATIVE REVIVAL AND RADICAL RESPONSE

*1579 Sept.* Arrival of Esmé Stewart
*Nov.* Forfeiture of Hamiltons
*1581 Jan.* Negative Confession
*June* Execution of Morton
*August* Esmé Stewart created Duke of Lennox
*1582* The Ruthven Raid
*1583 June* James escaped from Raiders
*1584 April* Ascendancy of James Stewart, Earl of Arran
*May* 'The Black Acts'
*1585 Nov.* Fall of Arran
*1586* League with England
*1587* Execution of Mary

Already in the interval after the end of Morton's formal regency in the spring of 1578 and before the abrupt termination of his political career when, on the last day of 1580, he was arrested on the charge of his part in the murder of Darnley, indications had appeared of foundations for a new alignment among Scottish politicians. The divisions which had emerged meant that there was no longer a coherent King's Party or even a coherent coalition combining the King's Party with some former Marians; while on the other hand, the conciliation of so many Marians, added to the elimination of the Hamiltons, meant that there was no longer a Queen's Party either. Interest focused not on King *versus* Queen but on the King and the influences which were going to be brought to bear on him as he emerged from tutelage. Even while Morton survived, he was now past 60 and men must have calculated and speculated about the future, whether they are moved by principles or by personal ambition. What was to prove most important in the short term was that a new figure appeared on the stage with the arrival from France of Esmé Stewart, Lord of Aubigny, the first cousin of Darnley. Darnley's younger brother, Charles, Earl of Lennox, had died in 1576, leaving only an infant daughter, Arabella; and Margaret Douglas, Countess of Lennox, mother of Darnley and Charles, had died in March 1578, creating problems about the destination of Lennox property. The King's male heir on his father's side was now his great-uncle, Robert, Bishop of Caithness, a brother of the late Regent Lennox and an aged bachelor, who succeeded Charles in the earldom of Lennox. Esmé, as the son of the Regent's next brother, was heir to the earldom, and he may have felt his prospects threatened by Bishop Robert's belated marriage in January 1579, although, at it turned out, the marriage was soon dissolved on the ground of impotence. Esmé obtained his passport for travelling to Scotland on 30 June 1579 and arrived at the end of September. Failing Arabella (who might have been thought disqualified as an English subject), Esmé was the inheritor not only of Lennox property but of the Lennox interest in the royal succession. As already explained, it was debatable whether James's heir was to be found on his mother's side (Hamilton) or his father's (Lennox), and the forfeiture of the Hamiltons, two months after Esmé's arrival in Scotland, may indicate that he had an eye to something more than the reversion of the earldom of Lennox. Yet, whatever Esmé's personal aims may have been, Morton's opponents found in him a rallying-point who was soon to become influential as he won the personal devotion of the adolescent King.

Initially at least, Esmé's faction, if it can be so called, had no ideological foundation but was a kind of Cave of Adullam for the disgruntled. Lord Ruthven, with his consistent Protestant and anti-Marian record, joined, apparently because he objected to the granting of the wardship of the earldom of Buchan, on the Earl's death in 1580, to Douglas of Lochleven.[1] Ruthven, however, was Treasurer, and the fact that Robert Pitcairn, the Secretary, also favoured Esmé suggested that office-bearers were preparing to salute one whom they evidently regarded as the rising sun and would continue to serve under him. Lindsay was another stout Protestant and King's Man who joined Esmé.[2] Others who turned to the newcomer were those who, as we saw, had their various quarrels with Morton and had joined with Atholl and Argyll against him – Maxwell and his kinsman Herries, Ker of Cessford and his kinsman the Commendator of Newbattle, and the Earl of Montrose.[3] It would be going too far to depict these connections as having any ideological basis, and the group soon split when ideological factors did emerge.

Yet Esmé may well have had a special appeal to those who had a lingering attachment to Mary and what Mary had stood for. The Lennox Stewarts had a connection with France going back to the early fifteenth century, when Sir John Stewart of Darnley was one of the commanders of a Scottish force which helped the French in their struggle against the English. He founded a French branch of the family which had a distinguished military record on the continent and was rewarded with various estates, including the seigneury of Aubigny, to which Esmé's father, John, succeeded in 1543. Earl Matthew, the later Regent (Esmé's uncle) had spent several years in France before returning to Scotland in 1543 to contest the succession with Arran, and, taking into account also Matthew's subsequent residence for nearly twenty years in England, he was a cosmopolitan figure who recalls the members of the international aristocracy – spanning France, England and Scotland – of the twelfth and thirteenth centuries. Thus Esmé, whatever political or ecclesiastical principles he may have held, represented a country of which Mary had been Queen, in which some of her supporters felt at home and to which her party looked for help and for refuge. It must be added that about the time of Esmé's arrival in Scotland there are signs (despite the general conciliation of ex-Marians) of something like a Marian resurgence on the part of a small minority. The francophile Lord Seton and his three sons were imprisoned for treason – which probably meant primarily opposition to Morton – in 1579, Ker of Ferniehirst was allowed to come back from France in February 1580 and Lord Ross, who had been taken prisoner when fighting at Langside for Mary but was subsequently listed as a King's Man, was described in 1578 (along with Livingston, Fleming, Home,

Lindsay, Traquair, Innermeath, Erroll, Saltoun, Sinclair and Cathcart) as an adherent of the Queen and 'not very attached to Calvinism'.[4]

While Esmé was thus probably attracting ex-Marians as well as those whom Morton had antagonised on various grounds, Morton's position must have become extremely precarious even before his arrest, and after his arrest it certainly turned out that he had few friends. The Earl of Mar, who had helped him to recover power in 1578, stood by him, but his mainstay lay in his own kinsmen. His nephew Angus made an attempt to rescue him, and that other, now aged, kinsman, Carmichael of that ilk, wept at his execution. Mar did not carry all the other Erskines with him and for a time Mar himself deserted Angus, though he returned to his side later. When, in the summer of 1581, Angus was forfeited, it was mainly Douglases who shared his fate and with him fled to England. It looked as if the Douglases, now isolated, were going to follow the Hamiltons into oblivion, so that the cores of the King's Party and the Queen's Party alike were for the time being eliminated. The persisting significance of the surname as a badge of affiliation came out in a curiously comprehensive act of 1581 against Morton 'and all utheris of the surnames of Hepburne, Hammiltoun and Douglas' for the murders of Darnley and the Regents Moray and Lennox.[5]

It was unmistakeable, viewing the situation in familial terms, that a Stewart ascendancy under the house of Lennox was going to replace that of the Douglases and to profit also by the ruin of the Lennoxes' ancient rivals the Hamiltons. It had been a straw in the wind that in April 1578 – immediately after the end of Morton's regency and not at the normal season for the election of burgh magistrates – George Douglas of Parkhead was succeeded as provost of Edinburgh by Archibald Stewart. The greatest Stewart of them all, Esmé, received a batch of grants from the crown in March 1580, including the earldom of Lennox, resigned by his uncle Robert, who became Earl of March instead. He was admitted to the privy council in June 1580, appointed keeper of Dumbarton Castle – that traditional channel for communication with France – in July, and chamberlain in September. After Morton's execution he was farther advanced, by promotion to a Dukedom of Lennox in August 1581. It was the solitary dukedom in the kingdom and it may not have escaped notice that the last dukedom created had been for the third husband of Queen Mary, the Earl of Bothwell. Another Stewart came on the scene in 1580 – James, of Bothwellmure, a younger son of that ardent Protestant and King's Man Lord Ochiltree and brother-in-law of John Knox. A man of education, culture and striking presence, he had served in continental armies before returning to Scotland in September 1580 and he was at once made one of the gentlemen of the chamber who were appointed under Lennox as chamberlain. It was he who, at the end of the year, dramatically accused Morton in the King's presence of the Darnley murder. He was admitted to the privy council in February 1581, made captain of the King's guard in the following month and on 22 April was advanced to the earldom of Arran. The earldom was of course rightfully held by the demented eldest son of Châtelherault, the one-time 'Young Arran', and the pretext for Stewart's elevation was the Hamilton forfeiture and his own descent from the first Hamilton Earl of Arran, two generations back. The

Stewarts had put down the Hamiltons with a vengeance. Bothwellmure's brother, Henry Stewart of Gogar, and his sister-in-law Margaret, widow of the Master of Ochiltree, also received gifts from the crown, and there were other Stewart beneficiaries.[6] Henry Stewart, the young Lord Methven, was recompensed for the service rendered by his father to the Regents in the civil war. Lord Robert Stewart, now the only surviving bastard of James V and so the King's uncle, was appointed captain of Blackness Castle in February 1581 and created Earl of Orkney in the following October. That other Lord Robert, the youngest son of James V, who had been Commendator of Whithorn, was succeeded, on his death in 1580, by Patrick, the son of the new Earl of Orkney. Sir James Stewart of Doune, who had been a Marian in 1568 and had married a sister of that other Marian, the 5th Earl of Argyll, was Morton's gaoler for the five months of his captivity in Dumbarton Castle, which involved him in the outlay of 'great sums of money'[7] and he was created Lord Doune in 1581 specifically because he was, as the King said, 'of our blood'.[8] It was Lord Doune's brother Archibald who had become provost of Edinburgh in 1578, and his son, by marrying the daughter of the Regent Moray in 1581, became 'the Bonnie Earl o' Moray' in right of his wife.

The composition of the party – or perhaps we should rather say group – who were in the ascendant after Morton's fall is further indicated in two lists. First, there were the members of the assize who condemned the ex-Regent: Eglinton, a former Marian with popish sympathies; Somerville, a former Marian once noted as a papist; Argyll, whose animosity against Morton had apparently not been cured by his appointment as Chancellor in 1579; Montrose, who had consistently supported the King's Party but had quarrelled with Morton; Glencairn (the 6th Earl, recently succeeded), whom it is odd to find in the company of his local rival Eglinton and taking part against Morton with whom his grandfather had collaborated for so long; Maxwell, who had always disputed Morton's right to his earldom because he was the son of the second daughter of the third earl while the Regent was the husband of the youngest daughter; Seton, that leading Marian, francophile and papist; Rothes, who had been a Protestant and had latterly supported the King's Party although he had signed the Hamilton Bond in Mary's favour in 1568; Sutherland, who had taken little part in affairs but had a Marian attachment and whose father had married a daughter of John, 3rd Earl of Lennox, so that he was a cousin of Esmé; Stewart of Innermeath, whose family tended to go with other Stewarts; Ogilvie, a former Marian sometimes suspected of popery; and the Master of Livingston, who had, like his father, been an active Marian and formed a close personal attachment to Esmé. So far as principles counted, most of them had what might be called a conservative record, but personal animosities were important.

The second list which is revealing is the catalogue of those who profited by the distribution of the possessions of Morton and other Douglases. Lennox got the escheat of the Regent's movables and lands which included Dalkeith, Aberdour and Whittinghame. To Stewart of Bothwellmure, the future Arran, there was transferred a pension of £500 from the abbey of Balmerino formerly held by Morton's illegitimate son James, as well as a 'tack' or lease of lead mines formerly belonging to Douglas of Parkhead. One of Bothwellmure's brothers, William Stewart of Monkton, got a tack of teinds previously held by Angus, and another brother, Henry, received teinds formerly held by Morton's son James. A pension of £500 from St Andrews Priory which had been held by Morton's son George was returned to the granter – Robert Stewart, now Earl of March. James Stewart, son of Stewart of Doune, got a pension of £500 from the bishopric of Aberdeen which had belonged to Morton's son Archibald. Alexander, son of Lord Seton, became Commendator of Pluscardin in succession to Morton's son James. Francis Stewart, son of Lord John (one of James V's bastards) and now Earl of Bothwell through his mother, received sheriffdoms held by Morton and Angus and the office of hereditary admiral which had previously belonged to the Bothwell family; Lord Maxwell was invested in the Morton earldom. Argyll became sheriff of Linlithgow in succession to Morton. Homes received various gifts, and Ruthven, besides less important grants, was created Earl of Gowrie in August 1581. Clearly the beneficiaries were mainly Stewarts or conservatives, but again personal animosities counted.

It might be debated whether importance should be attached to the list of 30 'gentlemen of the chamber' appointed in October 1580,[9] for it contains a number of lairds who were, as far as is known, political nonentities, and as eight of the 30 were heirs of peers there was probably an emphasis on youth for this largely honorific office; but some were sons of peers who had been Marians, some were Stewarts and Homes and others were members of families with a Marian background. All were required to profess the Protestant religion.

Not all the individuals in those lists need be regarded as committed supporters of any policies which Lennox might adopt, and some in fact left him, but, taken with other evidence, the lists suggest the formation of a party which had some foundation not only in opposition to Morton, personal greed and jealousies, or even a general conservatism, but an attachment or at least a leaning to the cause of Mary and perhaps to Rome. A month after Morton's execution that inveterate Marian Ker of Ferniehirst, along with the Kers of Cavers and Kerchester and their followers, received a respite for activities against the Regents, and Ferniehirst himself was fully rehabilitated. Other rehabilitations in 1581 were of John Maitland (brother of Lethington), the heirs of Kirkcaldy of Grange, and two minor figures, Adam MacCulloch the Marchmont Herald and James Cockie, son of the Edinburgh goldsmith executed in 1573. Probably Lennox and Arran found their principal ex-Marian collaborators in John Maitland, Maxwell, Seton, Ferniehirst and Melville of Murdocairny (whose estates had been restored in 1579 and who was knighted in 1581). Doune, Ogilvie and Seton were put on the council and Mark Ker became Master of Requests in March 1581.

What precisely Esmé's policies and intentions were has been a matter of debate. It is safe to say that the overthrow of Morton and the presence among those now conducting Scottish affairs of former adherents of Mary and of men of Roman Catholic sympathies aroused certain hopes and expectations as well as fears. All in all, it can be said that Lennox was a focus for foreign machinations and that opportunities seemed open for intrigues on behalf of the exiled Mary and the Roman Catholic interest. The details of those intrigues are not relevant here and in any event they are surrounded by the obscurity arising from the degree of secrecy which was involved. The essential facts are that there was some communication between James and his mother, between James and the militant Roman Catholic wing in France led by the Duke of Guise (who was, after all, James's cousin), and between James and various Roman Catholic agents, some of whom came to Scotland. The proceedings were connected with the important drive of the Counter-Reformation then being made in England by both secular priests and Jesuits, and Spain was much involved because the Spanish government was at that time a much more aggressive Roman Catholic agency than the French government was. Emissaries to Scotland optimistically reported that Huntly, Argyll, Caithness, Seton, Eglinton, Home, Ogilvie and Ferniehirst, as well as Lennox, would accept Spanish and papal help to bring about James's conversion or, should they fail, to transport him from the kingdom and even depose him. An ambitious proposal was hatched in Paris by papal agents and Scottish and English *émigrés* for sending a Spanish and papal army which Lennox would use to secure Scotland and then lead south to raise the English Roman Catholics.

Such fantasies went far beyond what responsible opinion would have countenanced. It is understandable that at a time when the Pope had recently declared that anyone assassinating the English sovereign 'with the pious intention of doing God service, not only does not sin but gains merit', King James, who did not seek martyrdom, was prepared to let it be believed that he might consider conversion. But to see zealots for a Roman Catholic revival, under Spanish auspices, in men who supported Mary and her liberal religious policy, was going much too far, and there was in fact singularly little Roman Catholic practice in Scotland, if only because of the scarcity of priests. The one strong centre of such practice seems to have been Dumfriesshire, under the aegis of Lord Maxwell, who protected the popish proclivities of Gilbert Brown, Abbot of New Abbey, but it is unlikely that at the end of the 1570s any other Scottish nobleman, except perhaps Lord Seton, had been a regularly practising Roman Catholic. Even when the mission to England began to have secondary effects in Scotland and when Jesuits occasionally appeared there to give both political and religious stimulus, there were few 'Roman Catholics' who did not accommodate themselves to the ecclesiastical situation by conforming outwardly, much in the fashion of the 'church papists' of England. This was true for example of the 6th Earl of Huntly, who had succeeded his father, the Marian leader, in 1576 and, now only 18, was to show himself much more inclined to Rome than his father had been. Other things apart, Esmé Stewart was a weak foundation indeed on which to build such fanciful schemes, for there is no reason to believe that he was a zealous supporter of either the Roman Church or Queen Mary. In the France from which he came, many influential men supported the reformed faith, and he made no difficulty about confessing it in Scotland. It may be added that if Lennox was indeed aiming at the restoration of Mary he must have been a singularly unselfish man. At it was, he dominated the young King and was not far from being his heir presumptive; but if Mary had come back she could hardly have failed to restore her old supporters, the Hamiltons, who had a better claim than he had to be her heirs presumptive. Besides, Mary had many friends who would expect to have her ear and enjoy rewards, whereas the King, it might almost be said, had no friend but his French cousin. There might, however, be some advantage, from Esmé's point of view, in an arrangement with Mary which would not impair James's rights as King – and indeed give his rule a legitimacy it could hardly otherwise have as long as his mother lived – and this notion may lie behind a revival of proposals for an 'Association' of Mary and James in sovereignty, though even this was received with more enthusiasm by Mary than by James or Esmé.

In the end, all the flurry of activity on the papal and Marian side amounted to very little when measured by its results. It did nothing at all for Mary and very little to strengthen French or Spanish influence in Scotland, and all it did for the cause of Rome was greatly to confirm Protestant hostility. The main effect of what leaked out and, more important, what was suspected, was to produce a kind of Popish Scare and a strong ultra-Protestant reaction against the rule of Esmé Stewart.

On the whole, Protestant fears seem rather forced in the light of the internal situation in Scotland, but had some justification in relation to the progress of the Counter-Reformation on the continent and the possibility that France or Spain might intervene. Lennox was denounced as an agent of the Counter-Reformation. It was in vain that he formally accepted the reformed faith and that the King, in January 1581, signed the Negative Confession, a document which, as a vigorous denunciation of everything papistical, could hardly be improved. When parliament met in October 1581 it certainly contained a goodly number of representatives of broadly conservative opinion – Huntly, Arran, Atholl, Crawford, Eglinton, Sutherland, Morton (that is, Maxwell), Home, Seton, Ogilvy, Oliphant, Somerville and Herries; but not many even of them were in any real sense Roman Catholics, and there were some strong Protestants as well – Glencairn, Gowrie, Rothes, Lindsay and Ochiltree, as well as Bishop Bothwell of Orkney and two more recently appointed Protestant bishops. The legislation included several strongly Protestant acts, so that if the administration was indeed under popish domination its actions hardly looked like it. Roman Catholic agents who reported that Lennox was untrustworthy and 'avowedly schismatic'[10] saw this, but nothing, it seemed, could reassure the ultra-Protestants among the nobility and the ministers, especially the latter. The reason was that they had a quarrel with Lennox which had nothing to do with popery but in which they could work up support through anti-popish agitation.

This new cause of dissension, while it is unlikely to have done much if anything in itself to create faction, probably made a certain contribution to a hardening of alignment. The reformed church had almost from the outset operated a kind of reformed episcopate, of an administrative but not sacramental nature, more akin to the system in some Lutheran countries than to the English model, and for such a system some claimed a divine mandate. Central authority had lain with a general assembly which, containing as it did the same three estates as a parliament – barons, burgesses and clergy – could have claimed to be roughly representative of the entire Christian, or at any rate Protestant, community. In 1572 it had been arranged that the titles and revenues of the ancient bishoprics should be conferred on ministers who would be appointed by the crown very much as English bishops were and would carry out the oversight of ministers. This arrangement was not in itself controversial – and was welcomed by John Knox among others – but it worked badly and created friction. About the same time the position of the general assembly was challenged on the ground that its functions could now be discharged by parliament, which, as it had been purged of unreformed bishops and operated under a sovereign committed to the reformed faith, had as good a claim as the assembly to represent the community. In the late 1570s the novel tenets of classical Presbyterianism appeared in Scotland for the first time. It was now contended that, as all ministers were equal, authority must lie not with individual overseers but with councils or courts, and that presbyteries should be introduced to take over episcopal duties. Central authority, it was argued, must be transferred to a kind of clerical oligarchy, for, while parliamentary power over the church was rejected, voting rights in the church courts should be confined to ministers and elders who were ordained for life and so constituted a branch of the ministry. These novelties were accompanied by sweeping claims to ecclesiastical revenues.

Clearly, whatever thoughts men may have had about the theological or theoretical merits of the two systems, the last point mentioned, with its effect on the material interests of the many laymen who held former church property, limited the appeal of the Presbyterian programme. Indeed, the crown and the landed classes had been manipulating the medieval endowments so successfully for decades that even the limited financial demands of the original reformers (in the first Book of Discipline) had been treated with something like ridicule, and the more comprehensive demands now made would have even less appeal. There were other grounds for dissension. It is not unreasonable to believe that the more traditional character of the quasi-episcopal system was attractive to men of a conservative cast of mind and that they looked askance at ministerial parity, which some thought 'the mother of confusion', while others may have thought it represented a dangerous precedent for secular society.[11] Not only so, but the anti-clericalism which is apt to stir the resentment of healthy-minded laymen against arrogant clergy could not take kindly to the proposal to exclude the laity from any voice in church affairs, while nobles and lairds stood to lose influence in another way by the proposal to abolish patronage.

Lennox's administration, instead of agreeing to make the changes in statute law necessary to authorise a Presbyterian revolution, took up the Presbyterians' challenge by making a fresh appointment to the archbishopric of Glasgow, which happened to be vacant. When the government's nominee was excommunicated by a presbytery the sentence was annulled by royal proclamation, so that a direct conflict arose between the government and the dominant party in the church.

Apart from disaffection caused by Lennox's policies and by suspicions of his motives, Scottish dissidents, not for the first time, received encouragement from south of the Border. There were English politicians and diplomats, like Francis Walsingham and William Davison, whose sympathy for Puritanism in England made them favourable to the Scottish Presbyterians who, they thought, should be supported not only as the best defence against French, Spanish and papal machinations but also on purely ecclesiastical grounds. They took the view that Scotland's relationship to England should be that of a satellite in the modern sense of the term: that is, not only should Scotland be denied the right to an independent foreign policy, but her government should consist only of men acceptable to England and that the two countries should share an ideology – the Puritan-Presbyterian ideology. Thus anglophile and Presbyterian opinion in Scotland tended to be identified. As early as April 1580 some English politicians thought that 'the ministers of Scotland which have credit and are wise may do much to abase the credit of D'Aubigny, who surely in the end if he prosper shall be the instrument to overthrow the religion there'.[12]

The opposition to Lennox therefore coalesced as a party based on militant Protestantism, political as much as religious in its emphasis, anxious for complete alignment with England against the papalist threat at home and abroad. It included noble and lairdly families which had been consistently Protestant and anglophile, with leaders in Lord Ruthven, now Earl of Gowrie, the 8th Earl of Angus (Morton's nephew and one-time ward) and the sixth Earl of Glencairn, and it had the backing of the Presbyterians, who were ever ready to use their pulpits for the political propaganda of ultra-Protestantism. Gowrie, who had at first sided with Lennox because of his irritation with Morton and his hopes of advancement (which he received handsomely in the shape of the only earldom created for a man not of royal blood since the reign of James IV) may be presumed to have taken the line he did partly because of his religious views, and he was not the only man who initially supported Esmé but later turned against him.

The reaction against Lennox came in a palace revolution called the Ruthven Raid, which took the shape of the seizure of the King's person in August 1582. Lennox, ousted from office, returned to France, and his lieutenant the new Earl of Arran was put under arrest. The motives for the Raid were not only religious, but in part personal and familial. The Lennox regime had been extravagant in its expenditure on the royal household and the King's Guard, and the deficit carried by Gowrie, who had been Treasurer since 1571, had risen within a few months from £36,000 to £45,000. To add insult to injury, after a dispute between Lennox and Gowrie over some patronage Lennox accused the Treasurer of misappropriating crown revenues, and there was a risk of violence between them. Thomas Lyon, Master of Glamis, who took a leading part with Gowrie, had a family feud with the Lindsay Earl of Crawford (who was inclined to popery) and had been fined £20,000 at the instance of Lennox. Whereas the Lennox regime had represented a Stewart ascendancy, the Douglases, out of favour under Lennox, now looked for restoration: Angus, their head, was still in England when the Raid took place, but, along with Morton's sons, was rehabilitated under the new administration, and about a dozen Douglas lairds were involved in the Raid. Other peers took part in the Raid or co-operated with the administration which the Raiders set up.

We have the names of some hundreds of persons associated in one way or another with the Gowrie faction,[13] and they formed a group which was heterogeneous in principles or ideology and broadly based socially. There were men whose personal or family affiliations pointed to support of Protestantism and the English alliance – Gowrie, Angus, Glencairn, Marischal and Lindsay. The old Earl of Caithness died just after the Raid, and his grandson was a ward of Gowrie. The Earl of Cassillis was a child, but his mother, a daughter of Lord Glamis, was in the Ruthven party. But the faction also included ex-Marians like Eglinton, Home, Boyd, Hay and three Hamilton lairds. The geographical basis was less broad than that of some other factions. The strong support which the Raiders had in Angus and Mearns owed little to any peer, but much to one man who stood in the line of succession to a peerage – Thomas Lyon of Baldukie, Master of Glamis, a forceful character who in October 1581 was able to muster about 250 'friends, tenants and servitors' in pursuit of a private quarrel;[14] and, as a number of the men so named are known to have been associated with the Raid – for example, Scrymgeour of Dudhope, Ogilvy of Inverarity, Ogilvy of Ballinshoe, John Lyon, apparent of Cossins, James Lyon of Easter Ogil and James Arbuthnot of Lentusk – it may be inferred that Glamis could rally a following of that order for the political *coup*. There were other Arbuthnots, Auchinleck of Balmanno, Grays, that veteran Protestant Haliburton of Pitcur and a brother of Wishart of that ilk. The Master of Oliphant was another Raider in this area, and Ruthven's own properties were almost adjacent, in eastern Perthshire. The Ruthven party found support, too, in the central area which had been somewhat cool to Mary's cause, and the reason is clear. The Earl of Mar, who had so recently been associated with Angus, this time had the support of the Erskine Commendators of Cambuskenneth, Dryburgh and Paisley, and the Erskines were out in force from their home ground, with 27 named servitors of Mar and men from Stirling, Alloa and Cambus, as well as Bruce of Powfoulis and his son. Murrays came in from nearby areas – Polmaise, Touchadam, Cockspow and Pardewis, and there were Drummonds of Carnock and Monzie, Mitchell of Bandeath and Mercer of Aldie. There were Colvilles, who now had a footing at Culross, only a few miles from the Erskine headquarters of Alloa, as well as their older properties at Cleish and Wemyss, and John Colville of East Wemyss was married to a Ruthven. From Mid and East Lothian came the bearers of names which have become familiar throughout the decades of Reformation history on the Protestant and anglophile side – Broun of Colstoun, Cockburns of Clerkington and Ormiston, Edmonstone of Newton, Fairlie of Braid, Foulis of Colinton, Heriot of Trabroun, Johnstone of Elphinstone, Wauchope of Niddrie, Richardson of Smeaton, Monypenny of Pilrig, Rig of Carberry, Hepburns of Bonhard and Whitecastle. One may detect three influences in this area: Francis, Earl of Bothwell, himself a Stewart but inheriting the Hepburn lordship of Hailes through his mother; the Earl of Angus, whose fortress of Tantallon was the mightiest stronghold in the Lothians; and Gowrie himself, who by marriage had become lord of Dirleton and built new residential quarters in a corner of the medieval castle there. Farther south, Lord Home was one of the Raiders, and eight lairds of his name, as well as some Kers, followed him. Lanarkshire supplied Carmichaels and other dependents of the Douglases, and Renfrewshire furnished Shaws and Sempill of Weitlandis. However, Ayrshire, that ancient Protestant stronghold, was inconspicuous this time. Glencairn was not well supported by his Cunninghams, though Drumquhassill and his brother stood by him; Eglinton was in the Raid, but no Montgomerys; Lord Boyd and his son were unsupported. There was a scatter of support for the Raid from more remote areas – MacCulloch of Ardwell and MacDowell of Garthland from the south-west, as well as one or two Leslies and the Master of Forbes (that anti-Marian champion) from the north-east. It was not only Ayrshire peers who lacked followers: Yester was there, but no Hays, Lord Lindsay but no Lindsay lairds. It may be that some of those magnates had followers who did not put their names to the bond of the Raiders or are otherwise unrecorded, but one must speculate that the issues now involved were such as to create breaches in old allegiances. Not one of the major offices changed hands, and officials seem generally to have acquiesced in the new regime, but whether this was because they had disapproved of Lennox is uncertain.

At first glance, and in so far as the object of the Ruthven Raid was to seize the person of an immature king, parallels are apt to be sought in episodes in the minorities of James II, James III and James V, when it had been almost a habit for a faction to seize a young king and rule in his name. But if the Ruthven Raid is looked at in a different context there are parallels already in Mary's own reign. In so far as the object was to separate the King from what was considered an undesirable influence, then there was a parallel in the proclaimed purpose of the confederates in 1567 to separate Mary from Bothwell, though the Raiders did not say that they thought it necessary to 'sequestrate the body' of the King from Esmé Stewart. But there was an earlier parallel in Mary's reign, probably a closer one. Only 16 years before the Ruthven Raid, a conspiracy had been hatched to separate the Queen from another undesirable influence, that of David Riccio. The motives of the conspirators were as various then as were those of the Raiders, for Darnley was involved as a supposedly wronged husband, but one of the motives for the general hostility to Riccio was that he was believed to be a papal agent. That meant that in the Riccio murder, as in the Ruthven Raid, there was a strong religious motive and explains why so many of the Raiders had in fact been involved in Riccio's murder. Admittedly, as Ruthven was a ringleader in each case, those who were attached to the Ruthven family naturally followed, but, as the Ruthven family had as consistent a Protestant record as any family in Scotland, it is very likely that those who habitually followed them shared their religious views. The other family mainly involved in both the Riccio murder and the Raid was that of Douglas. James Douglas, Earl of Morton, had been a leading conspirator against Riccio, and the Douglas element in the Raid was conspicuous. The Protestant – indeed ultra-Protestant and Presbyterian – emphasis was clear. Edinburgh decided to concur with the Ruthven faction and rejected an appeal by Lennox, from whom the burgesses were alienated because he had banished one of the ministers of the town for an attack on his administration. Besides, the general assembly, which found the religious and anglophile character of the new government congenial, referred to the Raid as 'the late action of the reformation' and contemplated asking the government to join it in an appeal to Elizabeth on behalf of the English puritans who were suffering under 'the tyranny of the bishops' and to urge the formation of a Protestant league.[15]

It is not difficult to see why some ex-Marians were in this camp. Protestants who had supported Mary because they considered that she represented lawful authority and did not threaten the reformed church, now opposed Esmé Stewart because they thought that he did threaten it, even though he, rather than the Ruthven Raiders, represented lawful authority. Their attitude, while intelligible, suggests that Mary's cause now had far less appeal than it once had had, because while Esmé might do something for Mary it was certain that the Ruthven party would do nothing. On the other hand, survivors of the Marian party or their successors were more numerous in the party opposed to the Raiders – Argyll, Elphinstone, Huntly, Gordon of Lochinvar, Ker of Ferniehirst, Crawford (whose family was in any event at feud with their pro-Ruthven neighbours, the Lyons), Livingston, Montrose, Seton, Maxwell (now Earl of Morton), Sinclair, Somerville and Sutherland, all of whom absented themselves from the convention held by the administration of the Raiders in October 1582, presumably because they disapproved of its radical attitudes. But how far had loyalty to Mary now given way to loyalty to James, representing lawful authority, and was this new loyalty a leading motive, in addition to disapproval of a radical ecclesiastical policy and of the subservience to England which the Raiders represented? Possibly the very fact that there was this threat to James, at the hands of a faction which had seized him by force, did something to encourage a transfer of loyalty from Mary to her son.

The Raiders had the same experience which had been fatal to Moray in 1565 and nearly so in 1567, namely the refusal of England to give effective help. It was all very well for radical English politicians to make promises and give encouragement, but only the Queen could order an army to march or loosen the purse strings, and Elizabeth declined to do either. Since her very limited intervention in 1573 to secure the fall of Edinburgh Castle she had steadfastly refused to make Scotland, effectively, a satellite. During Morton's regency she had disregarded suggestions that she should subsidise his administration and enter into a formal defensive league with Scotland. Once Morton's position was threatened by Lennox her action was limited to instructing her envoys to make representations and encourage propaganda, and when Morton was imprisoned and his life threatened she still refused to restore an anglophile faction in Scotland. Once Morton was gone, Elizabeth's attitude to Lennox was determined by her relations with France and Spain. The threat to England came not from France, but from Spain, which annexed Portugal in 1580, was in touch with disaffected elements in Ireland and at this time seemed likely to subdue the revolt in the Netherlands. Elizabeth was therefore anxious to preserve an understanding with France, and in 1579 and 1581 there were negotiations for her marriage with the Duke of Anjou, brother of the French king and leader of the French forces which were operating against Spain in the Netherlands. Now, Lennox represented France, not Spain, and there seemed no inherent reason why a French favourite in Scotland should be any more dangerous than a French consort in England. To that extent Elizabeth was justified in refusing to be stampeded by her Puritan politicians into intervening against Lennox.

In short, Elizabeth again rejected the satellite concept. Scotland was not to be denied an independent foreign policy, and in time James might be able to use negotiations with foreign powers to raise his value in the English market, although Elizabeth could at any time have checked such negotiations by conceding Scottish demands for a settlement of the succession and for financial subventions. Nor did the concept of ideological conformity ever appeal to her. There is no indication that in 1560 she had cared, as some had, that there should be uniformity of worship between the two kingdoms; although she later urged the Prayer Book on Mary that was with a view to weaning her from papistry and not to checking radical tendencies in Scotland; and Morton's policy, which some called one of 'conformity with England', did nothing to attract English support for his administration. It is doubtful if Elizabeth was much interested even in a common Protestantism, for she could ally with Roman Catholic France. Her frigid realism cut her off from the zealots, 'who beckoned her in vain to a crusade on behalf of the reformed faith'.[16]

The Ruthven administration thus found that Elizabeth, who had given encouragement before the Raid and approval afterwards, offered only a subsidy, so small that it would have been undignified to accept it. What was worse, she had again been considering the possibility of Mary's release and her 'association' in sovereignty with her son. Such a plan had much to commend it on paper: it was acceptable to France and therefore not contrary to Elizabeth's foreign policy; to James's government it offered a legality which otherwise his rule could hardly enjoy as long as his mother lived. But the interests of the parties concerned were not really reconcilable. Mary thought of the scheme as nothing less than a step towards her restoration as full sovereign; James welcomed the French ambassadors who arrived in the winter of 1582–3 because they gave him recognition and he hoped they would foster the opposition to the Ruthven Raiders; and Elizabeth's main concern was to hold the threat of Mary's release over the Ruthven party in order to keep it subservient to her. Although the Ruthven party obtained no effective English help, its critics made capital out of its English connection and spread rumours of a scheme to have the King transported to England.

James escaped from the Raiders in June 1583. Magnates like Huntly, Crawford, Argyll, Montrose, Rothes and Marischal – mostly northerners of conservative preferences – rallied to him, but the leading figure in the administration was soon James Stewart, Earl of Arran, who, after an imprisonment during the Ruthven ascendancy, reappeared on the council in August 1583 and was joined by Maitland of Thirlestane and Melville of Murdocairny. The King had to rely on conservative elements and after his recent humiliating experience had no taste for radicals. Reports that he was in the hands of 'favourers of the French and of the King's mother' caused such alarm in England that Walsingham himself was sent north at the end of August 1583.[17] With his ultra-Protestant prejudices, his Presbyterian sympathies and his hatred of Mary, he formed a very unfavourable impression of the situation. But his actions – lecturing James on the iniquity of changing his counsellors without Elizabeth's approval, taunting him with his inexperience and lack of power, and declining to deal with Arran – rather encouraged negotiations with continental powers. James had received a letter from Guise shortly after his escape from the Raiders, and in reply he professed to be ready to work for his mother's release and to operate against Elizabeth. In general, however, the change of policy was made slowly, with no immediate *volte face*. Gowrie himself remained on the council until the end of August and many of the Raiders received remissions, so that the coup made little impression in some ways. The almost fiercely reactionary character which Arran's administration was to assume would seem to have been the consequence, rather than the cause, of a challenge made to it in the spring of 1584, when it was threatened by a conspiracy encouraged by Walsingham and other English diplomats. Mar and Glamis, with Angus and Lords John and Claud Hamilton, seized Stirling Castle in April 1584 but they received no material English aid and when the King gathered a force which would have overwhelmed theirs they had to flee again to England. Gowrie, who had been arrested before this 'Raid of Stirling', was executed on 2 May: his ultimate fate was almost as exceptional as his earldom, for executions of unsuccessful rebels had been extremely rare. Thus Arran's position was strengthened, and after this success he felt that he had no more need to seek continental support. He could also afford to dispense with any Scottish faction other than his own supporters. There was a wholesale forfeiture of the leaders of the Ruthven group – the Erskine Commendators of Dryburgh, Cambuskenneth and Paisley, Angus, the Master of Glamis, and Mar himself; but with characteristic humanity the King took under his protection the old Countess of Mar, his one-time governess, and he still extended his favour to the Master of Mar and his son, who had been 'brocht up with his majestie in his tender aige the tyme of his discipline under his sculemaister', a phrase which strongly suggests that they had regarded themselves as fellow-sufferers under the rod of George Buchanan.[18]

There was now, but only now, a change of office-bearers. Arran became Chancellor on 15 May 1584 and three days later the office of Secretary went to John Maitland of Thirlestane, who resembled his brother Lethington in both his ability and his enthusiasm for England. On 13 May Montrose became Treasurer and Sir Robert Melville of Murdocairny Treasurer-Depute. Arran, besides becoming Chancellor, became keeper of the castles of Stirling and Edinburgh. His ascendancy was complete. Although the administration was a conservative reaction against the Ruthven Raiders, it did not go so far as the Esmé Stewart regime either in its flirtations with papal agents or in its disregard of England. Ecclesiastical policy was determined by the Presbyterians' association with the Ruthven party. The latter, favourable though they had been to the Presbyterians, never passed a statute in their favour, but there was a partial and strictly illegal

Presbyterian experiment in certain areas and the records reflect the antipathy of the Ruthven Raiders to episcopacy. Yet the law had not been changed, and when, in April 1584, the government clearly placed the emphasis on bishops once more it was acting in accordance with the law. However, in May it went farther, with the 'Black Acts', which asserted the power of King and parliament over all persons and estates, denounced 'the new pretended presbyteries' and reaffirmed the authority of bishops as commissioners of the crown. Nearly a score of ministers went to England, where they co-operated with the exiled lords in putting on a show of a 'godly' community, as an example and encouragement to the English, and intrigued with their sympathisers among English politicians. It was characteristic of the whole temper of Arran's administration that two old stagers, consecrated before 1560 – Bishop Crichton of Dunkeld, who had never conformed to the Protestant establishment, and Bishop Bothwell of Orkney, who had – were, so to speak, brought out of retirement to act as bishops once more.

The ultra-Protestant English diplomats, influenced by their contacts with the Presbyterian exiles, remained invincibly hostile to Arran, but the latter realised that those diplomats spoke neither for the whole of English official opinion nor for Elizabeth, and he had hopes that his anti-Presbyterian policy might facilitate an understanding with England if the diplomats could be by-passed. Archbishop Adamson of St Andrews, personally an enthusiast for Anglo-Scottish union, went to England in November 1583, partly to represent the Scottish government politically, partly to seek Anglican support for its ecclesiastical policy. The ecclesiastical side of the mission was a failure. The English Archbishop Whitgift was too Erastian to act without governmental approval, and the notion that a contribution could be made to Anglo-Scottish amity by conformity on an Anglican basis still made no appeal to Elizabeth. The political side of the approach to England was, however, more successful, for Elizabeth did not share the distrust of Arran which moved Walsingham and Davison, and she chose another agent in Lord Hunsdon, who was favourable to Arran and had a discussion with him in August 1584. There also appeared a new agent of Scottish diplomacy, the Master of Gray, who had been in France and returned in company with Esmé's son, Ludovick. Gray had been, and nominally still was, in the service of Mary, who was again pressing for an 'association', but he saw the weakness of Mary's plans. He therefore advocated an English alliance, which would ensure the retention of Mary in captivity, and in October 1584 James, who was personally attracted to Gray, sent him to London. He was to ask for the expulsion of the fugitive lords, and he did prevail on Elizabeth to make them withdraw from Newcastle to the south of England. But Gray was also to work for an Anglo-Scottish alliance, and he was successful in allaying Elizabeth's doubts about the reliability of the Scottish administration. In May 1585, after James had categorically repudiated any intention of approving of the 'association', Elizabeth sent Sir Edward Wotton to Scotland to offer £4000 down and £4000 yearly, and on the acceptance of those terms a league was formulated in July.

But although Arran's government had thus achieved a success abroad, its position at home had become insecure. His parliament in May 1584, which reaffirmed parliamentary and episcopal authority, had been well supported: there were eight bishops, 13 commendators, 14 earls and 15 lords. Figures are only part of the story. The earls were under strength because Gowrie was dead and forfeited and Angus and Mar were in England, but those who attended Arran's parliament included six peers who had been involved in the Ruthven Raid – Marischal, Bothwell, Eglinton, Glencairn, Yester and Home. The parliament extended the benefits of the 'Pacification' of Marians to John Maitland and Lord Fleming, as well as to Lethington's widow (Mary Fleming). It looked at that point as if Arran's regime might embrace all shades of opinion except the radicals. And there were in truth no ideological grounds for opposition. Anglophile opinion could hardly be rallied against an administration which was entering on a league with England, and although Andrew Melville could babble about a 'new popedom' there was nothing in Arran's policy to arouse Protestant suspicions, however hostile Presbyterians might be to his bishops. But Arran was personally unpopular, as something of an upstart, and English agents, with their Presbyterian bias, continued to work against him and were hand-in-glove with the Scottish lords and ministers who were in exile in England. The supple Gray was ready to listen to Walsingham's proposals for undermining Arran, and when Wotton came to Scotland he conspired with Gray and Maitland against the Chancellor, who found himself discredited on all sides. He had gone too far with England to retain the support of Roman Catholics but he had not gained the confidence of the ultra-Protestants, and he had bitter enemies in all who sympathised with the exiled ministers and lords. His opponents tried to sow in the King's mind the suspicion that Arran was not sincere about the league, and a Border affray in July 1585 was blown up by Wotton to accuse Arran of instigating the incident to break the league. James was persuaded to put Arran in ward, but he soon relented, whereupon Elizabeth, on the prompting of Gray, decided to 'let slip' the banished lords. They returned from England in October and were before Stirling on 2 November. As there was no force to resist them, the King surrendered and Arran fled.

The parliament which met shortly after this coup, in December, was much more poorly attended than Arran's parliament of May 1584 – which is creditable to Arran – for it contained only four bishops, 12 commendators, six earls and 11 lords, and it was obvious both that some of Arran's supporters (including Montrose, whom he had made Treasurer) were absent and that the ex-Raiders did not come flocking back either. However, among its proceedings was the restitution of a large group of peers and lairds who had been involved in the Raid of Stirling of April 1584, along with about 30 Hamiltons. The group contained recognisable elements on the usual pattern: the Douglas Earl of Angus with the Douglases of Drumlanrig, Parkhead, Cavers and Little Sauchy, and that Douglas client Carmichael of that ilk; the Erskine Earl of Mar with the Erskine Commendators of Dryburgh and Cambuskenneth and the Erskine parson of Campsie; Lyon of Baldukie, Master of Glamis, with the Lyons of Cossins and Easter Ogil and their neighbours Ogilvy of Ballinsho and Arbuthnot of Lentush; Lord

Home, Home of Cowdenknowes and their neighbour Ker of Cessford. The Hamilton detachment was headed by Lords John and Claud and, in addition to the 30 Hamilton lairds – making this list almost as impressive as the comprehensive remission to the Hamiltons after the Chaseabout Raid – there were the traditional Hamilton dependents, especially Baillies, Weir of Blackwood and Muirhead of Lauchope. Why precisely the Hamiltons were restored at this point, in the rather odd company of Douglases and Erskines, with whom they had usually disagreed in the past, and along with leaders of what had been a radical coup, is not clear. As part of a stroke designed to overthrow an essentially conservative government and restore a radical element it hardly seems to make sense. One may suspect the hand of Elizabeth, who always seems to have had a soft side for the Hamiltons and who may have insisted on their restoration – either as a matter of simple justice or to insert a counterweight to the influence of the former Raiders, with whom the Hamiltons had evidently reached some kind of accommodation in England.

At any rate, the restoration of the Hamiltons was one important aspect of what looked like a complete re-alignment in Scottish politics. Of course the Hamiltons were ex-Marians, and other ex-Marians got their restoration at this point – but they (Maitland and Fleming at any rate) were already acceptable to the Scottish administration, and Maitland continued in office after Arran's fall. The Hamiltons had been more or less in the wilderness ever since 1565, thanks to their unerring capacity for being on the losing side. While they had been formally restored after the end of the civil war, they had never been accepted by Morton, and when Morton was succeeded by Esmé Stewart, of the Lennox house, they had in effect fallen out of the Douglas frying pan into the Lennox fire.

The administration which succeeded that of Arran, in December 1585, has long been known as a coalition, and it deserves the name. Arran himself disappeared from the political scene and his office of Chancellor was declared vacant. Montrose, Treasurer since 1584, who had been on the assize which condemned his predecessor Gowrie and had been a strong supporter of Arran, was replaced by the Master of Glamis, from the Ruthven party, but Montrose remained on the council. No other changes were made in the officials, and in particular John Maitland of Thirlestane, Arran's choice as Secretary, retained his office. On the council, Angus, Mar and Glamis, leaders of the radical Ruthven party, sat with Huntly, Montrose, Crawford and Marischal, who can all be described as conservatives. The key office of Chancellor remained unfilled for a year and a half, possibly because the King was reluctant to take an irreversible step against Arran, possibly because the time was not considered ripe for conferring the office on the man who ultimately attained it – Maitland, to become the first Chancellor in the century who was neither a prelate nor a peer. What had been created was an uncommonly broadly based administration, and it must be concluded that the Marian party, which had ceased to be a fighting force with the fall of Edinburgh Castle in 1573 and had been undermined as a political force by conciliation in the 1570s, was now dead and buried. Individual Marians had come back to political influence, and some of them even to office, under

Lennox and Arran, and now in this coalition, but there was no longer a cohesive party with the objective of restoring Mary. As the focus of Scottish politics gradually shifted, the issue of James *versus* his mother faded into insignificance and had ceased to have any force before Mary was removed from the scene by her execution in February 1587. By that time James was approaching the age of twenty-one and the day could not be far distant when he would be the real ruler.

The fact that men of the same religious opinions had been on opposite sides need not be taken to mean either that religion was unimportant or that other inducements sometimes outweighed religious convictions. It is quite evident that men who shared religious views had to weigh up means as well as ends and did not all agree on the policies which could best further their aims. Convictions could therefore find expression in different policies as circumstances changed. This fact had helped to shape the response to Queen Mary's sometimes equivocal policy towards the reformed church, which was acceptable to some Protestants and not to others, and it continued to colour attitudes during James's minority. It would not be unreasonable to say that on the whole the records of the members of the Queen's Party suggest that most of them stood for the Reformation – perhaps a moderate reformation – within the framework of duly constituted authority in the state. To that extent one can see how their loyalty to lawful authority could be transferred to the Protestant James, if only because, whatever the initial foundation of his kingship, his prescriptive right grew ever stronger with each year that passed. While militant 'Roman Catholics' looked increasingly to intrigues with Spain, the Protestants and anglophiles who had made up the bulk of the Marian party found that their principles could be satisfied in a government led by Arran, then in a government led by Maitland and finally in one led by the King himself. Maitland himself showed how a former Marian could participate in the government as a loyal subject of James. One would hesitate to describe the quarrel between Queen's Men and King's Men as one between moderate and radical Protestants, for they had not been fighting specifically on the religious issue; but if, as seems likely, moderates were very largely aligned under the banner of the Queen, one can see how easily Marians could come to terms with the episcopalian policy of Arran and then the King, especially as Presbyterianism now provided a focus for their rivals the radicals.

Within the general framework of religious and political principles there had been various motives which may have led men to belong to the Queen's Party. Plenty of examples have been given of the significant part played by dynastic and personal objectives – in other words the desire for a place in the succession to the throne and for offices of power or profit. There is also a good deal of evidence that in this period as in others a considerable part was played by the judicious use of patronage, in the widest sense, with a view to appealing to secular ambitions. Henry VIII on his side, Cardinal Beaton, Governor Arran and the French government on the other, made their offers in the 1540s;[19] and Mary of Guise displayed tactical skill in bestowing favours on Protestants in the 1550s.[20] Queen Mary herself showed some of her mother's aptitude for 'management' in winning men to her side, for example in the crisis arising from the Darnley marriage.[21] During the period of the strife between Queen's Men and King's Men both sides used patronage. The Regents, who operated the government in a more or less normal manner in many parts of the country, had clear advantages over their opponents in that their offers may have seemed the more realistic. Moray was able to dispose of judicial offices, ecclesiastical revenues and gifts of forfeitures and escheats, and the material inducements he could hold out were one reason why he had the support of the Roman Catholic Lord Sempill.[22] During Mar's regency it became easier than before to use the bishoprics and their revenues as baits or rewards,[23] and Morton, while he used patronage largely to advance his own kinsmen, gave certain rewards to ex-Marians.[24] The Queen's supporters, clearly, had less to offer that promised immediate gain, but Huntly's administration in the north-east was strong enough *de facto* to be able to forfeit supporters of the King and reward those of the Queen.[25]

How far prospects of gain – or of loss – affected the attitude of the bulk of the population, and indeed what they thought about the issues at stake, can hardly even be guessed. The reformers had been able to appeal, on both material and ideological grounds, for the support of those whom Knox called (perhaps a little ungratefully) 'the rascal multitude'; but they had offered the prospects of loot of religious establishments and they proclaimed their tenderness for the injustices endured by 'the poor labourers of the ground', and even in the crisis of 1559–60 the lower classes among the insurgents were following the traditional leadership of the magnates. It was not until more than a century later that the lower orders for the first time took the initiative without aristocratic leadership.[26] In any event, neither Queen's party nor King's party could make an appeal at all comparable to that made by the reformers. There is no indication that there was any force in a 'No Popery' cry, such as there was to be later under Charles I, and indeed, apart from the specific issue of King *versus* Queen, there was little of political principle and none of religious to separate the moderates, at least, on the two sides. It is hard to see how even the most fervent supporters of the King could make a serious claim that either religion or national independence was threatened by the Queen's Party, and ultra-Protestant ministers may have thundered in vain from their pulpits, just as they had probably done in a frutiless attempt to rally support for Moray when he raised his rebellion in 1565. On the more material side, the prospect of raids (in which losses might be suffered) and counter-raids (in which losses might be made good) had no compelling attraction, though Borderers at least were inured to this as a way of life.

Much more study would have to be done to answer the question of how far the contest affected the general life of the country, and it might emerge that the majority of the people did not suffer heavily. Military operations were at worst sporadic, and many areas can have seen hardly any fighting at all. Tenants and clients would be obliged to turn out at the command of their lords, and even in the eighteenth century there was much talk of how tenants were 'forced out' for the Jacobite cause by their chiefs. But in the strife between King and Queen there are not likely to have been heavy calls on dependents to muster in arms except at the time of Langside, during the fighting around Edinburgh in 1571–2, the recurring activities in the north-east and perhaps the more intermittent operations in Clydesdale. So far as the evidence goes it gives the impression that the most serious damage to property was done in the course of Lennox's high-handed actions in 1571–2, in the incursions of Huntly into Angus and during the siege of Edinburgh Castle, when a number of houses in the burgh were destroyed and the adjacent countryside can hardly have been unscathed. Whether the lower classes were more affected than their lords by material considerations – either security on one hand or hope of loot on the other – is debatable; although in one sense they had less at stake, in another they had everything to lose, since their modest possessions represented the very means of survival.

If we knew more about how the administration functioned throughout the country it might emerge that conditions locally could be quite stable, under either one faction or the other. On the whole the central judicature was conducted by the Regents' administration in the name of James. Even in 1571–2, when the Queen's party held Edinburgh and there was an element of serious competition for control of the law courts, several clerks succeeded in carrying off their registers to the Regent's headquarters in Leith, and no doubt the King's party benefited from having so many lawyers in it.[29] But at that stage there must have been a good deal of dislocation of legal business. Equally, there was a period when large areas of the north-east were under a settled administration conducted by Huntly in the name of the Queen, and other magnates elsewhere, more intermittently, at least attempted to imitate him. But it is not conceivable that a Marian earl or lord, in effective control of his own vassals and tenants, would tamely submit to the paper or parchment claims of the officers of the Regents' government or that a King's Man would docilely accept the administration conducted in Mary's name by one of her supporters. The rank and file were not likely to act against their immediate landlords, but if they were not under direct dictation from them would very likely temporise and acquiesce in the *de facto* administration, whoever conducted it; the example of the townsfolk of Edinburgh, a good many of whom felt strongly enough to leave their homes rather than accept the rule of the Queen's Party, is hardly likely to have been often paralleled elsewhere.

One of the threads running through this book has been the extent to which an individual's religious or political principles might be either channelled or diverted by familial and personal influences. These influences could produce cohesion within families or create alliance between them, but equally they could involve persistent antagonisms between families. And in general the allegiance of the 'following' was determined by the party alignment of its head. Thus, whether the King's cause or the Queen's had the wider appeal to the nation at large, any express bids for support which either might have made could have been largely irrelevant, given the nature of Scottish society.

# APPENDIXES

## Appendix A. The Stewart Succession before Mary

The Scottish succession was defined by statute four or five times in the course of the fourteenth century: first of all in 1315 in favour of Robert I's brother Edward, to the exclusion of Robert's daughter, Marjory; in 1318 in favour of Robert the Steward, Marjory's son (showing that although a woman was rejected as queen she could transmit a right); then presumably in 1324 in favour of David Bruce, the new-born son of Robert I; in 1371, on the death of the childless David II, in the shape of an acknowledgement (in accordance with the act of 1318) of Robert the Steward as Robert II, the first Stewart king; and in 1373 in the shape of an entail on Robert II's descendants. The necessity for that entail arose from the fact that there was an irregularity in the first marriage of Robert II, to Elizabeth Mure. According to canon law, which forbade marriage between persons related within the fourth degree, there were two distinct impediments in the way of that marriage. In the first place, Robert had had as his mistress one Isabella Boutellier before Elizabeth Mure became his mistress, and as Isabella and Elizabeth were related within the forbidden degrees this connection furnished as firm a barrier to the Elizabeth Mure marriage as if Robert had been married to Isabella (with whom, in canon law, he was 'one person' or 'one flesh'). Secondly, Robert and Elizabeth were themselves related within the forbidden degrees, apparently because of a marriage in the previous century: Elizabeth's ancestor, Gilbert Mure (d. *c*. 1280), married Isabella, Countess of Buchan, and Isabella's sister married Walter, the third son of the 3rd High Steward, Robert II's ancestor. Despite this double impediment, Robert the Steward had a number of children by Elizabeth Mure and obtained a papal dispensation for their marriage only after three sons had been born. The dispensation, in 1347, legitimated children already born as well as any to be born, but this did not resolve all doubts, as the parallel case of the English royal house shows.

The House of Lancaster, like the House of Stewart, had a statutory or parliamentary title to the throne, but it was open to question whether it had the best hereditary right. The first Lancastrian king, Henry IV, had been acknowledged on the forced abdication of Richard II in 1399 and had been succeeded by his son and grandson, Henry V and Henry VI. Henry VI, however, had no child for the first eight years of his marriage and his heir within the Lancastrian family was to be found among his cousins the Beauforts, Earls and Dukes of Somerset. They were descended, as Henry was, from John of Gaunt, third son of Edward III, but their legitimacy was open to question, for John Beaufort, first of the line, had been born long before his mother had been married to John of Gaunt. True, he had been legitimated after the marriage, but it was not clear whether legitimation carried with it the right of succession to the throne; there was a subsequent declaration that it did not, and it was only by violence that the Beaufort line ultimately made good its claim in the person of Henry VII in 1485. If the Beauforts were disqualified, Henry VI's heir was the Duke of York, who was descended in the male line from a younger brother of John of Gaunt, the Lancastrian progenitor. As long as Henry VI was childless, York might have been content with recognition as heir, in preference to the Beauforts, along with the position meantime of protector to the feckless Henry. The situation changed when Henry's son was born on 13 October 1453, for York had another claim, which gave him priority over Henry's son, Henry himself and any other descendant of John of Gaunt, Edward III's third son. York was descended not only from Edward's fourth son but also from his second son, Lionel of Clarence. That descent came through a woman, Lionel's daughter Philippa, and this raised another point of debate – whether a woman, even if she could not herself inherit the throne, could transmit to a son the right to inherit. The title to the English throne had not yet been transmitted through a woman except in the case of Stephen, but his competitors had been, first Matilda, herself a woman, and then Matilda's son, who claimed through his mother and ultimately succeeded as Henry II. The point about succession through a woman was ultimately conceded later in the fifteenth century, when Henry VII advanced a claim through his mother, who was still alive when he became king and who indeed survived him. But in the 1450s York's secondary claim – if indeed it was secondary – was uncertain, though by no means without substance. It was in 1460, when York produced his pedigree with a formal demand for the crown worn by Henry VI, that what would later be called legitimist principles were first brought forward in England against the statutory right of a reigning monarch. York was killed in battle in the same year and it was his son, Edward IV, who became the first Yorkist king, largely because of the support of the Earl of Warwick, but Edward's reign was briefly interrupted in 1470–71 when Warwick changed sides and restored the imbecile Henry VI.

In Scotland it was the reigning line itself, and not, as in England, only the heirs presumptive, which was in an ambiguous position, because there was an irregularity in the first marriage of Robert II similar to that in the third marriage of John of Gaunt, and Robert III, like John Beaufort, had been legitimated only when his parents received a dispensation to marry, long after his birth. The ambiguity was twofold. For one thing, the validity of papal judgments in matrimonial causes could be challenged, and frequently was challenged. There was the very well known case of the first marriage of Henry VIII, who received a dispensation for marriage to Catharine of Aragon, widow of his brother Arthur, and much history flowed from the fact that the power of the Pope to grant such a dispensation was questioned. In Scotland there was the case of the 1st Earl of Arran, whose marriage to Janet Beaton followed a divorce the validity of which was open to question, with the consequence that the legitimacy of the 2nd Earl, later Duke of Châtelherault, could be challenged – and much history flowed from that too. Secondly, it was debatable, in Scotland as in England, whether legitimation carried with it the right to succeed to a lesser inheritance, let alone the crown. The *Corpus Juris Canonici* has nothing to say about the effect of papal dispensations on succession to property, and this is hardly surprising, for it was more concerned with their effect on entitlement to ordination and the tenure of ecclesiastical offices. So far as secular law is concerned, it might be hard to say exactly how it stood on this issue in fourteenth century Scotland, but in later times there was no ambiguity. Stair is quite explicit that legitimation conferred no right of inheritance; but bastards, like anyone else, could be included in an entail. To that extent the entail of the crown in the Succession Act of 1373 makes sense. But it might still remain uncertain whether the inclusion of bastards in an entail *of the crown* was lawful. Without an entail they were nowhere, and the title of the descendants of Robert II's first marriage depended squarely on the statute and not on the legitimation. It was true later in Scotland that James V's bastards, for example, were legitimated without thereby becoming eligible for the royal succession. Both Lord James and Lord John were legitimated in 1551, but no one thought that this gave them a place in the royal succession. The historians who have argued that because Robert II's dispensation legitimated his offspring by Elizabeth Mure, therefore there was no dubiety about the right of that offspring to succeed him on the throne, have really been extraordinarily naive.

The entail of the crown in 1373 designated as heirs the five surviving sons of Robert II, three by Elizabeth Mure and two by a second and unquestionably lawful marriage to Euphemia Ross, and the male heirs of each in turn, with an express exclusion of females. In the event of the extinction of all these lines, the succession was to go to 'the true and lawful heirs of the royal blood and kin', which presumably opened the possibility of a female or of a male inheriting through a female, and this made it possible in 1542, after the death of the last descendant in any male line from Robert II, for Mary, Queen of Scots, to succeed. Although she was a week-old infant, there are no indications that any counter-claim was made. The fact was that, as far as men could look, there was no one alive with a male descent from any earlier Scottish king, but even so this unprecedented acceptance of a baby girl is a strong indication that inheritance from parent to child was now regarded as indefeasible. The next male (though inheriting through a female) was the 2nd Earl of Arran, and one just wonders if he would have made a claim had his own birth been above reproach and had he not suffered from the same kind of shadow as hung over the Beauforts as heirs presumptive in England. It is to be noted that he took very good care to have statutory declaration of his position as second person in the realm and heir presumptive, which would hardly have been necessary if he had not been conscious of a possible defect of birth.

Returning to the parallel between Stewarts and Lancastrians, we see that James II (1437–60) had his statutory right, but it was open to challenge on the part of descendants of Robert II's second marriage. The male descendants of that marriage were already all extinct, but there were successors through females – Malise Graham, Earl of Menteith, who had the strongest claim but seems to have lacked capacity and ambition, and next his niece, the wife successively of the 8th and 9th Earls of Douglas, who lacked neither capacity nor ambition. When the 8th Earl of Douglas was murdered by the king in 1452, his brother, the 9th Earl, formally withdrew his allegiance from the King, took up arms and brought back to Scotland the Earl of Menteith, who had been a hostage in England for nearly 30 years. Close though Douglas himself stood to the throne in right of blood, as a result of a series of Douglas-Stewart marriages, he could hardly have advanced a convincing claim to the crown for himself – though yet another statute could have been passed, this time in his favour – and it looks rather as if he was cast for the part of a kingmaker. Certainly when he brought Menteith back from England in 1453 his action looks not unlike that of the English kingmaker, Warwick in 1470, when he produced the wretched Henry VI after ten years of oblivion. When Douglas threatened James II in 1455 he was actually in alliance with the Duke of York, while the Scottish government favoured the house of Lancaster, and curiously enough the battle between Douglas and the royal forces in 1455 took place exactly three weeks before the opening battle between York and Lancaster in England. James II, however, was a different proposition from Henry VI, and Douglas, deserted by some of his allies, was routed. He fled to England, whence he denounced 'him who calls himself king of Scots'. Thus Douglas was certainly disputing the claim of James II to be king, but was not explicit as to who had a better right to the title. No pretender from the Euphemia Ross line was put forward again (though as late as Charles I's reign an echo was heard of their possible claim), and Douglas was next associated with a different challenge to the reigning line, when Alexander, Duke of Albany, brother of James III, obtained Yorkist patronage and styled himself 'Alexander IV, King of Scots', but obtained little support from his fellow-countrymen. An invasion from England by Douglas and Albany in 1484 led to the latter's flight to France and the former's imprisonment for the rest of his life.

## Appendix B. Surnames and territorial titles

| | |
|---|---|
| Campbell | Earl of Argyll |
| Cunningham | Earl of Glencairn |
| Douglas | Earl of Angus |
| | Earl of Buchan (from 1574) |
| | Earl of Morton |
| Erskine | Earl of Mar |
| Gordon | Earl of Huntly |
| | Earl of Sutherland |
| Graham | Earl of Menteith |
| | Earl of Montrose |
| Hamilton | Earl of Arran |
| Hay | Earl of Erroll |
| | Lord Yester |
| Hepburn | Earl of Bothwell |
| Keith | Earl Marischal |
| Kennedy | Earl of Cassillis |
| Leslie | Earl of Rothes |
| Lindsay | Earl of Crawford |
| Lyon | Lord Glamis |
| Montgomery | Earl of Eglinton |
| Sinclair | Earl of Caithness |
| Stewart | Earl of Atholl |
| | Earl of Buchan (to 1574) |
| | Lord Innermeath |
| | Earl of Lennox |
| | Lord Methuen |
| | Earl of Moray |
| | Lord Ochiltree |

## Appendix C. The 'brainwashing expedition'

Persons who accompanied Mary of Guise to France on her 'brainwashing expedition' in 1550 (*Register of the Privy Seal of Scotland*, iv. 879, 880, 882, 883, 887, 893).

Lord James Stewart, Commendator of St Andrews
John Roull, Prior of Pittenweem
William Lauder of Haltoun
John Winram, Subprior of St Andrews
John Douglas, parson of Newlands
Patrick Cockburn, parson of Pitcox
David Henderson, vicar of Rossy
Henry Douglas, younger, of Drumgarland
Alexander Erskine, son of John, Lord Erskine
Robert Colville of Cleish
John Forret
Robert Winram in Ratho
James Somerville in Humbie
David Orme
Bartholomew Livingston
Robert, Lord Maxwell
James, Lord St John
John Spottiswoode, parson of Calder
Alexander Cochrane
Robert, Bishop elect of Caithness
Angus Murray, chantor of Caithness
William Murray of Tullibardine
Sir James Hamilton of Crawfordjohn
Archibald Hamilton of Lethame

## Appendix D. Lairds in the Party of Revolution, 1559–60*

*Aberdeenshire etc.*
James Crichton of Frendraught
Alexander Fraser, Lord Saltoun
Alexander Fraser of Phillorth
George Gordon, Earl of Huntly
George, Lord Gordon
Alexander Gordon of Abergeldie
John Gordon of Findlater
William Leslie of Balquhan
William Leslie, younger, of Wardis
Alexander Menzies of that ilk
George Ogilvy of Banff
John Strachan of Thornton

*Angus and Mearns etc.*
Robert Arbuthnot of that ilk
Sir Robert Carnegie of Kinnaird
John Erskine of Dun
Thomas Fotheringham of Powrie
Robert Graham of Morphie and his son
Patrick, Lord Gray
James Haliburton, tutor of Pitcur
George Haliburton of Pitcur
Walter Lundie of that ilk and his son
James, Lord Ogilvy of Airlie
James Ogilvy of Clova
Patrick Ogilvy of Inchmartin
John Ogilvy of Inverarity
David Ogilvy of that ilk
Andrew Straiton of Lauriston
Sir John Wishart of Pittarro
William Wood of Bonnington

*Fife and Kinross*
David Balfour of that ilk
Henry Balnaves of Halhill
William Douglas of Lochleven
John Kinnear of that ilk
Sir Patrick Learmonth of Dairsie
John, Lord Lindsay
Patrick, Master of Lindsay
John Melville of Carnbee
Sir Robert Melville of Murdocairnie
William Myreton of Cammo
Andrew Leslie, Earl of Rothes
James Sandilands of Cruvy
Robert Stewart of Rosyth

Henry Wardlaw of Torry
Thomas Scott of Abbotshall

*West Lothian*
James Dundas of that ilk
Robert Hamilton of Briggis
James Hamilton of Kincavill
Archibald Hamilton of Letham
William, Lord Livingston
Sir James Sandilands of Calder and his son

*Midlothian*
Sir John Cranston of that ilk
James Douglas, Earl of Morton
Robert Logan of Restalrig
William Sinclair of Roslin and his son
John Somerville of Drum
George Touris of Inverleith

*East Lothian*
George Broun of Colstoun
John Cockburn of Ormiston
Archibald Douglas of Kilspindie
William Douglas of Whittinghame
David Hamilton of Fingaltoun
Alexander Hamilton of Innerwick
Patrick Hepburn of Waughton
James Heriot of Trabroun
George Home of Spott
Andrew Johnstone of Elphinstone
William Lauder of Haltoun
David Ramsay of Broxmouth
Gilbert Wauchope of Niddrie-Marischal

*Eastern Borders*
William Douglas of Bonjedburgh
William Douglas of Drumlanrig
William, Lord Hay of Yester
Alexander, Lord Home
John Home of Cowdenknowes
Patrick Home of Polwarth
David Home of Wedderburn
Sir Walter Kerr of Cessford
Robert Kerr of Kersland
Andrew Kerr of Fawdonside
George Kerr of Linton
Sir John Kerr of Fernihirst
John Rutherford of Hunthill
Alexander Rutherford of that ilk
Thomas Scott of Haning

John and James Swinton of that ilk
James Tweedie of Drummelzier

*Ayrshire and Renfrewshire*
John Boswell of Auchinleck
William Campbell of Cessnock
Robert Campbell of Craigdow
William Campbell of Horsecleuch
Robert Campbell of Kinyeancleuch
James Campbell of Lochlee
Hugh Campbell of Loudoun
William Campbell of Skeldon
Alan, Lord Cathcart
John Cathcart of Gibsyard
James Chalmers of Gadgirth
Robert Chalmers of Martnaham
George Corrie of Kelwood
David Crawford of Kerse
George Crawford of Lefnoris
John Crawford of Walstoun
Alexander Cunningham, Earl of Glencairn
Robert Cunningham of Auchenharvie
John Cunningham of Caprington
William Cunningham of Carington
William Cunningham of Cunninghamhead
John Cunningham of Drumquhassill
John Cunningham of Glengarnock
Hugh Cunningham of Waterstoun
James Dalrymple of Stair
Sir Alexander Dunbar of Cumnock
Patrick Houston of that ilk
Thomas Kennedy of Bargany
Hugh Kennedy of Girvanmains
William Kennedy of Ternganoch
Patrick Montgomery of Giffen
Hugh Montgomery of Hesilheid
Neil Montgomery of Lainshaw
John Mure of Rowallan
Hugh Wallace of Carnale
John Wallace of Craigie

*Lanarkshire*
William Baillie of Lamington
John Carmichael of that ilk
John Carmichael of Meadowflat
John Hamilton of Broomhill
Sir James Hamilton of Crawfordjohn
Robert Hamilton of Garyn
Sir Andrew Hamilton of Goslinton

Sir William Hamilton of Sanquhar
John Lindsay of Covington
Robert Lindsay of Dunrod
John Lockhart of Bar
James Lockhart of Cleghorn
James, Lord Somerville
John Somerville of Cambusnethan
Thomas and George Weir of Blackwood
Gavin Hamilton of Roploch

*The South-West*
Robert, Lord Crichton of Sanquhar
Sir John Gordon of Lochinvar
John Jardane of Applegarth
John Johnstone of that ilk
Robert, Lord Maxwell
John Maxwell, Lord Herries
Robert Maxwell of Calderwood
Sir John Maxwell of Terregles
Sir Alexander Stewart of Garlies

*Perthshire*
Thomas Blair of Balthiok
Colin Campbell of Glenorchy
John Crichton of Ruthvens
John Graham, Earl of Menteith
William Murray of Tullibardine
Andrew Murray of Balvaird
George Ramsay of Bamff
Patrick, Lord Ruthven
John Stewart, Lord Innermeath
Sir James Stewart of Doune
John Stewart of Grandtully
James Stirling of Keir

*North and West*
John Grant of Freuchie
John MacLeod of Assynt
Robert Munro of Foulis
Alexander Sutherland of Duffus

*The names of certain peers, significant for either territorial or familial reasons, are inserted.

## Appendix E. The Hamilton and Dumbarton Bonds

| The Hamilton Bond, 8 May 1568* | The Dumbarton Bond, 12 September 1568† |
|---|---|
| *Earls* | |
| Argyll | Argyll |
| Crawford | Crawford |
| Cassillis | Cassillis |
| Eglinton | Eglinton |
| Huntly | Huntly |
| Rothes | Rothes |
| Montrose | |
| Sutherland | |
| Erroll | Erroll |
| | |
| *Lords* | |
| Herries | Herries |
| Fleming | Fleming |
| Boyd | Boyd |
| Seton | Seton |
| Ross of Halkheid | |
| Borthwick | |
| Maxwell | Maxwell |
| Livingston | Livingston |
| Somerville | Somerville |
| Ogilvy | Ogilvie |
| Oliphant | Oliphant |
| Sanquhar | Sanquhar |
| Hay of Yester | Hay of Yester |
| Drummond | Drummond |
| Elphinstone | |
| Carlisle | |
| Sinclair | |
| | |
| *Bishops* | |
| Ross | Ross |
| Dunkeld | Dunkeld |
| Moray | |
| Galloway | Galloway |
| Aberdeen | Aberdeen |
| St Andrews | St Andrews |
| Brechin | Brechin |
| The Isles | The Isles |
| Argyll | Argyll |
| | |
| *Commendators* | |
| Arbroath | |
| Paisley | |
| Inchcolm | Inchcolm |
| Lindores | Lindores |

| | |
|---|---|
| Glenluce | Glenluce |
| Holywood | Holywood |
| New Abbey | New Abbey |
| Dundrennan | |
| Soulseat | |
| Crosraguel | |
| Inchaffray | |
| Kelso | |
| Pluscardin | |
| Ardchattan | |
| | Jedburgh |
| | Kinloss |
| | Fearn |
| | Kilwinning |

\* Keith, ii, 807–10.
† Goodall, ii, nos. cxxxvii–cxxxix.

# GENEALOGICAL TABLES

# HAMILTON AND LENNOX

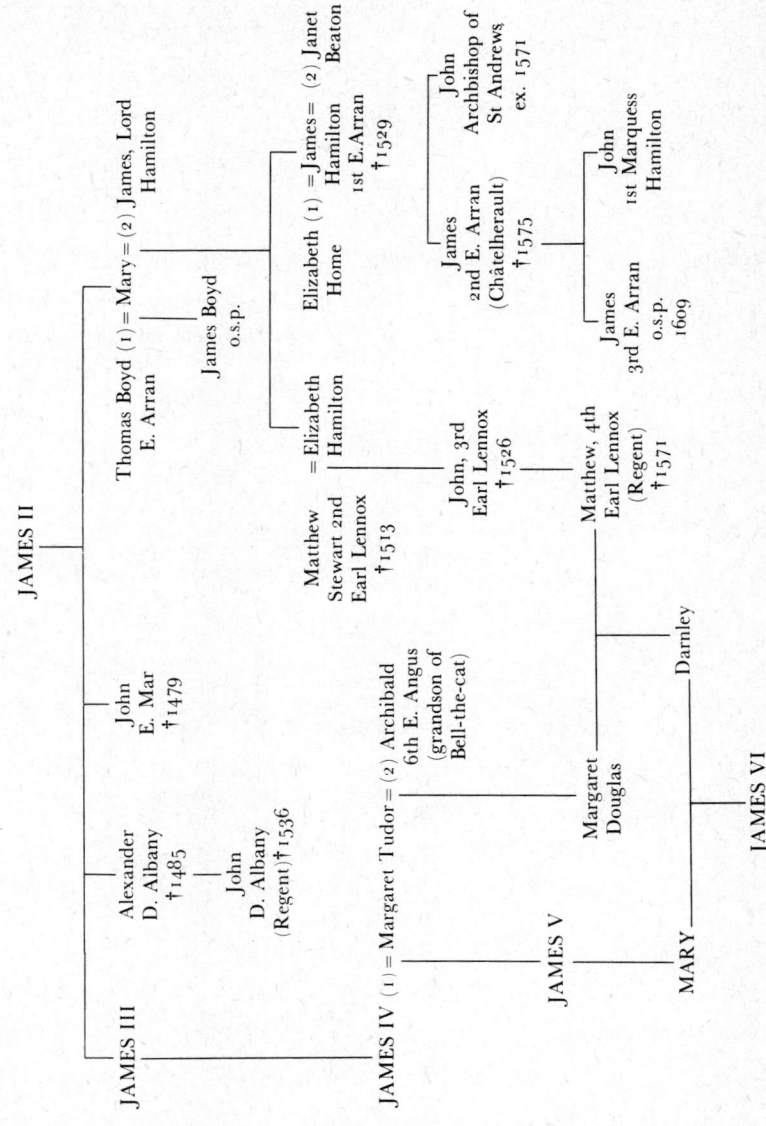

*Genealogical Tables*

# THE QUEEN'S MA[RIES]

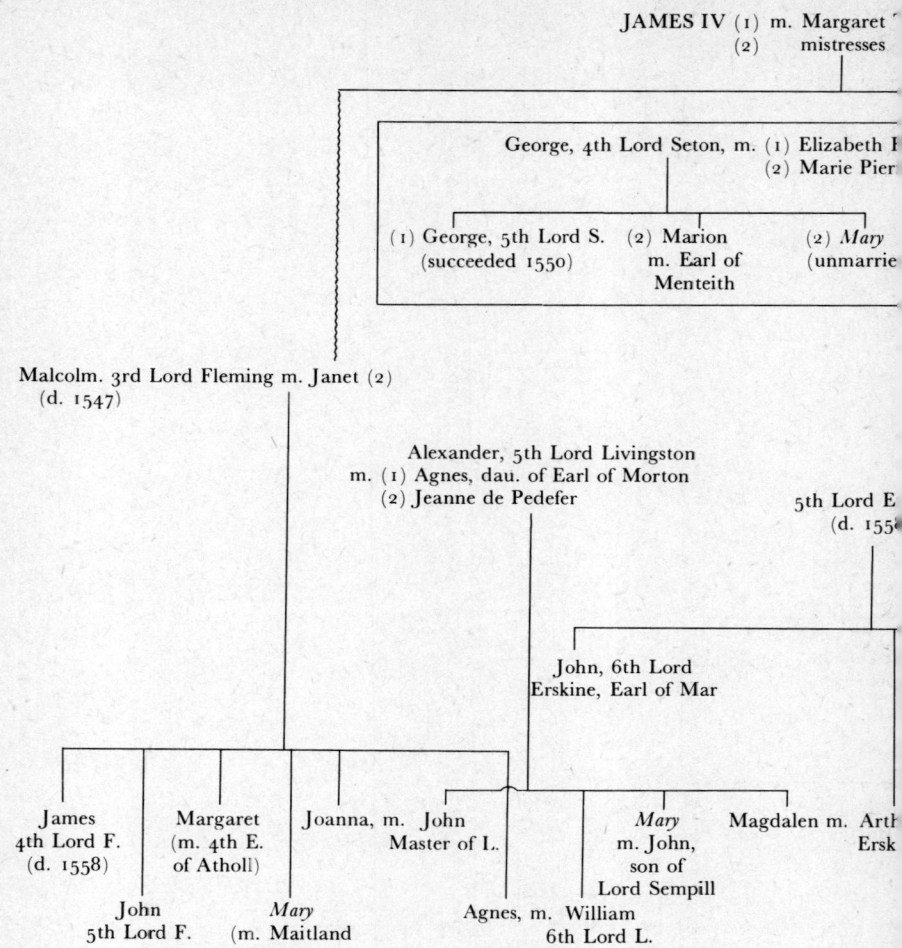

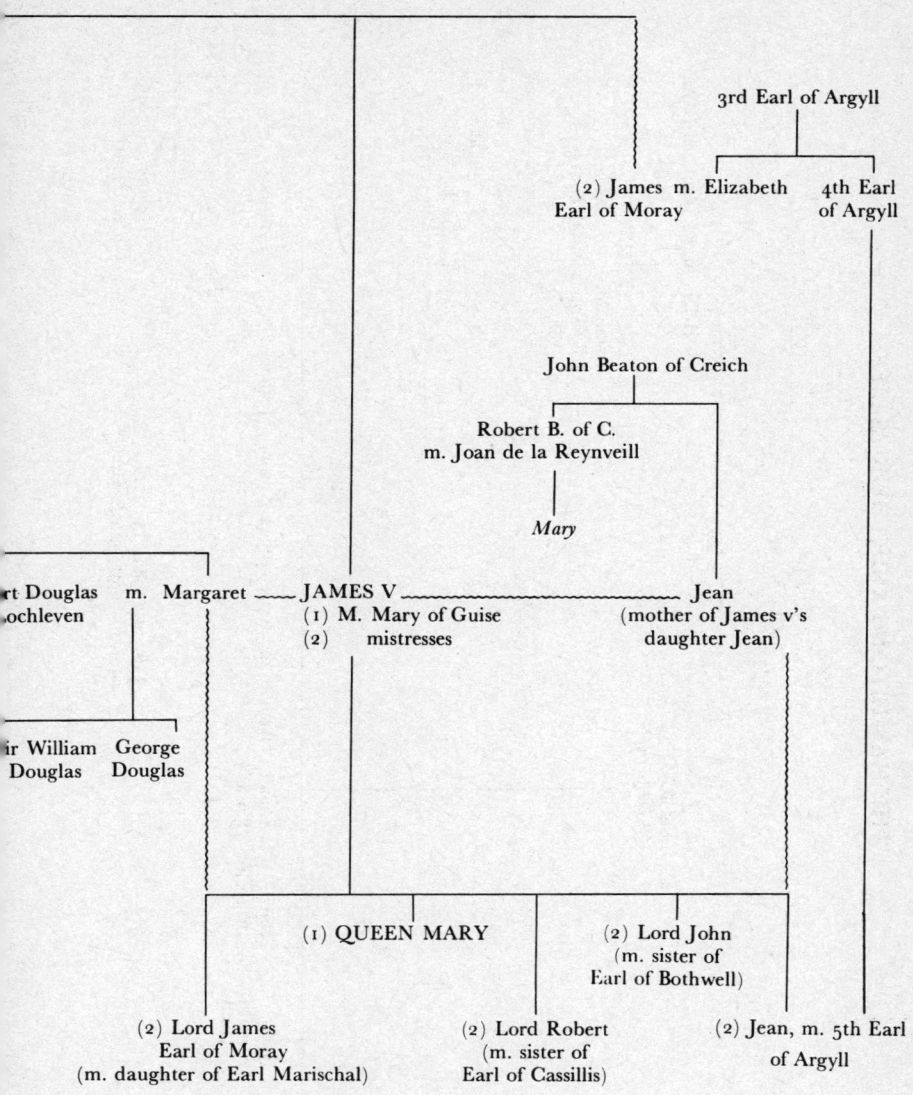

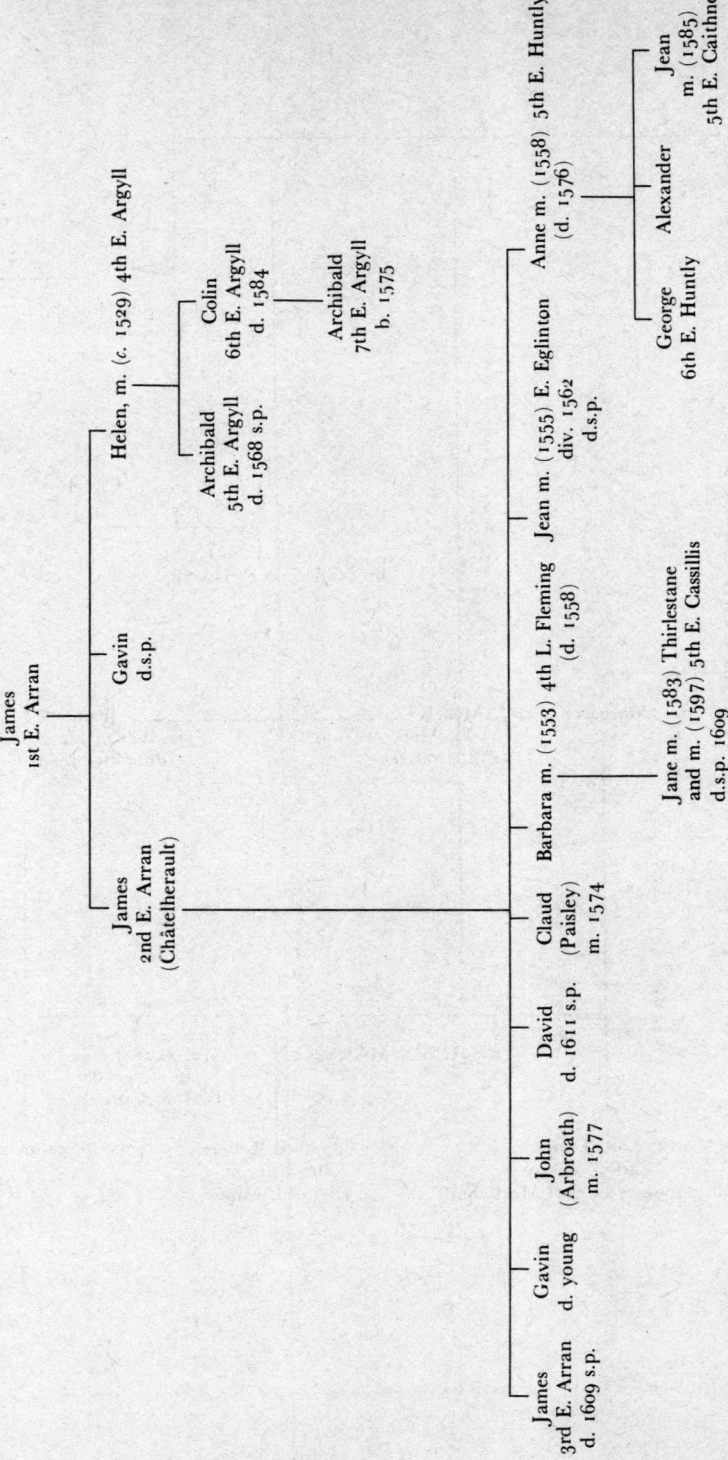

*Genealogical Tables*

# JAMES VI AND THE LENNOX FAMILY

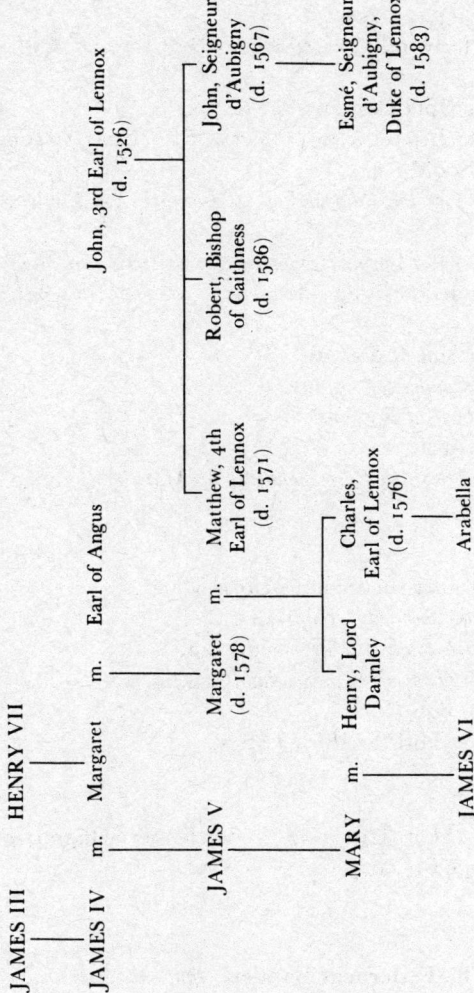

173

# NOTES

## Abbreviations:-

*APS*  Acts of the Parliaments of Scotland
Bannatyne  Richard Bannatyne, *Memorials of transactions in Scotland* (Bannatyne Club)
*CSP*  Calendar of State Papers relating to Scotland and Mary, Queen of Scots
*CSP For*  Calendar of State Papers, Foreign
Calderwood  David Calderwood, *The History of the Church of Scotland* (Wodrow Soc.)
HMC  Historical Manuscripts Commission Report
Keith  Robert Keith, *The History of the Affairs of Church and State in Scotland* (Spottiswoode Soc.)
Knox  John Knox, *History of the Reformation in Scotland* (ed. Dickinson, 1949)
*L and P*  Letters and Papers, Foreign and Domestic, of the Reign of Henry VIII
Melville, *Memoirs*  Sir James Melville, *Memoirs of his own life* (Bannatyne Club)
*RMS*  Register of the Great Seal of Scotland
*RPC*  Register of the Privy Council of Scotland
*RSS*  Register of the Privy Seal of Scotland
*SHR*  Scottish Historical Review
Scottish Correspondence  *The Scottish Correspondence of Mary of Lorraine* (Scottish History Society)

## Chapter 1

1 Appendix A, 'The Stewart succession before Mary'.
2 Annie I. Dunlop, *James Kennedy* (1950), 157.
3 Sir Ian Hamilton, *When I was a Boy* (1939), 22.
4 P. Hume Brown, *Early Travellers in Scotland* (1891), 128.
5 *L and P*, xii, pt. ii, No. 696 (i).
6 Appendix B, 'Surnames and territorial titles'.
7 Calderwood, viii, 248.
8 *RSS*, v, 2523.
9 *Chronicles of the Frasers* (Scot. Hist. Soc.), 206; Robert Chambers, *Domestic Annals* (1858–61), i, 70.
10 *RSS*, viii, 965.

## Chapter 2

1 David McRoberts, 'The Fetternear Banner', *Innes Review*, vii, 69–86.
2 Knox, i, 8–9.
3 Ibid., ii, 220–9.
4 The main sources are *RSS*, ii and iii and Robert Pitcairn (ed.), *Ancient Criminal Trials in Scotland* (Bannatyne and Maitland Clubs).
5 *APS*, ii, 342.
6 Ibid., 370–1.
7 *Gude and Godlie Ballatis*, ed. David Laing (1868) and ed. A.F. Mitchell (Scot. Text Soc.).

8 *L and P*, iv, pt. ii, 2903.
9 *Register of the Kirk Session of St Andrews* (Scot. Hist. Soc.), i, 96–7.
10 By Professor Philip McNair, author of *Peter Martyr in Italy*.
11 Melville, *Memoirs*, 60; Knox, i, 33–4, 42; Sir Ralph Sadler, *State Papers* (ed. Arthur Clifford, 1809), i, 47.
12 Melville, *Memoirs*, 67.
13 Quoted Annie I. Dunlop, *James Kennedy* (1950), 155.
14 *L and P*, xviii, pt. i, 324.
15 G. Donaldson, *Scotland: James V to James VII* (1965), 64.
16 Ibid., 65.
17 Cf. Appendix A.
18 *APS*, ii, 431–2, 443.
19 *RMS*, iv, 763; *St Andrews Formulare* (Stair Soc.), ii, No. 464; Register House Bulls, 65a.
20 *Scottish Correspondence*, 133.
21 *L and P*, xviii, pt. i, 974.
22 *Wodrow Soc. Miscellany*, i, 54.
23 *RPC*, i, 28–9.
24 Ibid., 61, 63, 65.
25 *Scottish Correspondence*, 188.
26 The best account of this episode is by Marcus Merriman, 'The Assured Scots', *SHR*, xlvii, 10–34.
27 *CSP*, i, 26.
28 Ibid., 71, 107.
29 Ibid., pp. 141–5.
30 *Scottish Correspondence*, 241.
31 Appendix C.
32 There is an example, damaged, in Morton Papers (GD 150), 332 (a), and a cast, not perfect, in the Laing Collection – both in H.M. General Register House. His Grace the Duke of Hamilton has the original matrix at Lennoxlove.
33 *RPC*, i, 89–90.
34 *APS*, ii, 485, 488–9.
35 Knox, i, 136–8.
36 *APS*, ii, 499–300.
37 Alexandre Teulet, *Relations politiques de la France et de l'Espangne avec l'Ecosse* (Paris, 1862), i, 319.
38 *CSP*, i, 457.
39 Ibid., ii, 54; Peter Lorimer, *John Knox and the Church of England* (1875), 298–300.

**Chapter 3**
1 *CSP*, i, 416.
2 *Scottish Correspondence*, 427.
3 Knox, i, 216, 224.
4 Ibid., 174.
5 *Scottish Correspondence*, 429.

6 *CSP*, i, 493.
7 Ibid., 821.
8 Knox, i, 314–15.
9 *Aberdeen Burgh Records*, i, 322.
10 Teulet, *op. cit.*, i, 325; cf. note 38 to Chapter 2.
11 Knox, i, 344–5, ii, 324.
12 *APS*, ii, 605; Keith, ii, 6–7n.; *CSP*, i, 885.
13 Calderwood, ii, 44–5.
14 Knox, ii, 55–6.
15 *CSP*, i, p. 609.
16 Ibid., 647, 690, 734, 736, 743–5, 747, 756.
17 Ibid., 455.
18 Ibid., 886.
19 *RMS* iii, 3029.
20 The list in Appendix C gives the names of the lairds.
21 *CSP*, i, 770.
22 Appendix C.
23 Knox, i, 338.
24 *CSP*, i, 886.
25 Keith, iii, 4.
26 Donaldson, *Scottish Reformation*, 57–8.
27 Knox, i, 339; *CSP*, i, 886.
28 *CSP*, i, p. 471.
29 Ibid., ii, p. 4.
30 Ibid., i, 838.
31 Ibid, 934.
32 Ibid., 983.
33 Ibid., 1023.
34 *The Buik of the Kirk of the Canagait* (Scot. Record Soc.), 38.

**Chapter 4**
1 *CSP*, iii, 142. There seems to be no contemporary evidence for the 'bogle'.
2 Keith, iii, 211; cf. *CSP*, i, 1004.
3 *CSP*, i, *1005*.
4 Ibid., 933, 949, 956.
5 Ibid., 603; cf. Donaldson, *Scottish Reformation*, 139.
6 *CSP*, ii, 163, 176.
7 Ibid., 757.
8 HMC, *Salisbury MSS*, i, 400. In Scotland then, as still in Scandinavia, a 'Psalm Book' was a book containing the services as well as the psalms.
9 *CSP*, ii, 821.
10 Ibid., 1070.
11 Ibid., 755.
12 *RPC*, i, 252.
13 *APS*, ii, 535.
14 *CSP*, ii, p. 35.

15 Knox, ii, 12.
16 *CSP*, ii, 67.
17 Ibid., i, 1035.
18 Melville, *Memoirs*, 150.
19 Keith, ii, 737.
20 Knox, ii, 86.
21 *CSP*, i, p. 622.
22 Ibid., ii, 93.
23 Knox, i, 174.
24 *RSS*, v, 1953, 1976.
25 *CSP*, ii, p. 2.
26 Ibid., 142.
27 *Inventaires de la royne descosse* (Bannatyne and Maitland Clubs).
28 Melville, *Memoirs*, 169.
29 Knox, ii, 82–3, 98.
30 Ibid., 147.
31 *CSP*, i, 886.
32 Ibid., ii, p. 138.
33 *CSP For, 1560–61*, 394.
34 *CSP*, ii, 142.
35 *RSS*, vii, 1882.
36 The indexes to *RSS* show these Murrays.
37 *CSP*, ii, 686.
38 Teulet, op. cit., ii, 268–81.
39 Knox, ii, 167.
40 *CSP*, ii, 987, 1194.
41 *RSS*, viii, 420.
42 Ibid., v, 2479.
43 *Maitland Club Miscellany*, i, pt. i.
44 *CSP*, ii, 1176.
45 HMC, *Salisbury MSS*, i, 400.
46 *CSP*, i, p. 619.

**Chapter 5**
1 *CSP*, ii, pp. 77, 85.
2 T.F. Henderson, *Mary, Queen of Scots* (1905), ii, 657; Teulet, op. cit., ii, 259; *CSP*, ii, 319, 335.
3 Keith, ii, 271–2.
4 *CSP*, ii, 141.
5 Ibid., 243.
6 Ibid., 316.
7 Ibid., p. 35.
8 *RSS*, v, 2523.
9 *RPC*, i, 363, 367, 378.
10 *CSP*, ii, 192.
11 *RPC*, i, 277; *CSP*, ii, 1197.
12 Keith, ii, 412–13.
13 *CSP*, ii, 274; Knox, i, 93, 97.

14 *CSP*, ii, 264.
15 Ibid., pp. 260–1.
16 Ibid., 319.
17 Ibid., 335.
18 The main evidence is the remissions in *RSS*, v, 3149 et seq.; cf. Michael Lynch, *Edinburgh and the Reformation*, 116.
19 *CSP*, ii, 400.
20 Ibid., 502.

**Chapter 6**
1 Keith, ii, 579–80.
2 Ibid., 582.
3 Ibid., 581–2.
4 *RPC*, i, 509–11.
5 *CSP*, ii, 582, 740.
6 Ibid., 740.
7 Ibid., 523.
8 Ibid., pp. 351, 356, 359.
9 Ibid., 536, 548, p. 376.
10 Hay Fleming, *Mary, Queen of Scots* (1898), 467; *RPC*, i, 537, 548.
11 Melville, *Memoirs*, 202, 257.
12 *CSP*, ii, 591.
13 Ibid., 618.
14 Ibid., 619.
15 E.g., Sir William Fraser, *Memoirs of the Maxwells of Pollok* (1863), ii, 1–2.
16 Melville, *Memoirs*, 200.
17 *CSP*, iii, 53.
18 *CSP*, ii, 836, 937.
19 *RPC*, i, 663; *CSP*, ii, 1075.
20 Donaldson, *First Trial of Mary, Queen of Scots*, 139.
21 Keith, ii, 807–10; *CSP*, ii, 650; Appendix D. In *CSP*, ii, 653, 655, there are some particulars of the Queen's army at Langside and the names of casualties.
22 Walter Goodall, *An examination of the letters said to have been written by Mary, Queen of Scots, to James, Earl of Bothwell* (1754), ii, Nos. cxxxvii–cxxxix; Appendix D.
23 *CSP*, ii, 744.
24 Ibid., iii, p. 54.
25 Ibid., ii, 588.
26 Ibid., i, 1010.
27 *Scots Peerage*, ii, 471.
28 *CSP*, ii, p. 555.
29 *CSP*, ii, 873.
30 *Historie of the Kennedyis* (ed. Robert Pitcairn, 1830), 25.
31 Knox, ii, 37–8.
32 *RSS*, vi, 681, 981, vii, 1062.
33 *APS*, iii, 112–14.

34 *RSS.*, viii, 1136.
35 Bannatyne, 314.
36 Ibid., 218–21; Michael Lynch, op. cit., 202.
37 E.g., John Campbell, provost of Kilmun and dean of Moray; Donald Fraser, archdeacon of Ross; and James Thornton, a notorious careerist who held a selection of choice benefices scattered from Ross to the Borders.
38 *Letter Book of John Parkhurst, Bishop of Norwich* (Norfolk Record Society), 62.
39 Calderwood, ii, 483. Calderwood thought the style of the letter to be that of Knox rather than the mild-tempered Spottiswoode.
40 Quoted J.E. Neale, *Elizabeth I and her Parliaments, 1559–81*, 270.

## Chapter 7

1 Bannatyne, 126–7. This *apologia* is echoed in a 'proclamation' obviously drafted by Maitland (*CSP*, iii, 181).
2 *CSP*, iii, 302.
3 Ibid., iii, 404; Scottish Record Office, GD 298/100/17 (to which Dr Athol Murray drew my attention and which he printed in 'Huntly's rebellion and the administration of justice in north-east Scotland, 1570–73,' in *Northern Scotland* (1981), 1–6).
4 *CSP*, iii, 190.
5 Cf. p. 89 ante.
6 Bannatyne, 132.
7 *CSP*, iii, 363.
8 Bannatyne, 348; *CSP*, iii, p. 438.
9 Bannatyne, 113–37.
10 *CSP*, iii, 805; Calderwood, iii, 102–3.
11 *CSP*, iii, 798.
12 Bannatyne, 125.
13 *CSP*, iii, 247.
14 Ibid., 897–8.
15 Bannatyne, 183; Calderwood, iii, 138.
16 Bannatyne, 188–90.
17 *CSP*, iii, 895.
18 Bannatyne, 197.
19 *Diurnal of Remarkable Occurrents* (Bannatyne Club), 263.
20 *RPC*, ii, 237.
21 *RSS*, vii, 1528.
22 *CSP*, v, 254.
23 Ibid., 305.
24 *CSP*, v, 254.
25 *Registrum Honoris de Morton*, i, 100.
26 Ibid., 108.
27 *CSP*, v, 363; *APS*, iii, 96; *RPC*, iii, 14–15.
28 Sir William Fraser, *The Douglas Book* (1885), iii, 269–70.
29 *APS*, iii, 125, 129–30.

## Chapter 8

1. *RPC*, iii, 312–13.
2. Ibid., 316.
3. Ibid., 323; *CSP*, v, pp. 511, 531, 534.
4. *CSP*, v, 397.
5. *APS*, iii, 227.
6. *RSS*, viii, Introduction.
7. Ibid., 323.
8. *APS*, iii, 234–5.
9. *RPC*, iii, 323.
10. Thomas Graves Law, *Collected Essays and Reviews* (1904), 229.
11. James VI, *Basilikon Doron* (Scot. Text Soc.), i, 77; Thomas McCrie, *Andrew Melville* (1899), 72.
12. Nat. Lib. Scot., Wodrow MSS, folio vol. 50, No. 47.
13. The names attached to the original bond of the Raiders (Calderwood, iii, 645–6), about 50 names of persons pardoned for their participation in the Ruthven Raid (*RSS*, viii) and the respites, remissions and forfeitures following on the Raid of Stirling (also in *RSS*, viii).
14. *RSS*, viii, 965.
15. Nat. Lib. Scot. MSS 6.1.13, fo. 42.
16. J.B. Black, *The Reign of Elizabeth*, 333–4.
17. *CSP*, vi, p. 538, cf. p. 558.
18. *RSS*, viii, 2480, 2741.
19. Pp. 19–20 above.
20. P. 27 above.
21. Pp. 74–5 above.
22. P. 99 above.
23. P. 123 above.
24. Pp. 127–8 above.
25. Pp. 101, 112, 119 above.
26. G. Donaldson, *Scotland: James V to James VII*, 367.
27. Lynch, op. cit., 133–4.

# GENERAL INDEX

Aberdeen, Aberdeenshire, 14, 27, 34, 42, 53, 110, 112, 119, 123-4
Ancrum, battle of, 20
Anglo-Scottish relations, *see* England
Angus and Mearns, 11, 14, 18, 20-21, 29, 41-2, 73, 102-3, 109-10, 119, 141
Argyll, 42
  Earls, 7, 40
Arran, earldom, 15, 134
'Association' of Mary and James in sovereignty, 119, 138, 144, 146
Atholl, Earls, 7
Ayr, Ayrshire, 18, 21, 27, 29, 39, 42, 75, 102-3, 119, 142
  Bond (1562), 36, 54, 103

'Beggars' Summons', 29
Berwick, Treaty of, 29, 33
Bible in vernacular, 13, 15, 16, 20, 23, 30
Bishops, 37, 44-5, 77, 99, 123-4, 127
Blackness Castle, 28
Book of Discipline (1561), 36, 48, 139
Borders, 42, 55, 84, 107-8, 124, 142
Brechin, 110, 120
Broughty Castle, 22, 28
Burghs,
  in Reformation, 31, 42
  in Queen's Party, 113-14, 118
Bute, 19

Calder (West Lothian), 40
Campbell families, 37, 41, 73, 100, 103
Carberry, encounter at, 81, 86
'Chaseabout Raid', 71
Collaborators with England, 22-5
Commendators, 37-8, 100-1, 124-5
Confederates (1567), 81-6
Corrichie, battle of, 53
Craibstane, action at, 112
Craigmillar Castle, 62
'Creeping Parliament', 121
Cunningham families, 18, 73, 75, 103

Dingwall, 111
Dornoch, 112
Douglas families, 2, 3, 8, 18, 41, 73, 79, 142
Doune Castle, 120
Dumbarton, 87-8, 90, 96, 120
  Bond, 90-1
Dumfriesshire, 42, 108-9
Dunbar, 28, 84

Dundee, 11, 16, 21-3, 27, 29, 110
East Lothian, 20-1, 42, 82, 84, 104-5, 120, 141
Edinburgh, 16, 27, 76, 90, 114, 119-20, 124-6, 142-3
  Siege of, 120 ff
  Treaty of, 29, 35
England, influence on Scottish Reformation, 13-14, 22, 25, 30, 48
  policy towards Scotland, 5, 28-30, 33, 35, 48, 51, 70-1, 76, 90, 116, 140, 143-5
Episcopal system, 138-9, 146
Erskine family, 37, 82, 129-30, 141, 145, 147
Eyemouth, 28

Familial structure of Scottish society, 5-7, 56
Feuds, 7, 17, 23, 32, 41-2, 55, 71, 95, 97, 107-8, 111, 128
Fife and Kinross-shire, 18, 21, 42, 73, 75, 106-7
'First Bond' of Lords of Congregation, 27
'Followings' of Scottish magnates, 5-7, 53, 72-4, 91, 102, 105, 111, 113, 125
Forbes families, 53, 111-12
Forbidden degrees of matrimony, 6, 155
France, relations with Scotland, 5, 25, 27-9, 32, 52, 126, 133, 137
French servitors of Queen Mary, 66-7

General Assembly, 36, 139
Geneva, 25, 28, 48-9
Gordon families, 37, 41, 53, 110
Guise family in France, 61

Hamilton, 87, 102
  Bond, 90-1
  family, 4, 7, 15-17, 19, 25, 33, 35, 41-2, 74, 79, 84-8, 91-2, 131, 148
  following, 74, 91
Hepburn families, 7, 79, 84, 104-5, 107-8, 141
Heresy, action against, 10-12, 17, 20, 21, 26
Highlands, 19, 21, 22, 24, 55, 112
Home families, 7, 18, 108
Huntly, Earls, 7, 37, 53, 110

## General Index

Illegitimacy and royal succession, 2, 17, 33, 55–7
Inchkeith, 28

James VI's coronation, 85
Justice, administration of, 7, 55, 119

Kennedy families, 18, 41, 103
Ker families, 107–8

Lanarkshire, 42, 102
Langside, battle of, 87–8, 93
Legitimation and royal succession, 2, 33, 156–7
Leith, 20, 29
  Bond at (April 1560), 33–4, 36–7, 103
Lennox family, 7, 17, 70, 132–3
Leslie families, 110–11
Lethington Tower, 120
Lochleven Castle, 64, 81
Lollardy, 10
'Lords of the Congregation', 27, 29, 34
Lutheran influence on Scotland, 10–11, 20, 48, 77

'Management' and patronage, 19–20, 23, 25, 27, 74–5, 88, 99, 127–8
Maries, the Four, 58–61
Marriage laws, 2, 6
Mary, Queen of Scots,
  behaviour and personality, 60, 66–8
  French friends, 61, 66–7
  kinsfolk, 56–8
  religious views and policy, 50–2, 54–5, 59, 64, 71, 76, 78, 80–1
Midlothian, 42, 104, 141
Montgomery families, 103
Moray, 42, 112
  earldom, 73
  Earls, 7

Niddrie Castle, 87, 120

Pacification of Perth, 125–6, 130–1
Paisley, 32, 102, 120
Papacy, see Rome
Parliament, see 'Creeping Parliament' and 'Reformation Parliament'
Patronage, see 'Management'
Perth and Perthshire, 16, 18, 29, 42, 79, 106

Pacification of, 125–6, 130–1
Pinkie, battle of, 22, 32, 37–8
Prayer Book, 24, 30, 51
Presbyterianism, 139–40, 146
Professional men in Queen's Party, 114–15
Protestantism, strength of, 9 ff., 15, 23, 27, 31, 34, 42–3, 50, 72–3

'Reformation parliament', 29–30, 35–6, 44
Regency, practice relating to, 16, 84–5, 91
Religious thought in Scotland, see Protestantism, Roman Catholicism
Renfrewshire, 32, 42, 102
Resistance to rulers, reasoning on, 8, 33–4, 116, 121
Riccio murder, 57–8, 78–9, 142–3
Roman Catholicism, extent of, 43–7, 54, 70, 136–7
Roman Catholic intrigues, 137–8
Rome, relations with, 26, 57, 71, 76
Ruthven Raid, 140–1

'Sacramentaries', 21
St Andrews, 21, 27–8, 39
'Servitors', 5–7
Seton House, 60, 84, 120
Solway Moss, battle of, 14, 16
Stewart families, 106, 134–6
Stirling, 105, 122
  'Raid' of, 145
Succession to throne, 1, 8, 17, 32–3, 91, Appendix A
Succession to James VI, 91–2, 132–3
Surnames in Scottish society, 6, 7, 56, 134

Tenure and society, 6–7
Thirds of benefices, 51, 76
Towie Castle, 126
Trent, Council of, 47, 51

'Wagers', 7, 113
West Lothian, 42, 104
Wigtownshire, 42

York-Westminster Conference, 89, 90

Zwinglian influence, 21, 24, 48

# INDEX OF PERSONS

ABERCROMBY, Alexander, of that ilk, 111
  Alexander, of Pitmedden, 111
  Andrew, of Pettelpie, 111
Adamson, Patrick, Archbishop of St Andrews, 146
Aikman, Matthew, 113
Albany, Dukes of, *see* Stewart, Alexander *and* John
Angus, Earls of, *see* Douglas, Archibald
Arbuthnot, James, of Lentush, 141, 147
  James, 113
  Robert, of that ilk, 20, 41, 161
Ardchattan, Commendator of, *see* Campbell, John
Argyll, Earls of, *see* Campbell, Archibald *and* Colin
Arran, Earls of, *see* Hamilton, James *and* Stewart, James
Atholl, Earls of, *see* Stewart, John
Auchinleck, George, of Balmanno, 141

BAILLIE, Alexander, of Litilgill, 125, 131
  Thomas, of Ardneily, 53
  William, of Lamington, 75, 102, 125, 163
Bairdy, Peter, 'wager', 113
Balfour, David, of that ilk, 18, 161
  Gilbert, of Westray, 106
  Michael, of Burleigh, 81
  Sir James, of Pittendreich, 77, 80, 82, 88, 106, 115, 118–21, 126, 131
  Robert, 131
Balmanno, Henry, in Auchtertool, 107
Balmerino, Commendator of, *see* Hay, John
Balnaves, Henry, of Halhill, 39, 115, 161
Bannatyne, John, of Corehous, 102
  Ninian, of Kames, 19
Bannerman, —, of Wattertoun, 111
Barclay, David, of Cullerny, 111
  David, of Ladyland, 103
  George, of that ilk, 53, 111, 125
  George, of Mathers, 111
  William, of Peirstoun, 103
  William, of Towy, 111
Bassandyne, Thomas, 114
Beaton, David, Archbishop of St Andrews and Cardinal, 16–21, 39–40, 73, 93, 95, 111
  David, of Creich, 106
  James, Archbishop of Glasgow, 44, 99, 116
  John, of Creich, 108
  Mary, 59–60, 66
  Robert, of Creich, 59–60
  Robert, of Westerhall, 106
Bellenden, Sir John, of Auchnoule, Justice-Clerk, 79, 86, 118
  Patrick, of Stennes, 112
Bissett, Patrick, of Lessindrum, 53
Blacader, John, of Tulliallan, 106
Blackie, Robert, in the mill of Heriot, 104
Blair, Thomas, of Balthiok, 109, 164
Borthwick, John, 6th Lord, 43–5, 74
  Sir John, 13
  John, of Raschaw, 104
  Michael, of Craigengelt, 104
  Thomas, of Castellaw, 104
  William, 7th Lord, 82, 84–5, 88, 97, 104, 119, 124
  William, of Wattterstoun, 104
Boswell, John, of Auchinleck, 75, 103, 163
Bothwell, Earls of, *see* Hepburn, James *and* Stewart, Francis
  Adam, Bishop of Orkney, 37, 83, 85–6, 99–100, 115, 118, 123–4, 129–30, 138, 146
Boyd, James, Archbishop of Glasgow, 128
  James, collector depute, 128
  Robert, 5th Lord, 73, 78, 82–7, 96–7, 103, 115, 118–25, 128, 130–1, 141–2
Boyle, Archibald, son of B. of Kelburn, 103
Brechin, Bishop of, *see* Campbell, Alexander
Brody, Alexander, of that ilk, 53
Broun, George, of Colstoun, 23, 40, 105, 141, 162
Brown, Gilbert, Commendator of New Abbey, 101, 121, 137
  John, of Carsluith, 109
  John, in Land, 109
Bruce, Alexander, of Airth, 59, 106
  Archibald, of Powfoulis, 141
  Captain James, 113
  Robert, of Clackmannan, 106
Buchan, Earl of, *see* Douglas, Robert
Buchanan, George, 65, 115
  John, of that ilk, 59

CAIRNCROSS, James, of Allaneschaw, 102
Robert, of Colmslie, 113
Caithness, Earl of, *see* Sinclair, George
Cambuskenneth, Commendator of, *see* Erskine, Adam
Cameron, Gilbert, in Birkinshaw, 102
Camerons of Lochiel, 19, 55
Campbell, Alexander, Bishop of Brechin, 99, 118
Archibald, 4th Earl of Argyll, 20, 25, 27, 40, 92, 118
Archibald, 5th Earl of Argyll, 27, 31-2, 37, 40-1, 50, 58, 71, 73-4, 78, 80, 81, 85-8, 90, 92-5, 106, 115, 120, 122-5, 127-8, 131
Colin, 6th Earl of Argyll, 128-30, 133, 135-7, 143-4
Colin, of Glenorchy, 41, 164
Donald, Commendator of Coupar, 37
Hugh, of Loudoun, 39, 75, 103, 163
James, of Ardkinglas, 112
James, of Lochlee, 163
John, Bishop elect of the Isles and Commendator of Ardchattan, 37, 45, 100
Robert, of Craigdow, 163
Robert, of Kinyeancleuch, 40, 103, 163
Thomas, Commendator of Holywood, 100, 121
William, of Cessnock, 163
William, of Horsecleuch, 163
William, of Skeldon, 163
Cant, Thomas, of St Giles Grange, 104
Carkettle, John, of Fingland, 105
John, of Markle, 105
Carlyle, Michael, 4th Lord, 85, 98, 123
Carmichael, John, of that ilk, 79, 102, 127, 134, 147, 163
John, younger, of that ilk, 102
John, of Meadowflat, 40, 79, 163
Carnegy, Sir Robert, of Kinnaird, 18, 40, 75, 110, 161
Carswell, John, Bishop of the Isles, 99, 100, 118
Cassillis, Earls of, *see* Kennedy, Gilbert *and* John
Cathcart, Alan, 4th Lord, 37, 74, 85, 88, 102, 118-19, 123, 129-31, 134, 163
Alan, of Drumsowane, 102
John, of Gibsyard, 163
Chalmers, David, of Ormond, 80

James, of Gadgirth, 40, 163
Robert, of Martnaham, 163
Charteris, John, of Kinfauns, 18
Châtelherault, Duke of *see* Hamilton, James
Cheyne, Gilbert, of Cruvie, 111
Mr John, of Fortre, 111
John, apparent of Straloch, 111
Patrick, of Essilmont, 111
William, of Arnage, 111
William, of Straloch, 53
Chisholm, John, captain of artillery, 113
William, Bishop of Dunblane, 44-5, 76, 83
Clanranald, Captain of, 19
Clerk, William, in Coustoun, 107
Cochrane, Alexander, 160
John, of that ilk, 102
Cockburn, James, of Langton, 46, 84, 105
James, of Skirling, 108
John, of Clerkington, 18, 141
John, of Ormiston, 21, 24-5, 27, 40, 79, 84, 141, 162
Mr Patrick, parson of Pitcox, 160
Cockie, James, and his son, 125, 136
Coldingham, Commendators of, *see* Home, Alexander, *and* Maitland, John
Colville, Alexander, Commendator of Culross, 82, 101, 118, 131
Sir James, of Easter Wemyss, 86
John, of Easter Wemyss, 141
Robert, of Cleish, 18, 160
Congiltoun, Patrick, of that ilk, 105
Corrie, George, of Kelwood, 163
Coupar, Commendators of, *see* Campbell, Donald *and* Leslie, Leonard
Coutts, Alan, of —, 113
Captain Alexander, 113
Captain John, 113
Craig, John, minister, 121
Craigingelt, John, of that ilk, 86
Cranston, Cuthbert, of Thirlestane Mains, 108
Sir John, of that ilk, 162
John, of Moriston, 108, 130
Crawford, Earls of, *see* Lindsay, David
David, of Kerse, 163
Hugh, of Kilbirny, 113
George, of Lefnoris, 39, 163
John, of Walston, 163
Crichton, Alexander, of Drylaw, 131
Alexander, brother of Brunstane, 79
Edward, 7th Lord C. of Sanquhar,

## Index of Persons

74, 82, 85, 98, 108, 126
James, of Frendraught, 161
John, of Brunstane, 21, 25, 27, 79
John, of Ruthvens, 164
Robert, 6th Lord C. of Sanquhar, 98, 164
Robert, Bishop of Dunkeld, 44–5, 99, 121–2, 125, 127, 146
Robert, of Eliok, Queen's Advocate, 115
William, 5th Lord C. of Sanquhar, 59
Crosraguel, Commendator of, *see* Kennedy, Quentin
Culross, Commendator of, *see* Colville, Alexander
Cunningham, Alexander, 5th Earl of Glencairn, 25, 27, 29, 32, 37–8, 41, 50, 73–4, 78, 80–1, 85, 88, 93, 103, 118–19, 122, 124, 131, 163
Hugh, of Watterstoun, 163
Captain James, 113
John, of Caprington, 39, 75, 103, 163
John, of Drumquhassill, 79, 102, 123, 125, 128, 142, 163
John, of Glengarnock, 75, 163
Robert, of Auchenharvie, 163
William, 4th Earl of Glencairn, 11, 17–18, 23
William, 6th Earl of Glencairn, 130, 135, 138, 140–2, 147
William, of Carington, 163
William, of Craigans, 75
William, of Cunninghamhead, 73, 75, 79, 103, 163

DALRYMPLE, James, of Stair, 18, 39, 73, 163
Dalyell, Robert, of that ilk, 102, 113
Danellourt, Sebastian, 66, 77
Darnley, Lord, *see* Stewart, Henry
Dawling, Thomas, 113
Deer, Commendator of, *see* Keith, Robert
Douglas, Archibald, 6th Earl of Angus, 13, 16–18, 25
Archibald, 8th Earl of Angus, 38, 81–2, 122, 124, 127–30, 134, 140–1, 145, 147–8
Archibald, of Kilspindie, 162
Archibald, parson of Douglas, 73
George, Bishop of Moray, 123, 125, 129
Sir George, of Pittendreich, 18, 33
George, of Parkhead, 127, 134, 136, 147

George, brother of laird of Lochleven, 64, 69, 87, 107
Henry, younger, of Drumgarland, 160
Hugh, of Borg, 18
Hugh, of Longniddry, 21, 23–4
James, 3rd Earl of Morton, 18, 38
James, 4th Earl of Morton, 27, 37–8, 41, 50, 73–4, 77–81, 85, 88, 90, 110, 116, 119–32, 134, 136, 144, 162
James, of Drumlanrig, 147
John, Archbishop of St Andrews, 123–4
John, of Pumpherston, 18
John, of Tilwhillie, 53
John, Captain of Tantallon, 127
John, parson of Newlands, 160
Malcolm, of Mains, 127
Margaret, Countess of Lennox, 17–18, 70, 132
Robert, Earl of Buchan, 82, 85, 118–19, 122, 124, 130–1, 133
Sir Robert, of Lochleven, 64
Sir William, of Lochleven, 64, 133, 161
William, of Bonjedburgh, 162
William, of Cavers, 147
William, of Drumlanrig, 18, 39, 73, 162
William, of Hawick, 73
William, of Whittinghame, 18, 162
—, of Little Sauchy, 147
Drummond, Alexander, of Conze, 53
David, 2nd Lord D., 37, 74, 82, 98, 106
James, Commendator of Inchaffray, 100
Patrick, of Monzie, 141
Robert, of Carnock, 141
Dryburgh, Commendator of, *see* Erskine, David
Dunbar, Sir Alexander, of Cumnock, 39, 103, 163
Archibald, of Pennik, 53
Dunblane, Bishops of, *see* Chisholm, William *and* Graham, Andrew
Dundas, James, of that ilk, 18, 40, 162
Dundrennan, Commendator of, *see* Maxwell, Edward
Dunfermline, Commendators of, *see* Durie, George, *and* Pitcairn, Robert
Dunkeld, Bishop of, *see* Crichton, Robert
Durham, William, of Grange, 73
Durie, George, Commendator of Dunfermline, 101

George, brother of laird of Durie, 107

ECHLENE, Henry, of Pettadro, 131
Edmonston, John, younger, of that ilk, 79
    James, of Newtoun, 141
Eglinton, Earl of, *see* Montgomery, Hugh
Elphinstone, Nicol, of Schank, 86
    Robert, 3rd Lord, 98, 123, 143
Erroll, Earls of, *see* Hay, George *and* Andrew
Erskine, Adam, Commendator of Cambuskenneth, 37, 82, 101, 129–30, 141, 145, 147
    Alexander, of Gogar, Master of Mar, son of 5th Lord E., 129–30, 145, 160
    Arthur, son of 5th Lord E., 59
    David, Commendator of Dryburgh, 37, 82, 101, 125, 130–3, 141, 145, 147
    John, 6th Lord Erskine, Earl of Mar, 37, 50, 74–5, 80–1, 85, 88, 90, 105, 119, 122
    John, 7th Lord Erskine, Earl of Mar, 129–30, 134, 141, 145, 147–8
    John, of Dun, 21, 27, 39, 41, 62–4, 75, 86, 109, 131, 161
    Margaret, Lady Lochleven, 64
    Robert, of Little Sauchy, 105
    William, Commendator of Paisley, 141, 145, 147

FAIRLIE, Robert, of Braid, 141
Fearn, Commendator of, *see* Ross, Nicholas
Fergushill, John, of that ilk, 103
Fleming, James, 4th Lord, 58
    John, 5th Lord, 45, 72, 75, 78, 80, 82–9, 92, 94–7, 102, 118, 120, 123, 126
    John, 6th Lord, 131, 133, 147–8
    John, of Boghall, 102
    Malcolm, 3rd Lord, 20, 58
    Malcolm, Commendator of Whithorn, 45
    Mary, 58–9, 66, 147
    Captain Patrick, 113
Forbes, Alexander, of Pitsligo, 111
    Arthur, of Balfour, 111
    Arthur, of Reres, 107
    Duncan, of Monymusk, 111
    John, Master of F., 111–12, 142
    John, of Aberiatrie, 111
    John, of Towie, 126
    William, 7th Lord, 37, 53, 74, 82, 111, 123–4
    William, of Keithmore, 53
    William, of Tolquhon, 53
Forrest, David and George, 24
Forrester, Sir James, of Corstorphine, 104, 125
Forret, John, of that ilk, 75, 160
Fothringham, Thomas, of Powry, 161
Foulis, James, of Colinton, 141
Francis II, King of France, 25, 29, 32, 46, 48
Francisco de Busso, Sir John, 66, 77
Fraser, Alexander, 6th Lord Saltoun, 118–19, 124, 130, 134, 160
    Alexander, of Phillorth, 39, 160
    Hugh, 5th Lord Lovat, 74, 119, 123
Fullerton, John, of Dreghorn, 73

GALLOWAY, Bishop of, *see* Gordon, Alexander,
Gibson, Alexander, servitor of Lord Ruthven, 113
Glamis, Lord and Master of, *see* Lyon
Glasgow, Archbishops of, *see* Beaton, James, *and* Boyd, James
Glen, James, of Bar, and his son, 125
Glencairn, Earls of, *see* Cunningham, Alexander *and* William
Glenluce, Commendator of, *see* Hay, Thomas
Goodman, Christopher, 72
Gordon, Adam, of Auchindoun, 111–12, 122–7
    Alexander, 11th Earl of Sutherland, 90, 94, 111, 122, 135, 138, 143
    Alexander, Bishop of Galloway, 37–8, 45, 77, 80, 83, 85, 87, 99–100, 119, 121–2, 125, 127
    Alexander, of Abergeldie, 161
    George, 4th Earl of Huntly, 18, 20, 25, 37, 41, 45–6, 50–3, 71, 78, 80–5, 160
    George, 5th Earl of Huntly, 53, 71, 73–4, 77, 80, 86–90, 92, 94, 110, 118–22, 124–5, 127, 131, 137–8, 143–4, 148, 161
    George, of Gight, 110
    George, of Lesmoir, 110
    George, 119
    James, of Creich, 110
    John, 10th Earl of Sutherland, 37, 46, 53, 60, 82–4, 94
    Sir John, of Lochinvar, 75, 85, 109, 120, 124, 127, 143, 164
    Sir John, 52–3, 69

## Index of Persons

John, of Carnburrow, 69, 110
John, of Findlater, 161
Robert, of Haddo, 110
William, of Auchindoir, 110
William, Bishop of Aberdeen, 37, 53, 99, 122
Gormson, Donald 123
Gowrie, Earl of, *see* Ruthven
Graham, Andrew, Bishop of Dunblane, 128-9
  David, of Fintray, 105
  John, 4th Earl of Menteith, 37, 60, 164
  John, 3rd Earl of Montrose, 85, 118-19, 122, 124, 128-31, 133, 135, 143-5, 147-8
  John, in Saltcoats, 105
  Robert, of Morphie, 39, 41, 161
  William, 5th Earl of Menteith, 82, 85, 88, 90, 119, 129, 130
  William, 2nd Earl of Montrose, 45, 50, 53, 72, 74, 81, 90, 94, 105
Grant, John, of Freuchie, 112, 164
Gray, Patrick, 4th Lord, 18, 20, 37, 39, 41, 44, 74, 82, 109, 119, 124, 161
  Patrick, Master of, 146-7
Guthrie, Alexander, town clerk of Edinburgh, 80

HACKET, George, Conservator in Flanders, 114
Haldane, John, of Gleneagles, 18
Haliburton, George, of Pitcur, 41, 110, 141, 161
  Mr James, provost of Dundee and tutor of Pitcur, 41, 73, 78, 86, 131, 161
Hamilton, Alexander, of Innerwick, 19, 40, 105, 162
  Sir Andrew, of Goslinton, 163
  Andrew, of Heleis, 131
  Archibald, of Lethame, 40, 131, 160, 162
  Lord Claud, 26, 37, 87-8, 100, 120-1, 125, 131, 145, 148
  David, of Fingalton, 19, 40, 162
  David, of Monkton Mains, 131
  Gavin, Commendator of Kilwinning, 84, 86, 91, 100, 115, 120-2
    Gavin, of Roploch, 131, 164
  James, 2nd Earl of Arran and Duke of Châtelherault, 15-16, 18, 20, 25-7, 33, 35-6, 40-1, 46, 50, 69, 71-3, 78, 80, 82, 86, 91, 116-18, 120-2, 125, 131

  James, 3rd Earl of Arran, 32-3, 35-6, 38, 48-9, 55, 69, 71, 91, 99, 134
  James, Bishop of Argyll, 26, 37, 45, 99
  Sir James, of Crawfordjohn, 19, 40, 75, 160, 163
  James, of Bothwellhauch or Woodhouselee, 89, 131
  James, of Kincavill, 162
  James, of Livingston, 113
  James, of Samuelston, 105
  James, of Sprouston, 108
  Lord John, 26, 37, 83-4, 86, 91, 100, 115, 120, 122-3, 125, 131, 145, 148
  John, Archbishop of St Andrews, 17, 26-7, 32, 44-5, 54, 76, 81, 83-4, 89, 91, 99, 102, 122
  John, of Broomhill, 163
  John, of Haggs, 19
  John, of Kilbowie, 113, 131
  John, of Millburn, 19
  John, of Orbiston, 19
  John, of Shawtoun, 131
  Patrick, 11
  Robert, of Briggis, 19, 40, 162
  Robert, of Dalserff, younger, 131
  Robert, of Garyn, 163
  Thomas, of Priestfield, 104
  Sir William, of Sanquhar, 75, 85, 164
  William, of Humbie, 19
  —, of Nesbit, 108
  —, of Tweedside, 108
Harlaw, James, writer, 115
Hay, Andrew, 8th Earl of Erroll, 95, 130, 134
  Mr Andrew, parson of Renfrew, 79
  George, 7th Earl of Erroll, 18, 37, 50, 53, 74, 82, 95, 124, 130-1
  John, 4th Lord Hay of Yester, 20
  John, Commendator of Balmerino, 101, 118
  John, of Tallo, 108
  Peter, of Melginch, 109
  Thomas, Commendator of Glenluce, 100
  William, 5th Lord Hay of Yester, 37, 72, 74, 84, 98, 105, 108, 122, 141-2, 162
Henderson (or Henryson), David, vicar of Rossy, 160
  James, 23
Henry VIII, 13-15, 18-19
Hepburn, Adam, of Bonhard, 141
  Adam, of Kingistoun, 104

## Index of Persons

Adam, of Smeaton, 84, 104
Alexander, Bishop of Ross, 128
Sir Alexander, of Whitsome, 105, 108, 130
Alexander, of Bolton, 104
Henry, of Fortune, 104, 131
James, 4th Earl of Bothwell, 43, 50, 55, 57, 71, 75, 77–84, 86, 104, 107–8, 131
Patrick, Bishop of Moray, 99–100, 111, 122
Sir Patrick, of Luffness, 104
Patrick, of Kirklandhill, 104, 131
Patrick, of Waughton, 40, 84, 104, 162
Patrick, of Whitecastle, 104–5, 141
Patrick, 84
Robert, of Stevenson, 104
Thomas, parson of Oldhamstocks, 83–4, 105, 114, 130
William, of Gilmerton, 84, 104
Heriot, James, of Trabroun, 23, 40, 105, 141, 162
Walter, of Ramorny, 73
Herries, Lord, *see* Maxwell, John
Hertford, Earl of, *see* Seymour, Edward
Hislop, Sir John, in Crichton, 104
Holyrood, Commendator of, *see* Stewart, Robert
Holywood, Commendator of, *see* Campbell, Thomas
Home, Alexander, 5th Lord, 37, 39, 41, 44, 46, 74–5, 82, 85, 88, 98, 108, 118–21, 125–6, 130–3, 162
Alexander, 6th Lord, 133, 137–8, 141–2, 147–8
Alexander, Commendator of Coldingham, 125
Andrew, Commendator of Jedburgh, 37, 46, 75, 100
David, of Wedderburn, 84, 162
Ferdinando, of Brumehouse, 108
George, of Spott, 73, 108, 162
Sir James, of Cowdenknowes, 148, 162
John, of Blackadder, 84
Mr John, provost of Dunglass, 108
Patrick, of Polwarth, 162
Houston, John, 102,
Patrick, of that ilk, 39, 102, 163
Robert, 102
Howard, Thomas, Duke of Norfolk, 52, 69, 116
Huntly, Earls of, *see* Gordon, George

INCHAFFRAY, Commendator of, *see* Drummond, James *and* Gordon, Alexander
Innermeath, Lord, *see* Stewart, John
Innes, James, of Drany, 112
Robert, of Innermarky, 112
Irvine, Alexander, of Drum, 53
Isles, Bishop of, *see* Campbell, John *and* Carswell, John

JAMES V, King of Scots, 13–15, 58
James VI, 80 ff.
Jardine, John, of Applegarth, 40, 75, 164
Jedburgh, Commendator of, *see* Home, Andrew
Jennet, Corporal, 113
Johnstone, Andrew, of Elphinstone, 18, 40, 162
James, of Elphinstone, 79, 141
John, Commendator of Soulseat, 100, 131
John, of that ilk, 109, 120, 164

KEITH, George, 5th Earl Marischal, 141, 144, 147–8
Robert, Commendator of Deer, 37, 74, 101, 130–1
William, 3rd Earl Marischal, 94
William, 4th Earl Marischal, 11, 18, 37–8, 41, 44–5, 50, 73–4, 77, 80, 81
William, Lord Keith, 119
Kelso, Commendator of, *see* Ker, William
Kelso, Archibald, of Kelsoland, 103, 113
Kennedy, George, of Barclannoquhan, 103
Gilbert, 3rd Earl of Cassillis, 17, 18, 27, 31, 93
Gilbert, 4th Earl of Cassillis, 41, 44–5, 72, 74–5, 78, 80, 82, 93, 102, 118–19, 122–5, 131
Gilbert, of Dalquharran, 103
Hugh, of Girvanmains, 103, 163
John, 5th Earl of Cassillis, 141
Quentin, Commendator of Crosraguel, 46
Sir Thomas, of Culzean, 103
Thomas, of Bargany, 5, 75, 103–4, 123, 163
William, of Ternganoch, 163
—, of Bennane, 103
—, of Lambie, 103
Ker(r), Sir Andrew, of Hirsell, 84
Sir Andrew, of Cessford, 46, 107
Andrew, of Fawdonside, 79, 89,

## Index of Persons

107, 162
George, of Linton, 162
Sir John, of Ferniehirst, 23, 40, 107, 162
John, of Carchesters, 107, 136
Mark, Commendator of Newbattle, 37, 75, 125, 129–31, 133, 136
Robert, of Kersland, 73, 162
Sir Thomas, of Ferniehirst, 107, 120, 124, 126, 133, 136–7, 143
Thomas, of Cavers, 107, 136
Captain Thomas, 113
Sir Walter, of Cessford, 18, 23, 40–1, 46, 75, 107, 129, 133, 148, 162
William, Commendator of Kelso, 75
William, parson of Roxburgh, 46
—, of Greenhead, 46
Kilwinning, Commendator of, see Hamilton, Gavin
Kinloss, Commendator of, see Reid, Walter
Kinnaird, Walter, of Culben, 112
Kinnear, John, of that ilk, 161
Kirkcaldy, James, brother of K. of Grange, 125
Sir William, of Grange, 27, 73, 78, 82, 86, 90, 107, 113–14, 119–23, 125, 136
Kirkpatrick, Roger, of Closeburn, 85, 109
Thomas, of Alisland, 85
William, of Kirkmichael, 85
Kneland, Arthur, of Knowbottill, 102
John, of Foscane, 102
William, of that ilk, 102
Knox, John, 24, 28–9, 39, 46, 49, 55–6, 75–6, 79, 121, 125, 134, 139

LAUDER, Captain Hugh, 113
Sir Robert, of Popill, 105, 113
Robert, of Bass, 84, 105, 113, 125
Captain Robert, 113, 130
William, of Haltoun, 79, 160, 162
Learmonth, George, of Balcomie, 73
Sir Patrick, of Dairsie, 18, 161
Leith, Patrick, of Harthill, 111
Lennox, Countess of, see Douglas, Margaret
Earls of, see Stewart, Esmé, Matthew and Robert
Leslie, Andrew, 5th Earl of Rothes, 7, 37, 40–2, 51, 73–4, 78, 80–83, 95, 110, 123, 130–31, 135, 138, 144, 161
George, 4th Earl of Rothes, 7, 11, 18, 20, 40–1

John, Bishop of Ross and Commendator of Lindores, 77, 80, 83–4, 89, 99, 115, 122
John, of Parkhill, 110
Leonard, Commendator of Coupar, 101
Patrick, Commendator of Lindores, 100
William, of Balquhan, 110, 181
William, of Wardis, younger, 161
Lindores, Commendator of, see Leslie, John and Patrick
Lindsay, David, 9th Earl of Crawford, 18, 44, 63
David, 10th Earl of Crawford, 37, 74, 77, 80–1, 83, 86–7, 93, 109, 118, 122–4, 131
David, 11th Earl of Crawford, 130–1, 138, 140, 143–4, 148
John, 5th Lord Lindsay of Byres, 7, 18, 20, 37–8, 42, 51, 161
John, of Covington, 164
John, of Evelik, 109
Patrick, 6th Lord L. of Byres, 74–5, 78–9, 82, 85, 88, 95–6, 106, 118–19, 128–31, 133–4, 138, 141–2, 161
Robert, of Dunrod, 39, 164
Livingston, Alexander, 7th Lord, 135 (as Master)
Bartholomew, 160
Mary, 59
William, 6th Lord, 37, 59, 72, 74, 78, 82–3, 86–7, 95, 104, 126, 133, 143, 162
Lockhart, Gavin, of Kirkwood, 102
Sir James, of Lee, 102
James, of Cleghorn, 102
John, of Bar, 39, 73, 102, 164
Robert, 24
Stephen, of Wicketschaw, 102
Logan, Robert, of Restalrig, 60, 162
Lovat, Lord, see Fraser, Hugh
Lundy, Walter, of that ilk, 41, 64, 73, 161
Lyon, James, of Easter Ogill, 141, 147
John, 7th Lord Glamis, 18, 20
John, 8th Lord Glamis, 74, 82–4, 88, 93, 109–10, 118–19, 123, 128–31, 141
John, apparent of Cossynis, 141, 147
Thomas, of Baldukie, Master of Glamis, 140–1, 145, 147–8

MACBRAIR, Thomas, in Dumfries, 109
MacCalyean, Thomas, of

Cliftonhall, 115, 118
MacCulloch, Adam, Marchmont herald, 115
   Gothray, of Ardwell, 142
   Thomas, of Cardoness, 85
MacDonald of Glen Nevis, 55
MacDowall, John, in Airis, 109
   Uthred, of Garthland, 109, 142
MacGill, Sir James, of Rankeillor Nether, Clerk Register, 51, 79, 82, 115, 118
Macilwrayth, Gilbert, in Trolorg, 109
Macintosh, Lachlan, of Dunnachtan, 112, 123, 125
Mackay, Y, of Far, 112
Mackenzie, Colin, of Kintail, 112
Mackeson, Robert, canon of Cambuskenneth, 105
Mackinnon of Strathordale, 19
Macleans of Coll, Ardgour, Lochbuie and Duart, 19
MacLellan, Thomas, of Bombie, 84, 109
MacLeod, John, of Assynt, 164
MacLeods of Harris and Dunvegan, 19
MacNeil of Barra, 19
   of Gigha, 20
MacQuarrie of Ulva, 19
Maitland, John, of Auchingassill, 130
   John, of Thirlestane, Commendator of Coldingham, 101, 105, 115, 118–22, 125–6, 136, 144–8
   Sir Richard, of Lethington, 105, 120
   Thomas, 122, 126
   William, of Lethington, 49–51, 58–9, 71, 79, 82, 86, 89, 94, 105, 115–16, 118–22, 125
Mar, Earls of, *see* Erskine, John
March, Earl of, *see* Stewart, Robert
Marischal, Earls, *see* Keith, George *and* William
Mary of Guise, 25, 27–9, 33–4, 49
Maule of Panmure, Robert, 18
   Thomas, 86, 109
Maxwell, Edward, Commendator of Dundrennan, 100
   John, 8th Lord M. and Earl of Morton, 98, 102, 108–9, 118, 120–21, 123–4, 127–9, 133, 135–8, 143, 160, 164
   John, 4th Lord Herries, 37, 74, 80–6, 89, 96, 108–9, 118, 120–1, 123–4, 129–30, 133, 138, 164
   Sir John, of Terregles, 77, 164
   John, of Pollock, 18, 102
   Robert, 5th Lord M., 15–17, 19, 108
   Robert, of Calderwood, 164
   William, 5th Lord Herries, 124, 131
Mayne, John, wager, 113
Meldrum, Sir George, of Fyvie, 24
Melville, Andrew, of Garvock, 106
   Captain David, of Newmill, 106, 113
   James, of Halhill, 62, 106
   Sir John, of Raith, 25, 106, 131
   John, of Carnbee, 161
   Robert, of Murdocairnie, 73, 106, 125, 127, 131, 136, 144–5, 161
   Walter, 106
Menteith, Earls of, *see* Graham, John *and* William
   John, of Kerse, 79
Menzies, Alexander, of that ilk, 161
   Thomas, of Petfoddellis, 110
Mercer, Gabriel, of Adie, 141
Methven, Lord, *see* Stewart, Henry
Mitchell, Thomas, in Edinburgh, 125
   William, of Bandeath, 141
Moffat, Captain Hugh, 113
Moncrieff, William, of that ilk, 18
Montgomery, Hugh, 3rd Earl of Eglinton, 41, 44–6, 72, 74–5, 78, 80–1, 92, 97, 102, 119, 122–4, 129–31, 135, 137–8, 141–2, 147
   Hugh, of Hesilhead, 163
   Neil, of Lainshaw, 163
   Patrick, of Giffen, 163
Montrose, Earls of, *see* Graham, John *and* William
Monypenny, David, of Petmillie, 73
   Patrick, of Pilrig, 141
Moray, Bishops of, *see* Douglas, George *and* Hepburn, Patrick
   Earls of, *see* Stewart, James
Morton, Earls of, *see* Douglas, James *and* Maxwell, John
Moscrop, Mr John, advocate, 115
Mossman, James, goldsmith, 125
Moubray, Robert, of Barnbougle, 104
Moutray, George, of Seafield, 75–6
Muirhead, James, of Lauchope, 125, 131, 148
Munro, Robert, of Foulis, 112, 125, 128, 164
Mure, John, of Rowallan, 75, 79, 103, 163
Murray, Andrew, of Balvaird, 79, 164
   Angus, chantor of Caithness, 160
   Sir Charles, of Cockpool, 109, 141
   Captain David, 113
   James, of Cobairdie, 53
   James, of Pardewis, 106, 141

Patrick, of Tibbermure, 79, 106
Thomas, of Polmais, 141
Sir William, of Tullibardine, 18, 39, 40, 76, 79, 86, 106, 118, 160, 164
William, of Touchadam, 79, 106, 141
Muschet, John, commissary clerk of Dunblane, 115
Myreton, William, of Cammo, 161

NAPIER, Sir Archibald, of Merchiston, 86, 104
New Abbey, Commendator of, *see* Brown, Gilbert
Newton, William, of that ilk, 84, 105
Norfolk, Duke of, *see* Howard, Thomas

OCHILTREE, Lord, *see* Stewart, Andrew
Ogilvy, Alexander, of Boyne, 112
David, of that ilk, 161
Sir George, of Banff and Dunlugus, 60, 161
James, 4th Lord O. of Airlie, 20, 37, 41, 161
James, 5th Lord O. of Airlie, 74, 98, 109, 119, 126–7, 129–30, 135–8
James, of Clova, 161
James, of Findlater, 20, 59, 81, 112
John, of Balgro, 110
John, of Ballinsho, 141, 147
John, of Inverarity, 141, 161
John, of Inverkeilor, 110
Patrick, of Inchmartin, 161
Oliphant, Laurence, 3rd Lord 45, 98, 110, 124
Laurence, 4th Lord, 82–4, 98, 110, 119, 124, 130, 138
Master of, 141
Orkney, Bishop of, *see* Bothwell, Adam
Orme, David, 160
Ormiston, James, of that ilk, 46, 84, 108

PITBLADO, Alexander, of that ilk, 107
Pitcairn, Robert, Commendator of Dunfermline, Secretary, 82, 85, 115, 118, 125, 133
Pittenweem, Commendator of, *see* Balfour, Sir James
Prior of, *see* Roull, John
Pluscardin, Commendator of, *see* Seton, Alexander
Preston, Sir Simon, of that ilk, 62, 76–7, 80, 83

RAIT, William, of Halgreen, 110
Ralstoun, Hugh, of that ilk, 102
Ramsay, Cuthbert, parson of Crichton, 104
David, of Broxmouth, 162
George, of Banff, 110, 164
George, of Dalhousie, 81, 104
Reid, Adam, of Barskimming, 41
Walter, Commendator of Kinloss, 100, 112, 118, 125
Riccio, David, 78
Richardson, James, of Smeaton, 141
Robert, Commendator of St Mary's Isle, Treasurer, 51, 85, 118, 125
Rig, James, of Carberry, 141
Roberton, James, of Ernock, 102
Robertson, John, in Braidwodsyd, 113
Ross, Bishops of, *see* Leslie, John, *and* Hepburn, Alexander
Alexander, of Balnagown, 112
Hucheon, of Kilravock, 112
James, 4th Lord R., 72, 74, 84, 97, 123, 133
Nicholas, Commendator of Fearn, 101
Rothes, Earls of, *see* Leslie, Andrew *and* George
Rough, John, 24
Roull, John, Prior of Pittenweem, 160
Rutherford, Alexander, of that ilk, 162
John, of Hunthill, 75, 162
Nicol, of Hundolie, 46
Richard, of Edgarstoun, 41
Ruthven, Patrick, 3rd Lord, 37, 46, 51, 63, 164
William, 4th Lord, Earl of Gowrie, 68, 72, 74–5, 77, 79–80, 82, 85, 95, 109, 113, 118–19, 122, 124, 128–30, 133, 136, 138, 140–2, 145, 148

ST ANDREWS, Archbishops of, *see* Beaton, David, Hamilton, John, Douglas, John, *and* Adamson, Patrick
St John, Lord, *see* Sandilands, James
St Mary's Isle, Commendator of, *see* Richardson, Robert
Saltoun, Lord, *see* Fraser, Alexander
Sandilands, Sir James, of Calder, 39, 40, 162
James, his grandson, 79
James, preceptor of Torphichen, otherwise Lord St John and later Lord Torphichen, 40, 49, 82, 85, 88, 124, 160, 162
James, of Cruvie, 161

James, of St Monans, 18, 107
Sanquhar, Lord, *see* Crichton, Edward, Robert *and* William
Scott, Thomas, of Abbotshall and Pitgorno, 73, 79, 162
   Thomas, of the Haining, 162
   Sir Walter, of Buccleuch, 23
   Sir Walter, his grandson, 41, 75, 108, 120
   William, of Balwearie, 107
Scrymgeour, James, of Dudhope, 141
Sempill, John, of Bultreis, 127
   John, son of Lord S., 59
   Robert, 3rd Lord, 32, 45, 59, 74–5, 80–2, 85, 88–9, 99, 118–19, 123, 131
Seton, Alexander, son of Lord S., Commendator of Pluscardin, 100, 131, 136
   David, of Parbroath, 73
   George, 4th Lord, 60
   George, 5th Lord, 43–5, 55, 60, 74, 78, 80, 82–4, 87, 95–6, 104–5, 113, 120, 123, 125–6, 130, 133, 135–8, 143
   Mary, 60, 66
Seymour, Edward, Earl of Hertford and Duke of Somerset, 19, 21, 23
Shaw, Andrew, of Sornebeg, 102
   James, of Sauchy, 102
   James, in Chalmerstoun, 103
   John, of Grymett, 102
   William, in Munnok, 102
Sinclair, George, 4th Earl of Caithness, 44, 72–4, 77–8, 80–4, 94, 118, 122, 129–30, 137, 141
   Henry, 5th Lord S., 119 (as Master), 124, 130, 134, 143
   Henry, Lord President, 51
   William, 4th Lord S., 74, 98, 107
   William, of Roslin, 104, 162
Skea, James, 24
Somerset, Duke of, *see* Seymour, Edward
Somerville, Alexander, of Tarbrax, 102
   Hugh, 4th Lord S., 17–18
   Hugh, 6th Lord S., 98, 102, 121, 123–4, 127, 129–31, 135, 138, 143
   James, 5th Lord S., 44–5, 74, 97, 102, 164
   James, younger, of Cambusnethan, 102
   James, in Humbie, 160
   John, of Cambusnethan, 79, 164
   John, of Drum, 162
Soulseat, Commendator of, *see*

Johnstone, John
Spence, David, of Wormiston, 107, 131
Spens, John, of Condie, King's Advocate, 51
Spottiswoode, Mr John, 40, 160
Stewart, Lord Adam, 56, 58
   Alexander, Duke of Albany, 2, 3
   Sir Alexander, of Garlies, 40, 75, 120, 164
   Alexander, tutor of Castlemilk, 109
   Allan, Commendator of Crosraguel, 93, 100, 125
   Andrew, 2nd Lord Ochiltree, 37, 39, 51, 56, 73, 78, 82, 85, 88, 118–19, 123, 130–1, 138
   Archibald, provost of Edinburgh, 134
   Esmé, seigneur d' Aubigny, Earl and Duke of Lennox, 130–44
   Francis, Earl of Bothwell, 57–8, 61, 136, 141, 147
   Henry, Lord Darnley, 70–2, 78, 80–1, 91
   Henry, 2nd Lord Methven, 20, 25, 73, 119, 123
   Henry, 3rd Lord Methven, 135
   Henry, of Gogar, 135–6
   Lord James, Commendator of St Andrews priory, Earl of Moray and Regent, 27, 33, 37, 46, 49–50, 52, 55–7, 61–2, 64, 71–2, 78–82, 88–9, 116–18, 160
   James, of Bothwellmure, Earl of Arran, 134, 138, 140, 144–8
   Sir James, of Doune, 20, 37, 75, 79, 82, 106, 135, 164
   James, Commendator of Inchcolm, 100, 129, 131, 136
   James, of Cardonald, 102
   James, sheriff of Bute, 19
   Jean, Countess of Argyll and of Moray, 58–61, 128
   John, Duke of Albany, 15–16
   John, 4th Earl of Atholl, 44–5, 50, 53, 59, 72–4, 77, 80–1, 83–6, 93–5, 98–9, 118, 123, 126, 128–31, 133
   John, 5th Earl of Atholl, 138
   John, Lord Innermeath, 18, 37–9, 74, 82, 85, 88, 119, 129–30, 134–5, 164
   Lord John, 37, 55, 57, 157
   Sir John, of Minto, 86
   Sir John, of Traquair, 134
   John, of Grandtully, 164
   Margaret, wife of Master of

## Index of Persons

Ochiltree, 135
Matthew, 4th Earl of Lennox, 17–20, 55–6, 70–4, 77, 82, 89–90, 119–22, 132–5
Patrick, Commendator of Whithorn, 135
Robert, Bishop elect of Caithness, Earl of Lennox and of March, 70, 99, 118, 124, 130, 132, 134, 136, 160
Lord Robert, Commendator of Holyrood, Earl of Orkney, 37, 55, 57, 61, 72, 75, 135
Robert, Commendator of Whithorn, 58, 88, 131, 135
Robert, of Rosyth, 161
Walter, Commendator of Blantyre, 131
William, of Dunduff, 106
William, of Monkton, 136
Stirling, James, of Keir, 18, 79, 106, 164
William, of Ardoch, 79
Strachan, John, of Thornton, 161
Straiton, Andrew, of Lauriston, 39, 161
Sutherland, Earls of, *see* Gordon, Alexander *and* John
Alexander, of Duffus, 112, 164
Swinton, James and John of that ilk, 162–3

TORPHICHEN, Lord, *see* Sandilands, James
Touris, John, of Inverleith, 104, 162
Turnbull, Sir Thomas, of Bedrule, 75
Tweedie, James, of Drummelzier, 40, 79, 163

UDNY, Walter, of that ilk, 111
Walter, sheriff of Cromarty, 112

VILLEMORE, Bartholomew, Comptroller, 51, 66

WALLACE, Hugh, of Carnale, 40, 73, 163
John, of Maynefurde, 102
John, of Craigie, 75, 163
John, brother of W. of Elderslie, 102
Wardlaw, Henry, of Torry, 39, 162
Warnour, Thomas, of Auchendinny, 104
Wauchope, Adam, of Caikmuir, 105
Gilbert, of Niddry Mariscbal, 162
Gilbert, of Stottandcleuch, 105
William, of Niddry, 141
Captain William, 113
Wedder[burn], James, 110
Weir, George, monk, 114
George, of Blackwood, 164
James, of Blackwood, 102, 148
Thomas, of Blackwood, 164
Wemyss, Captain David, 113
Sir John, of that ilk, 18, 75, 107
Wetherspune, James, of Brighous, 59
Whiteford, John, of that ilk, 102
Robert, 102
Whitelaw, Alexander, of Newgrange, 24–5, 79
Sir Patrick, of that ilk, 84, 105, 131
Whithorn, Commendators, of, *see* Fleming, Malcolm *and* Stewart, Patrick
Wilkie, George, in Saughtonhall, 104
Williamson, Patrick, in Airth, 106
Winram, John, superintendent of Fife, 121, 160
Robert, in Ratho, 160
Winyet, Ninian, 46
Wishart, George, 20–1, 24, 38–9
Sir John, of Pittarro, 20, 21, 39, 51, 73, 76, 78, 128, 161
Thomas, brother of John W. of that ilk, 141
Wood, Walter, of Bonnington, 79, 161
William, in Newmyln, 102

YESTER, Lord, *see* Hay
Young, James, in Dysart, 107